POSTCARD HISTORY SERIES

Cleveland

And the Western Reserve

IN VINTAGE POSTCARDS

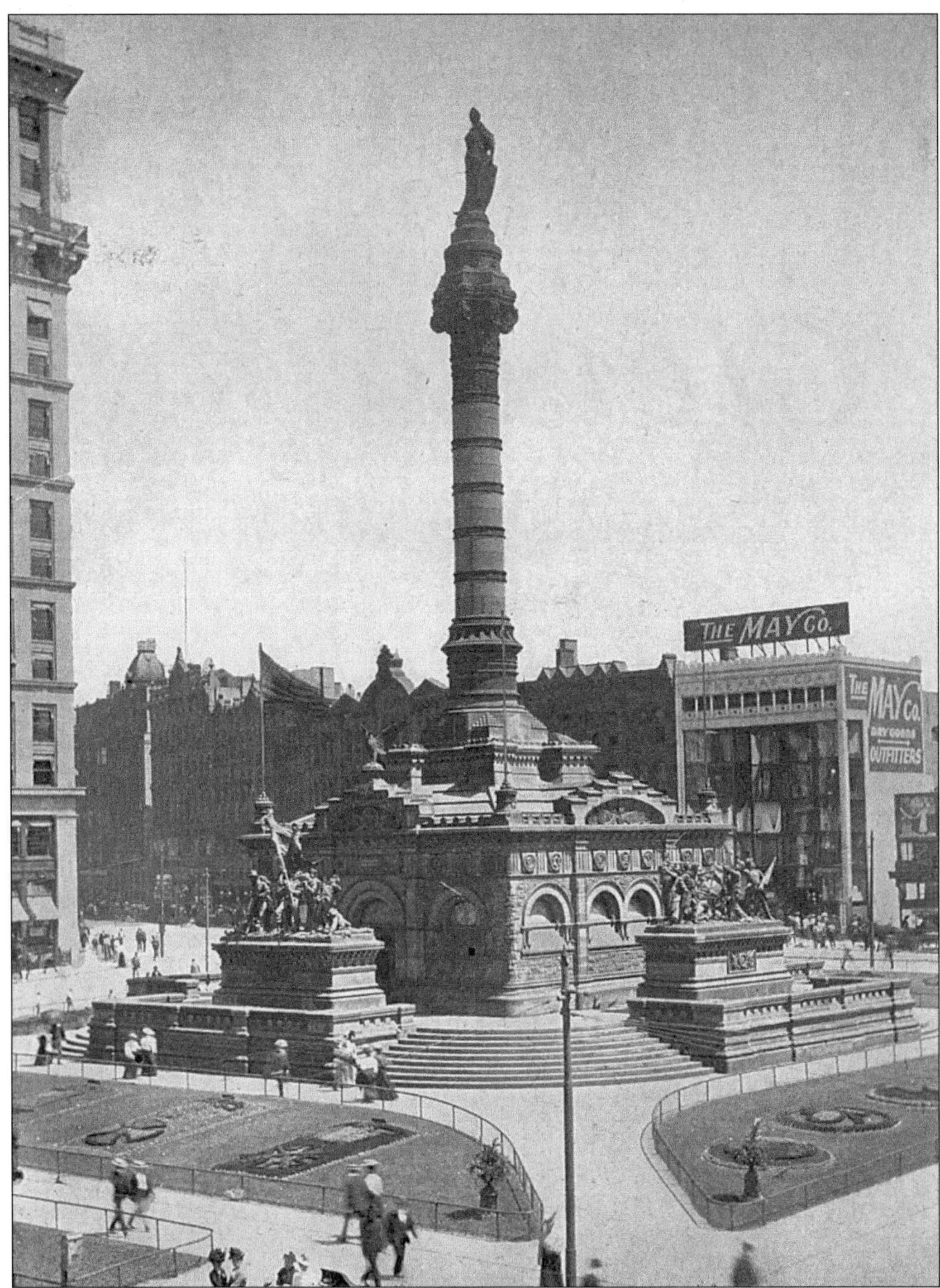

The Soldiers and Sailors Monument, Cleveland's most well-known monument, was dedicated on July 4, 1894 to honor Civil War veterans. This huge, beautifully-detailed structure, designed by noted Cleveland architect Levi T. Scofield, is the focal point of Public Square.

POSTCARD HISTORY SERIES

Cleveland

And the Western Reserve

IN VINTAGE POSTCARDS

R. Wayne Ayers

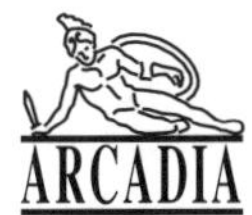

ISBN 0-7385-0737-7

Published by Arcadia Publishing,
an imprint of Tempus Publishing, Inc.
3047 N. Lincoln Ave., Suite 410
Chicago, IL 60657

Printed in Great Britain.

Library of Congress Catalog Card Number: 99-63433

For all general information contact Arcadia Publishing at:
Telephone 843-853-2070
Fax 843-853-0044
E-Mail sales@arcadiapublishing.com

For customer service and orders:
Toll-Free 1-888-313-2665

Visit us on the internet at http://www.arcadiapublishing.com

Dedication

To Nancy:

My partner on this project, my partner in life.

Contents

Acknowledgments		6
Introduction		7
1.	Cleveland Beginnings	9
1.	Lakes, Rivers, and Parks	13
2.	The Flats and Harbor	37
3.	Public Square	49
4.	Downtown	59
5.	University Circle	83
6.	Residential Cleveland	95
7.	Western Reserve	107

ACKNOWLEDGMENTS

The author consulted a number of sources in writing the captions for the images in this book. He found the following two books to be particularly helpful, and would recommend them to anyone wanting a fascinating and comprehensive history of the city:

Rose, William Ganson. *Cleveland, The Making of a City*. Ohio: Kent State University Press, 1990 (1950).

Van Tassel, David D. and John J. Grabowski. *The Encyclopedia of Cleveland History, Second Edition*. Indiana: Indiana University Press, 1996.

INTRODUCTION

The Cleveland area began as part of the Western Reserve, originally a strip of land stretching from Western New York westward to Ohio, claimed by Connecticut and set aside for Revolutionary War veterans. Connecticut subsequently gave up most of this territory to the United States, and by the late 18th century the Reserve had shrunk to what is now essentially Northeastern Ohio.

Land companies were formed in Connecticut to survey and parcel out the rich lands bordering Lake Erie, which offered bountiful opportunities for Connecticut farmers frustrated with poor soil conditions in the East. One such survey party was headed by Moses Cleaveland, who traveled by land across New York, then by boat across Lake Erie, until the party decided to disembark at the mouth of the Cuyahoga River. The site was expected to offer attractive possibilities for commerce and agriculture.

While surveyors laid out lands stretching east from the Cuyahoga River, Moses Cleaveland and a small party established the settlement of Cleaveland at the mouth of the river. The Cuyahoga was the western boundary of the United States at the time, and lands west of the river were still in the hands of Indian tribes.

The town grew slowly into the early 1800s, as growth was hampered by a harbor that was often clogged by sandbars. Additionally, malarial fevers plagued the swampy bottom lands bordering the river.

Settlers from Connecticut and other New England states nevertheless continued to pour in, claiming and clearing the fertile lands. Cleaveland prospered modestly during the early 1800s as a typical New England mercantile town. Settlers built white clapboard houses patterned with some modifications after the New England styles they had left behind. Outlying villages such as Hudson, Chagrin Falls, Painesville, Solon, and Aurora sprouted up, and stores and houses took on the distinctive Western Reserve architectural style which is still predominant in the area today.

By the time a local newspaper dropped the "a" from Cleaveland in 1833 to fit its masthead, the thriving town of Cleveland was on its way to prominence. The decision in the 1830s to make Cleveland the terminus of the Ohio-Erie Canal was the impetus to rapid growth. By the 1840s, the town had become the leading commercial center of the region. Growth of rail transportation further added to Cleveland's reputation as a transportation hub.

The discovery of rich iron ore deposits in the upper Great Lakes, combined with a rise in the number of steamboats that delivered the iron pellets, led to development of smelters along the banks of the upper Cuyahoga. The metalworking industry, feeding the nation's growing demand for manufactured goods, was born in the 1850s. By the outbreak of the Civil War, Cleveland had become an industrial powerhouse and the leading city in Ohio.

Industry continued to grow after the war, as business giants like John D. Rockefeller, Mark Hanna, and others made their fortunes in oil, iron, steel, and all sorts of manufactured goods. By the turn of the century, that included the automobile.

Cleveland exploded to become the nation's fifth largest city by 1920. The city's industrial expansion continued well into the 20th century, as two world wars and post-war prosperity fueled demand for a diversified array of products including automobiles, machine tools, sewing machines, and light bulbs, among other products. As one observer proclaimed early in the century, "If you can buy it, it's probably made in Cleveland."

Cultural and recreational pursuits also flourished during this period. Cleveland's wealth was channeled into the development of such excellent institutions as the Cleveland Orchestra, the museums of University Circle, outstanding educational facilities such as Case Institute of Technology and Western Reserve University, the Emerald Necklace park system that circled Cleveland, and waterfront parks such as Edgewater and Gordon Park.

Today, Cleveland's industrial might has been somewhat diminished by the recession of the 1970s. The city is changing its identity, and evolving toward a service and light industrial economy. Medical care and financial services lead the way. Tourism and entertainment are prominent features of the new Cleveland. The Rock and Roll Hall of Fame, the Great Lakes Science Museum, the restored Playhouse Square theaters, the Flats, the Warehouse District, and new structures for professional sports headline the attractions that draw record numbers of tourists to the city.

One

Cleveland Beginnings

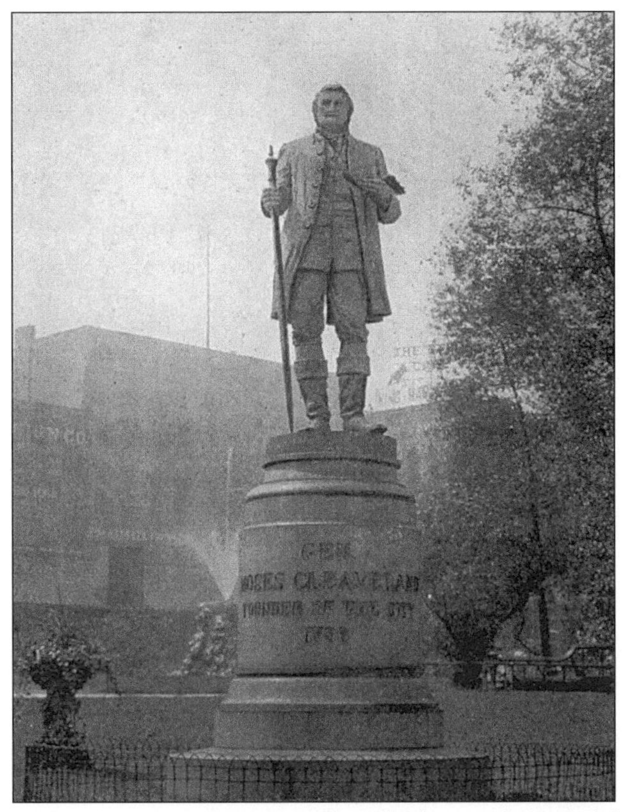

Cleveland, or Cleaveland as it was originally called, was founded by General Moses Cleaveland when his surveying party, representing the Connecticut Land Company, landed at the mouth of the Cuyahoga River on July 22, 1796. This monument on Public Square commemorates the city's founding.

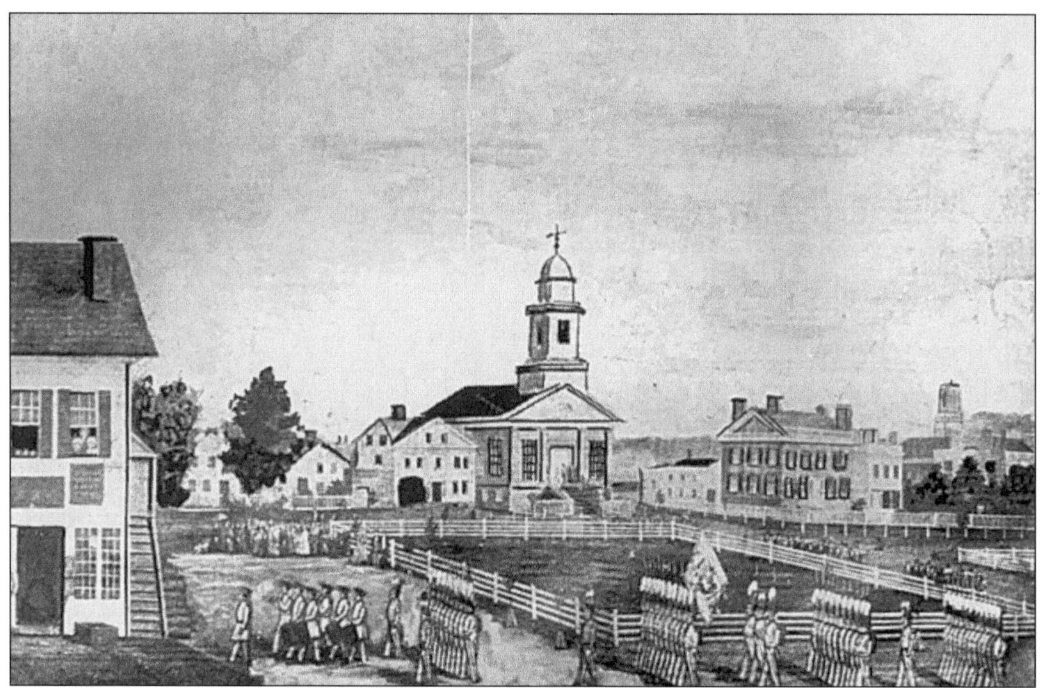

Cleveland in the 1830s was a pretty, New England-style mercantile village laid out on a public square, reflecting the heritage of its Connecticut forebears. The impact of the opening of the Ohio Canal in 1825 was just beginning to be felt. Pictured here is the northwest corner of the Square, including the original Old Stone Church.

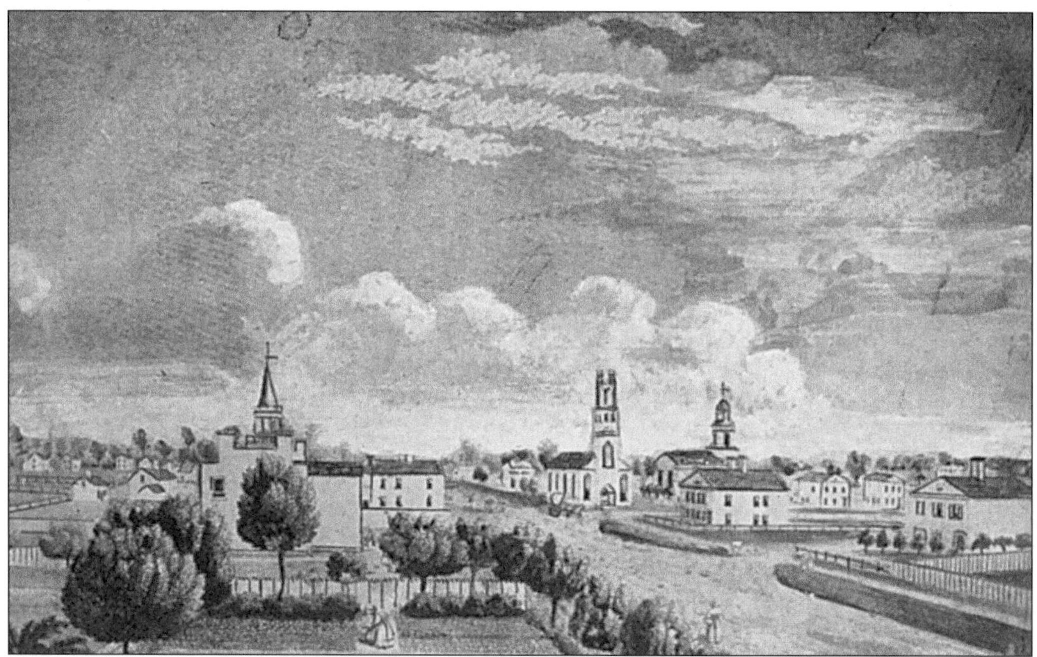

As the 1840s approached, the Ohio Canal spurred growth of the city, turning it into a regional commercial center for trade and shipping, second in Ohio only to Cincinnati.

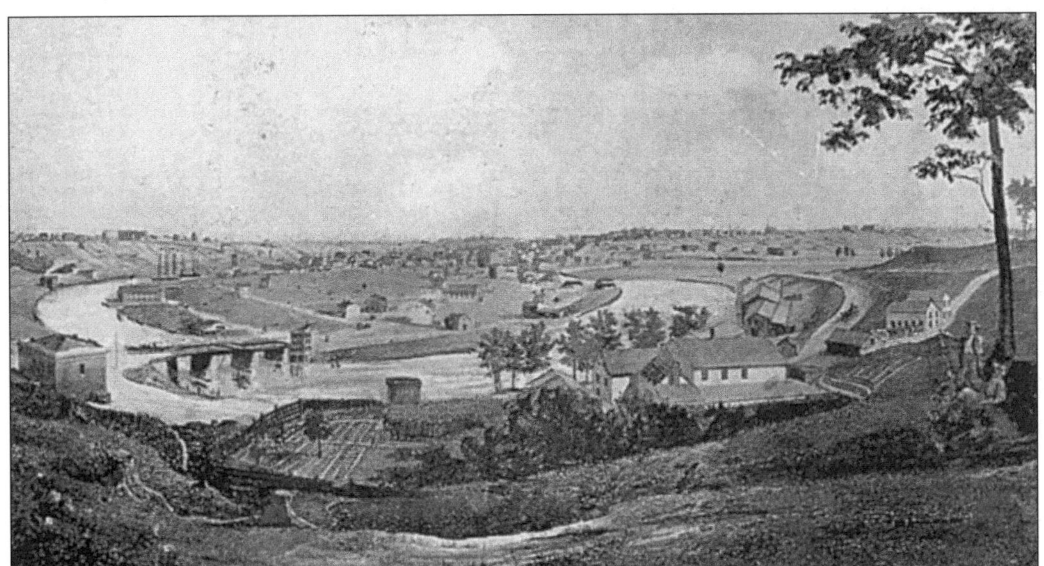

By the 1850s, industrialization had begun and the city was expanding up the hill from the Cuyahoga River, and eastward from Public Square. The city was now the leading town in the Western Reserve, and with an 1850 population of 17,034, was almost as large as Milwaukee (20,000) and Detroit (21,000). The Cincinnati Gazette that year proclaimed Cleveland "the most desirable town in the Great West to live in."

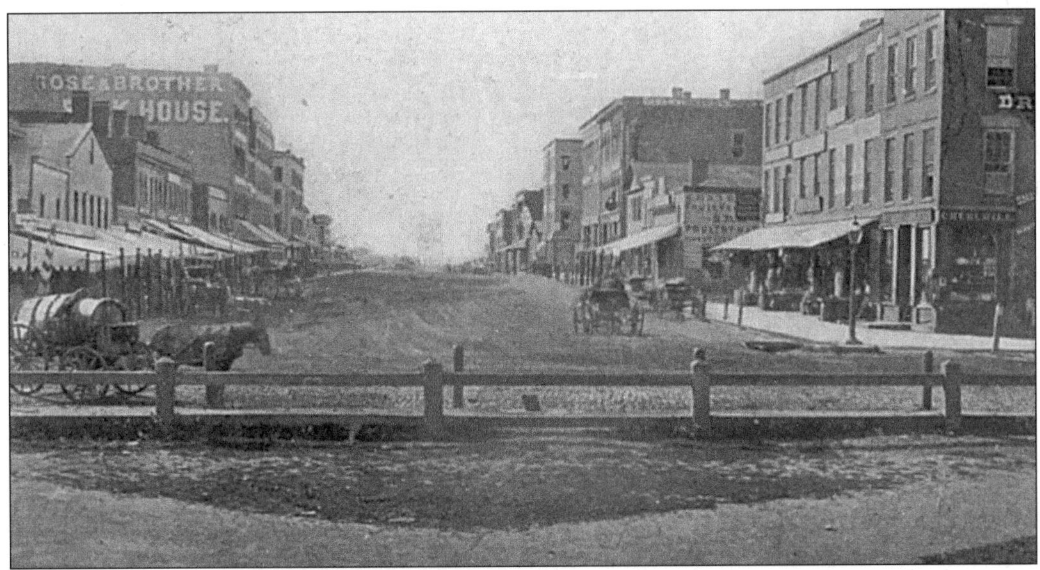

By 1860, on the eve of the Civil War, Cleveland had become a major commercial and industrial metropolis with a population of 43,417, more than doubling in a decade. Tycoons such as John D. Rockefeller, Jay Gould, and Mark Hanna ushered in a new industrial era, and a flood of immigrants arrived to take advantage of the jobs being created. A new era of growth and prosperity, not halted until the Great Depression, signaled Cleveland's rise to become the nation's "Fifth City" in the 1920s. This scene shows a bustling Ontario Street from Public Square, now replete with fencing (to keep livestock out) and hitching posts.

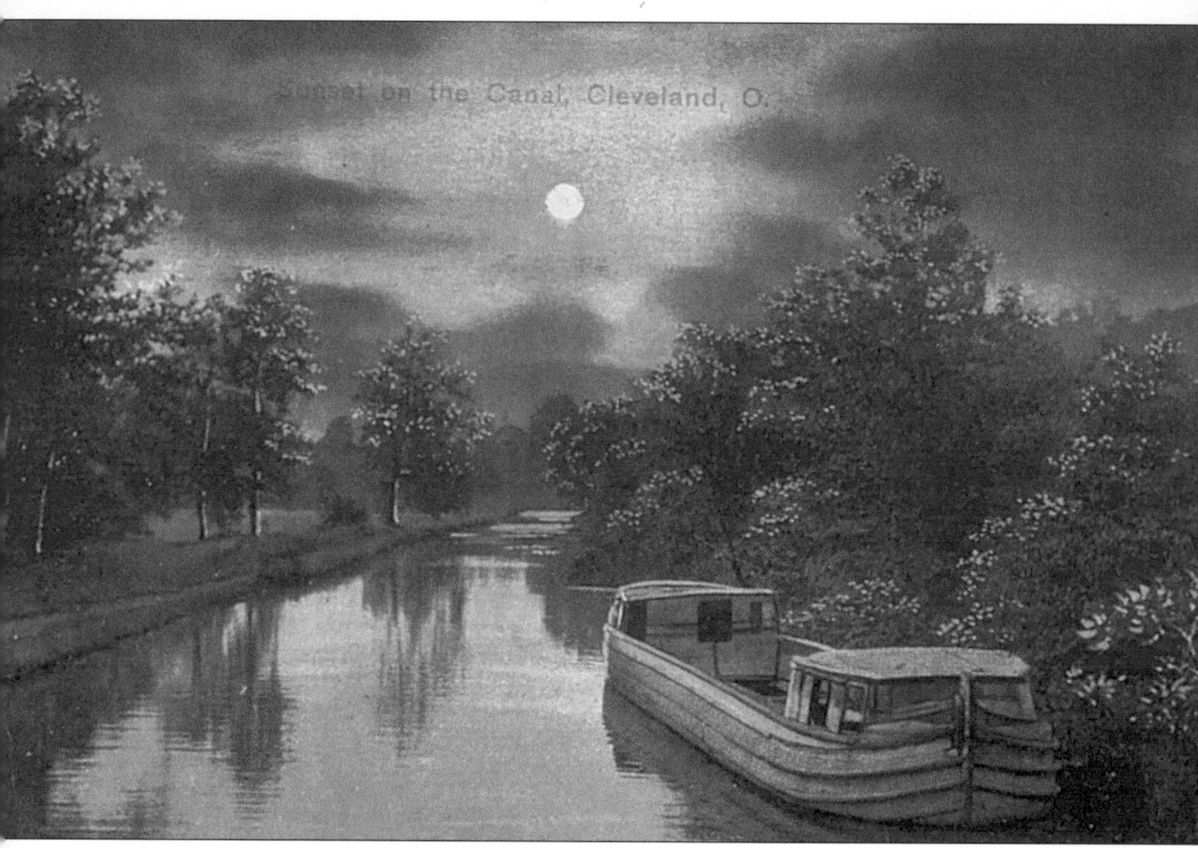

Completion of the Ohio Canal transformed Cleveland from a sleepy "New England" village into a bustling, mercantile city. Water transportation continued to be the major factor in the progress of the city, leading to Cleveland's explosion as an industrial giant in the late 1800s.

Two

Lakes, Rivers, and Parks

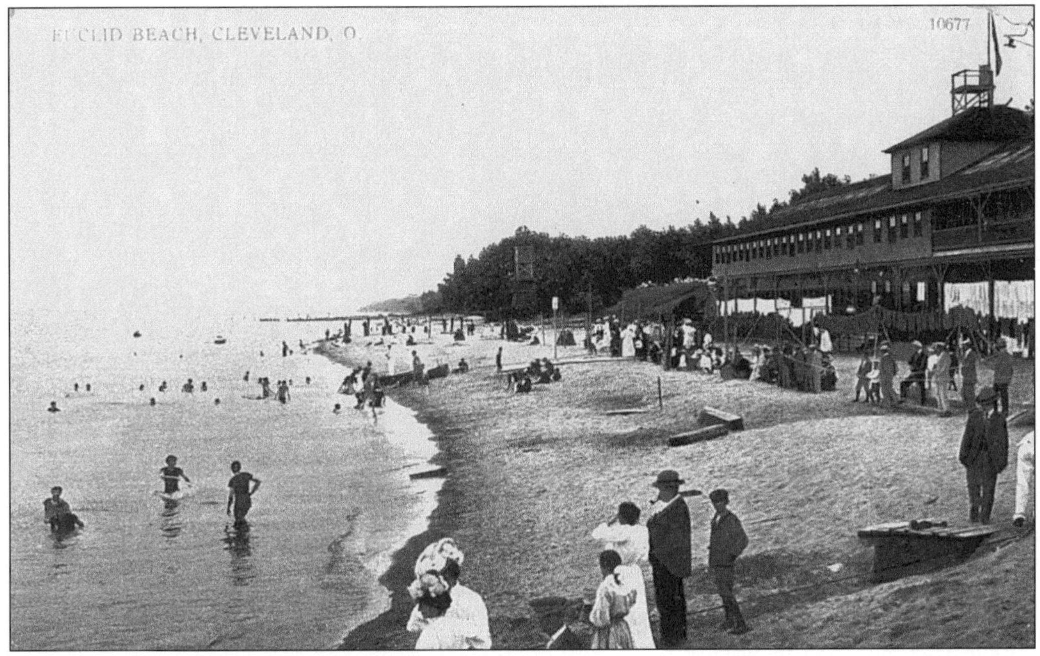

The superb beach at Euclid Beach Park has attracted crowds for over one hundred years. "Clotheslines" of drying beach garb can be seen in front of the bathhouse.

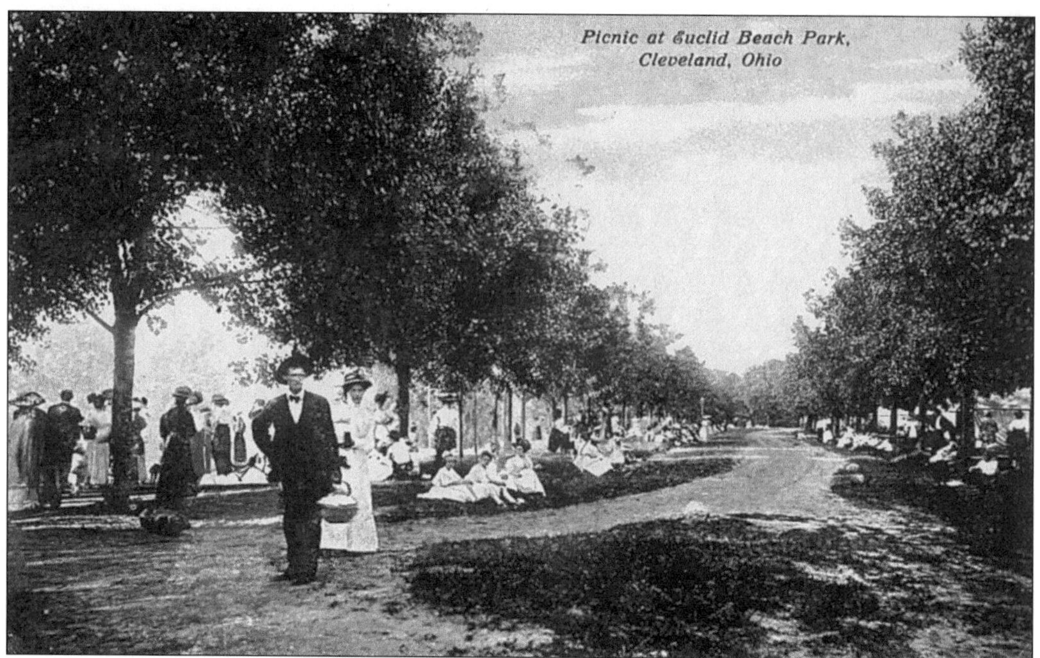

Victorians dressed formally for virtually every occasion, including picnics, as this scene at the picnic grounds at Euclid Beach Park shows.

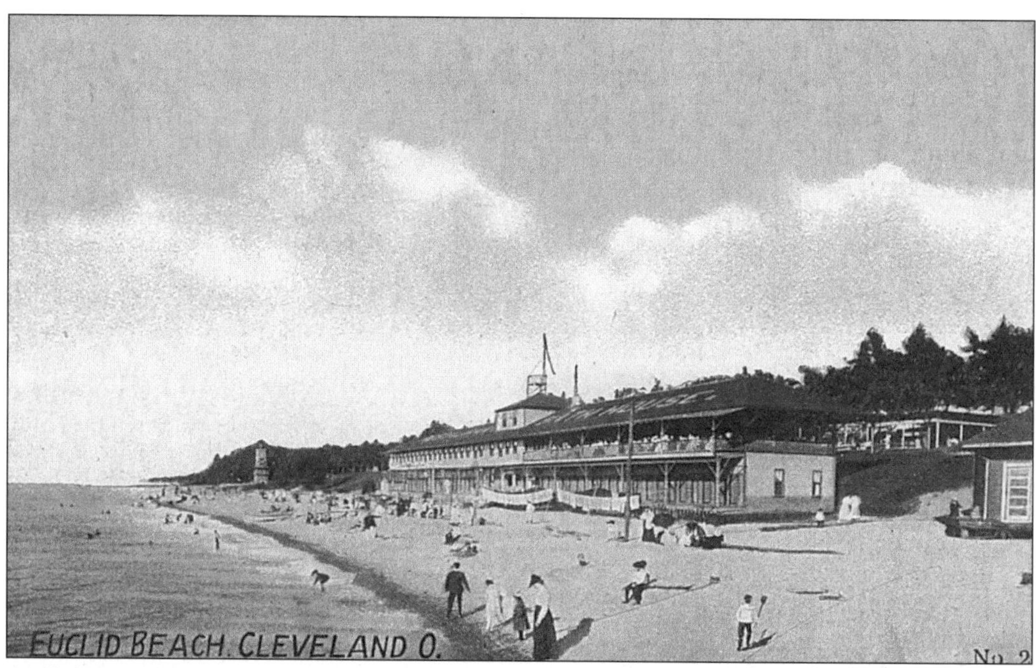

Euclid Beach opened with the new century in 1900, and became the most successful amusement park in America. The Humphrey family operated the park continuously from its inception until its dismantling in 1969. Shown here in 1908 is the Bath House, built to accommodate the large number of bathers visiting the park each summer.

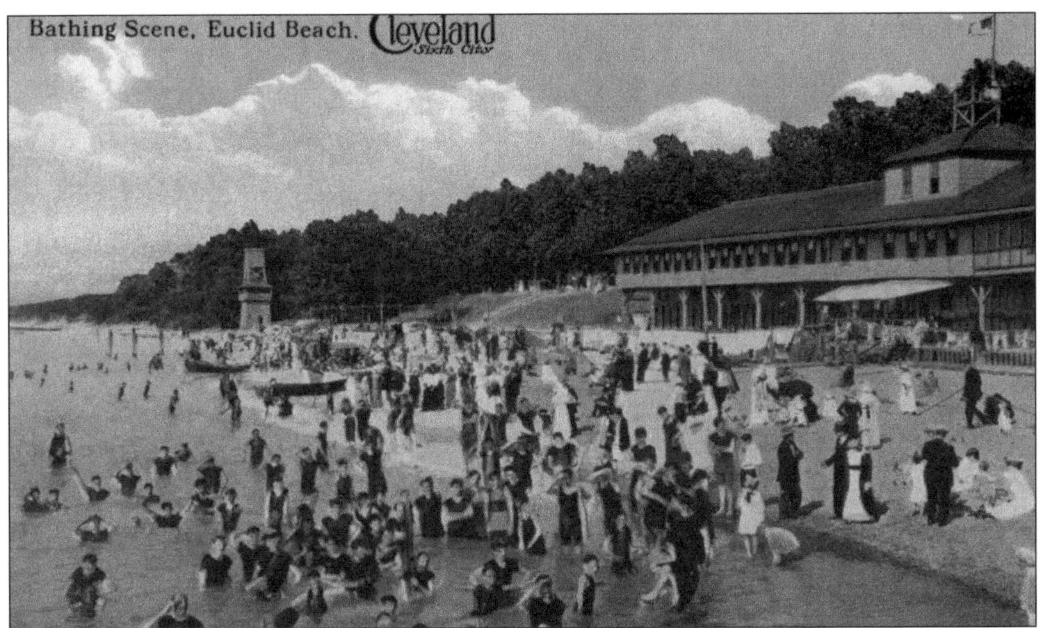

This early Euclid Beach scene shows a close-up of the crowds. Note the difference in dress between the bathers and the people on the beach. It certainly helps explain the need for large bathhouses!

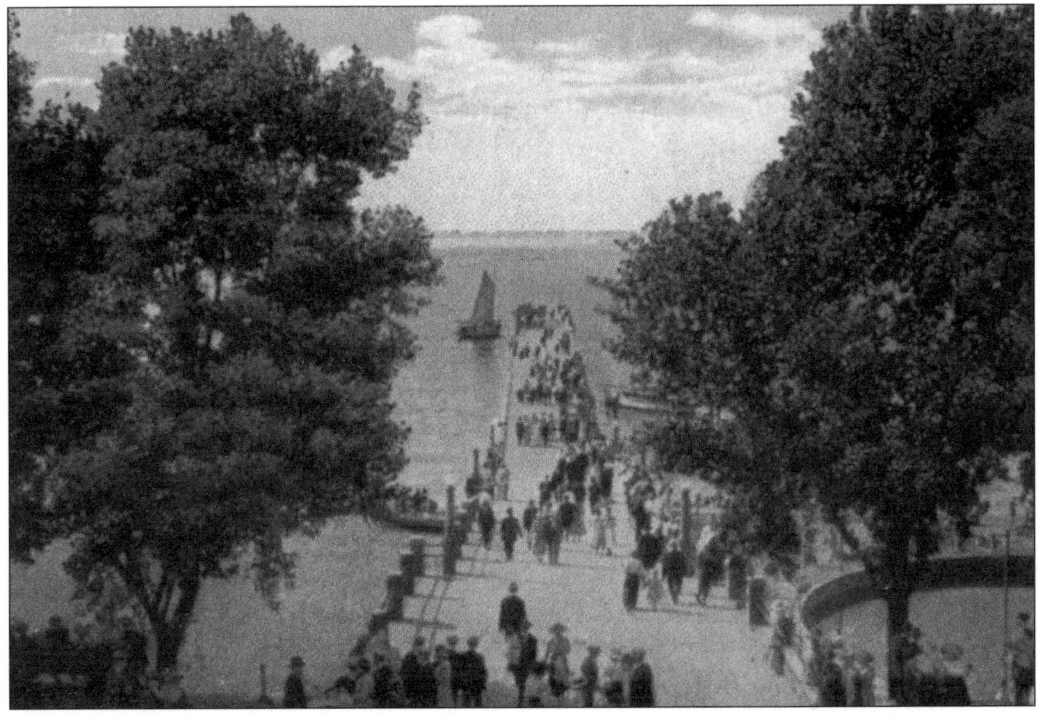

The concrete pier was a popular attraction at Euclid Beach in the mid-1920s.

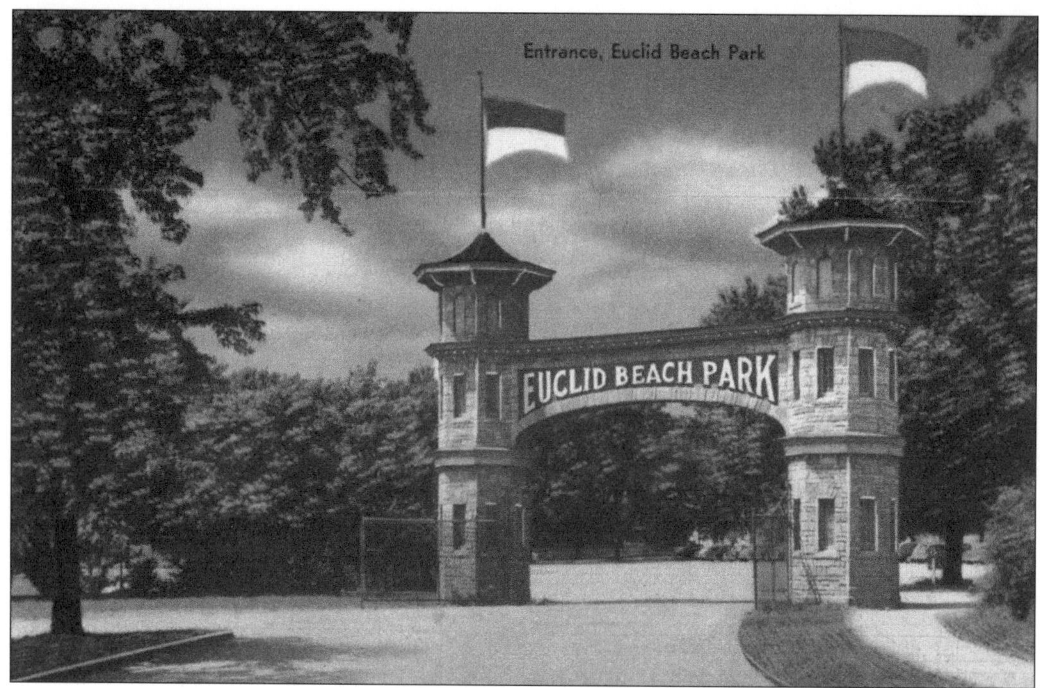

All that remains today of Euclid Beach Park is this landmark entrance arch and a small parcel of land designated as Euclid Beach State Park.

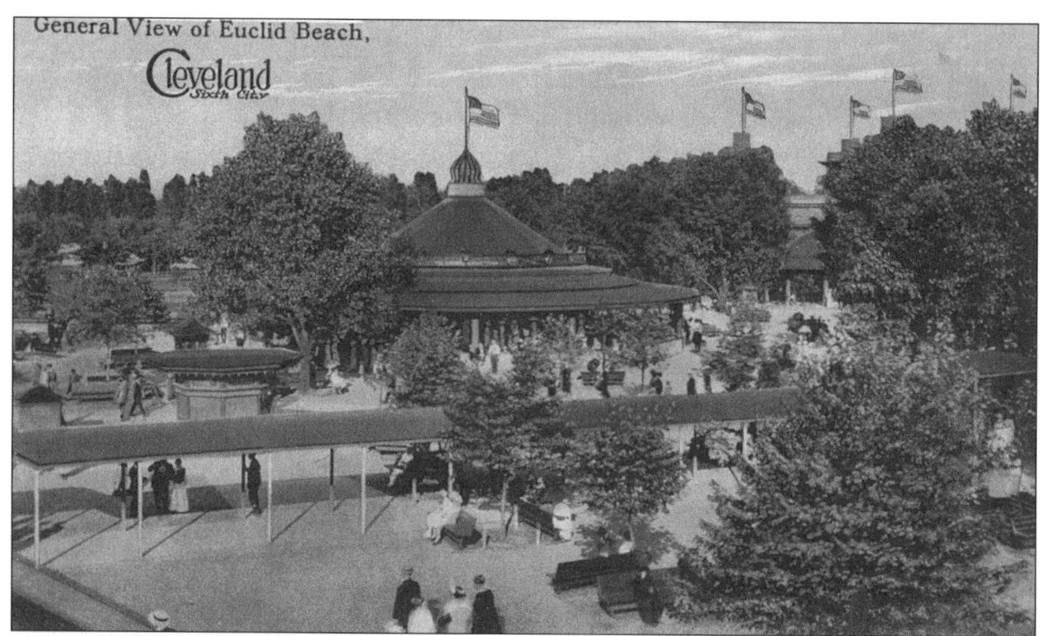

Euclid Beach Park became an amusement park in the mid-teens, when rides and arcades were added.

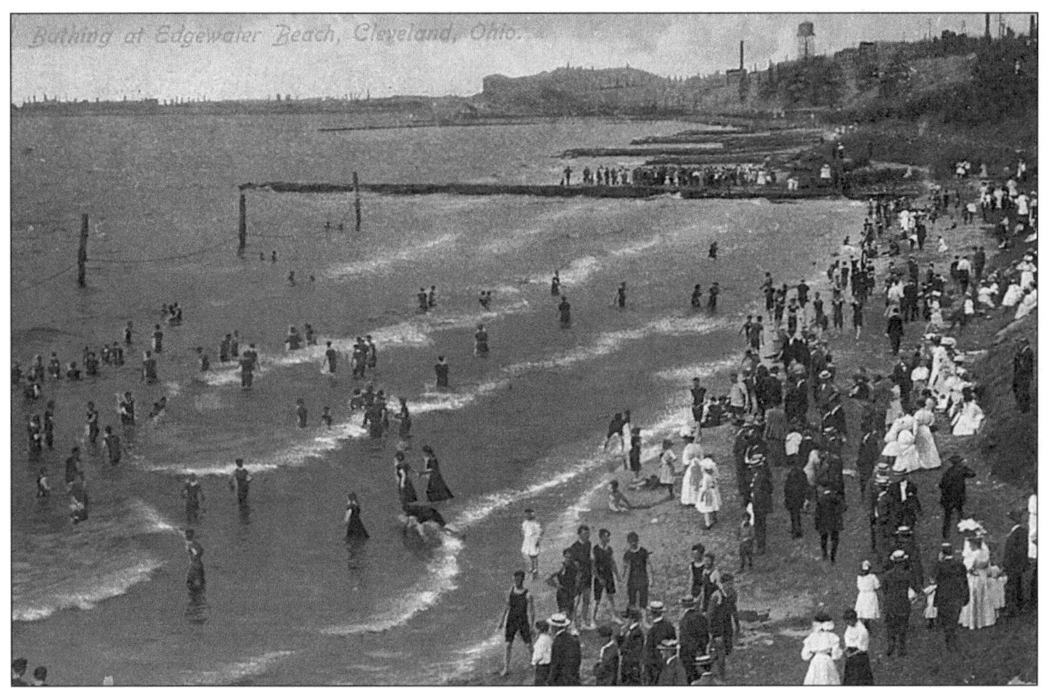

Edgewater Park, on the city's west side, opened in 1894 on land purchased by the city from industrialist Jacob B. Perkins. The park was later home to bathhouses, a pavilion, and picnic and playground areas. The area is now Edgewater Beach State Park, and a turn-of-the-century bathhouse is home to Don's Lighthouse restaurant. The scene here is of a crowded day in 1908.

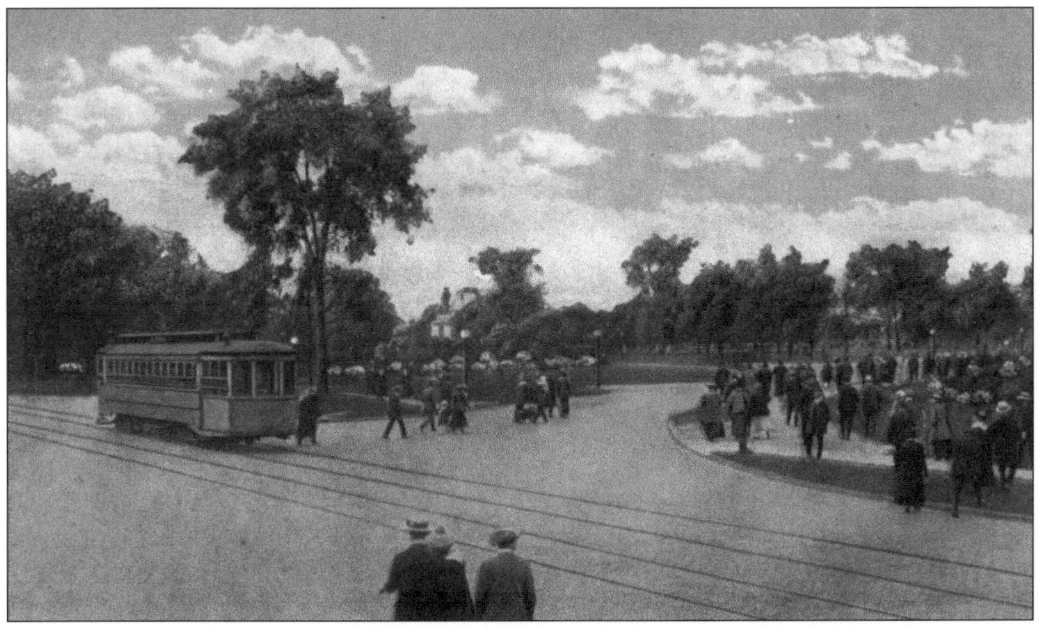

The trolley provided a cheap and easy means to a brief vacation at Edgewater Park.

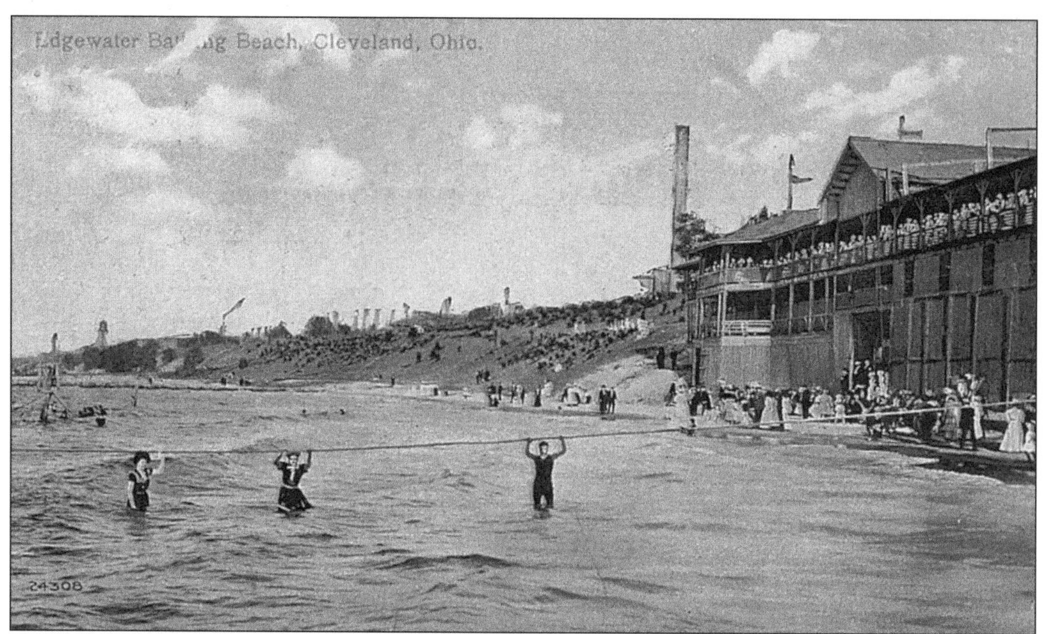

The "rope" appears to be a popular gathering spot at Edgewater in the summer of 1913. Note the crowds on the balcony in the pavilion.

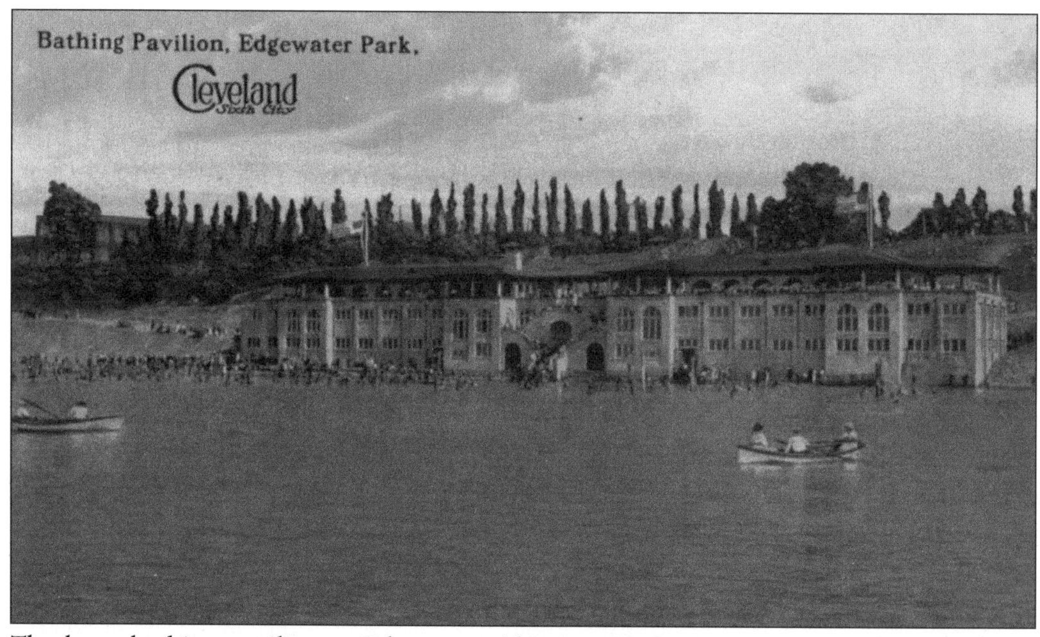

The large bathing pavilion at Edgewater (this is a 1918 view) attests to the popularity of the park, with its spacious grounds and wide, sandy beach.

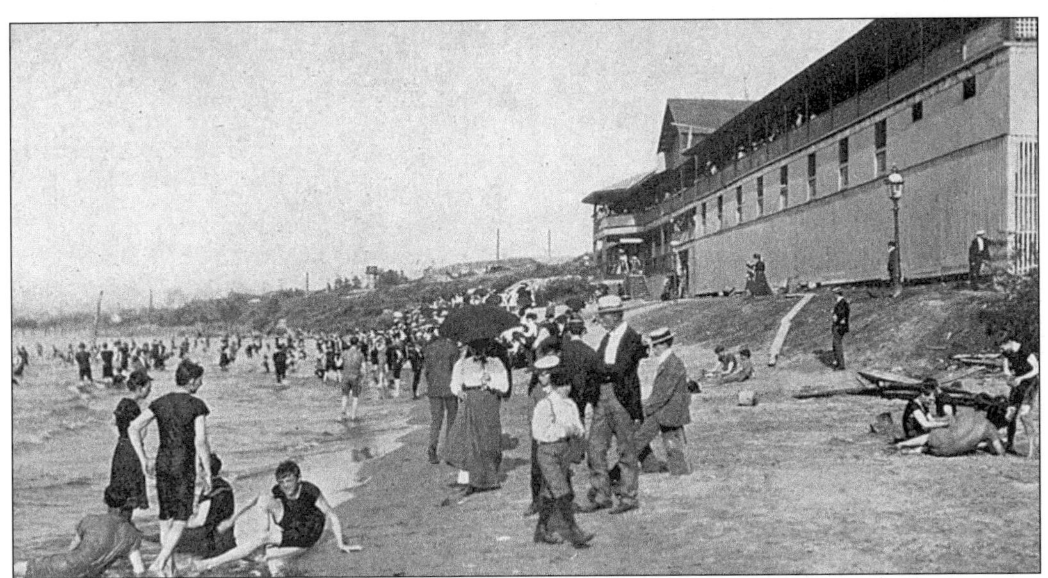

Crowds fill the beach and bathhouse at Edgewater Park on a hot summer's day.

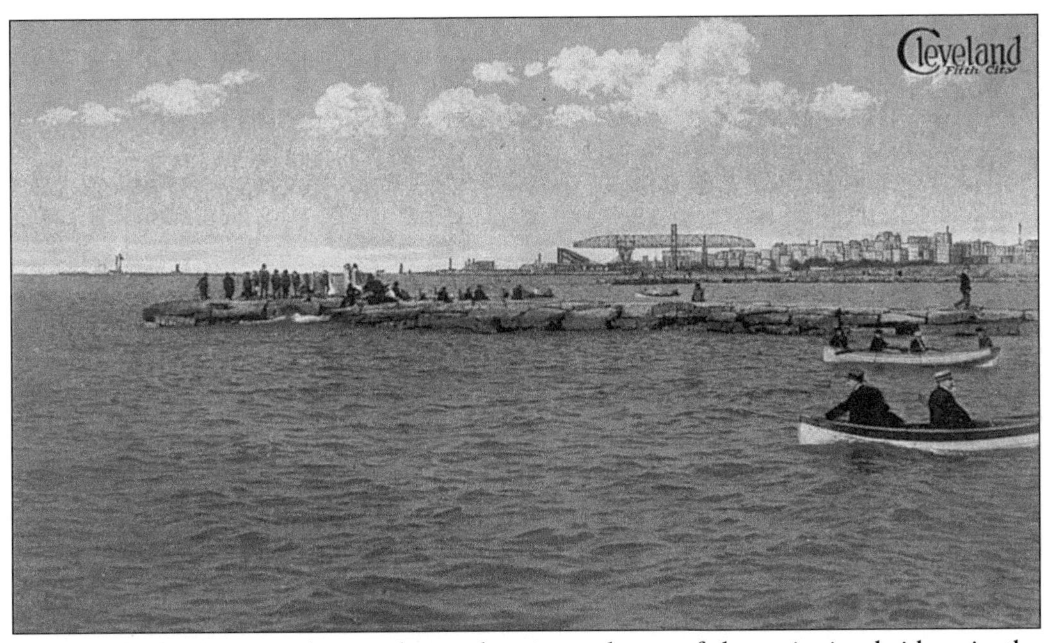

A view of Edgewater Park Pier shows the city and one of the swinging bridges in the background.

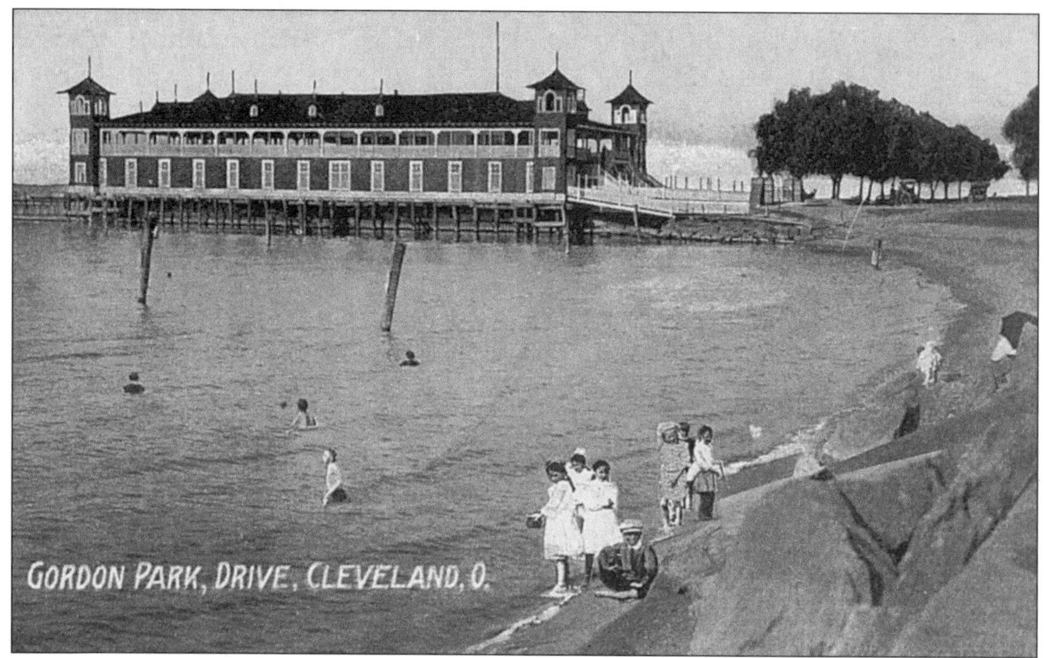

Gordon Park, on the lakefront on Cleveland's East Side, was once the estate of wholesale grocer William J. Gordon. It was deeded to the city for use as a public park upon his death in 1893. The scene shows the bathhouse and rocky shore as they appeared in the early 1900s.

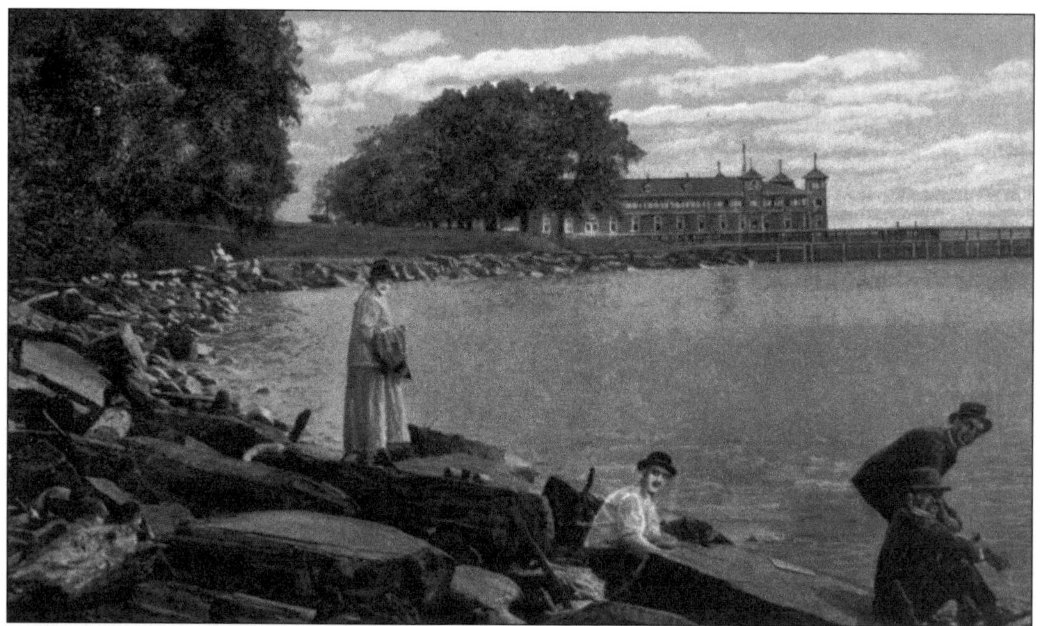

A diverse group fishes at Gordon Park. The bathhouse is in the background. The fishermen seem none too happy at being disturbed.

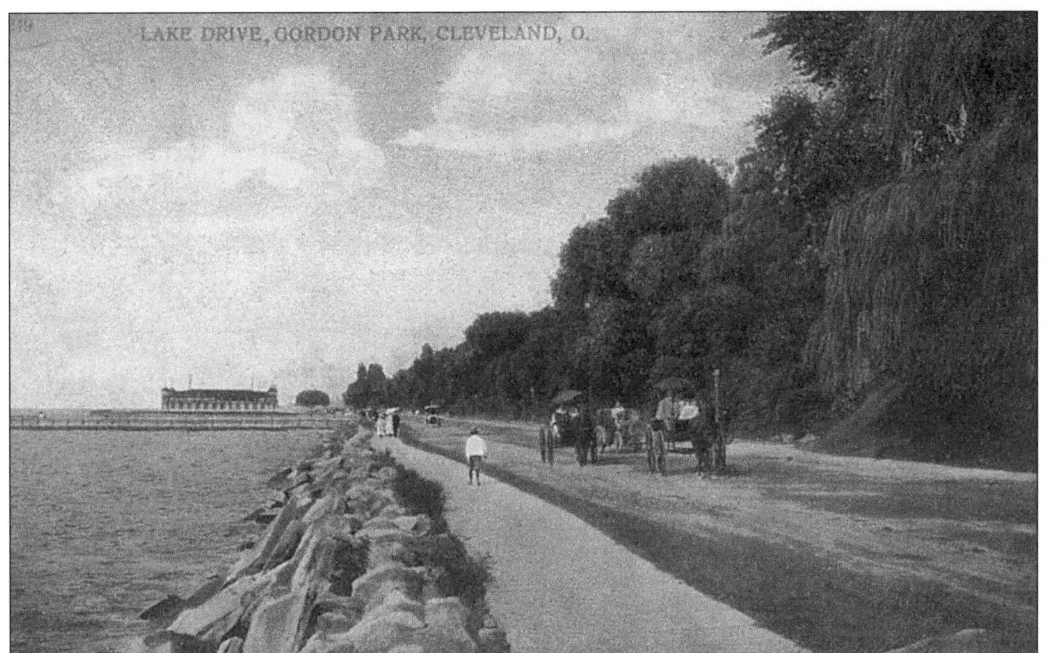

Gordon Park became a famous playground for Clevelanders, with activities that included fishing, boating, bathing, picnicking, and, as this 1908 scene shows, promenading.

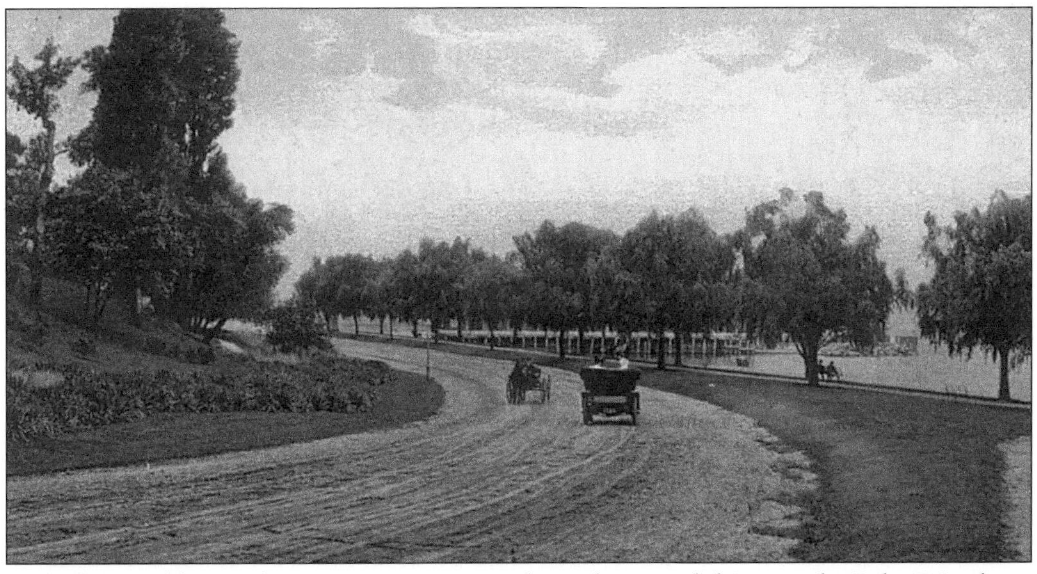

Horseless and horse-drawn carriages meet along the gravel drive on the Lake Erie shore at Gordon Park.

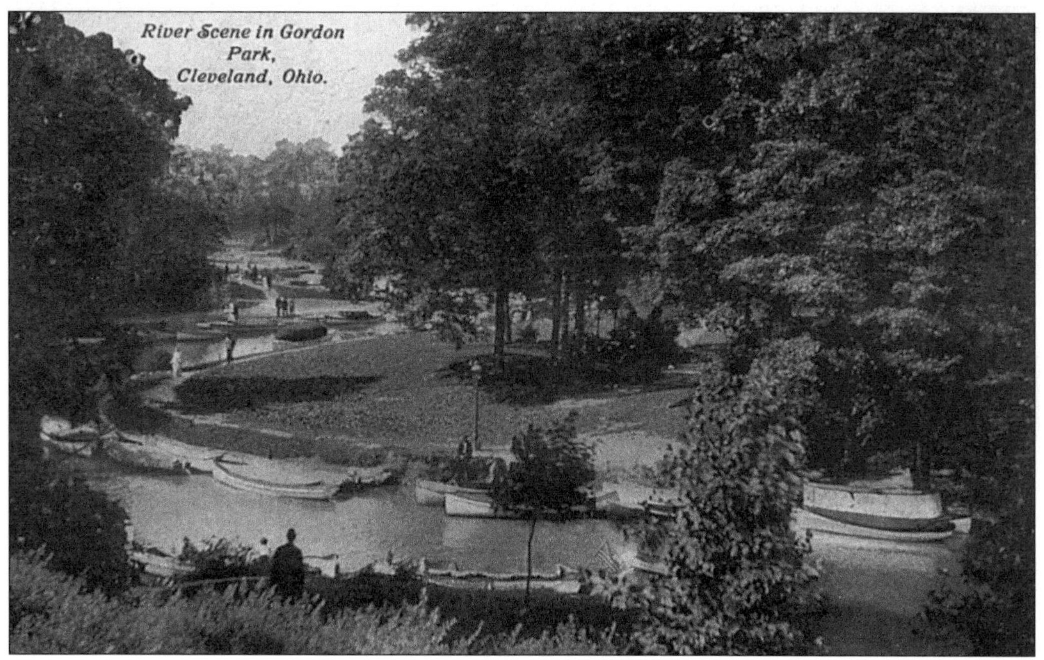

Boats galore crowd Gordon Park at Doan Brook.

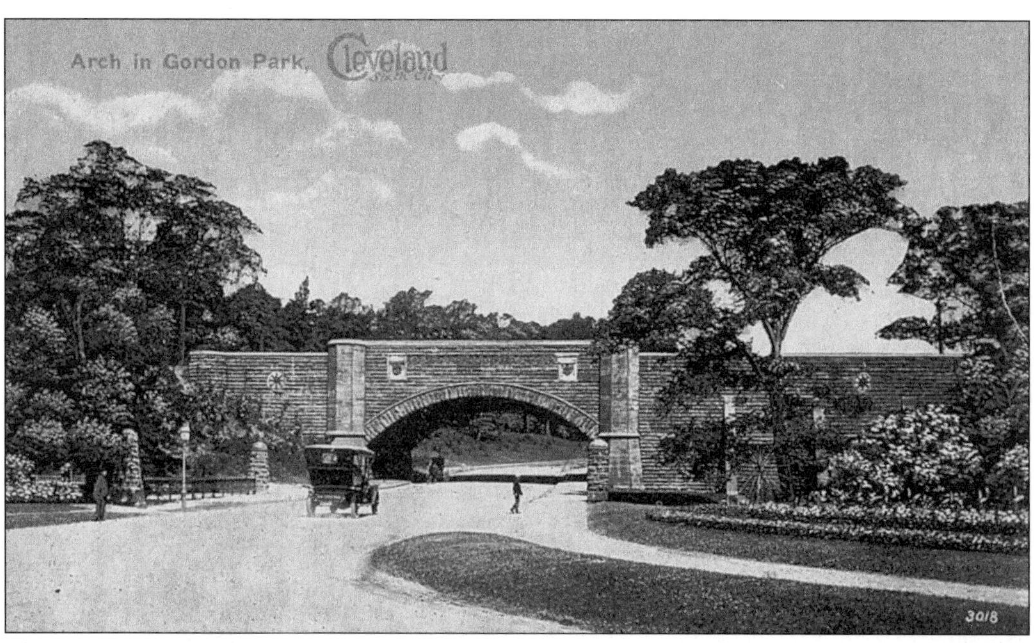

This concrete arch bridge at Gordon Park is typical of many such bridges spanning the roadways in Cleveland parks.

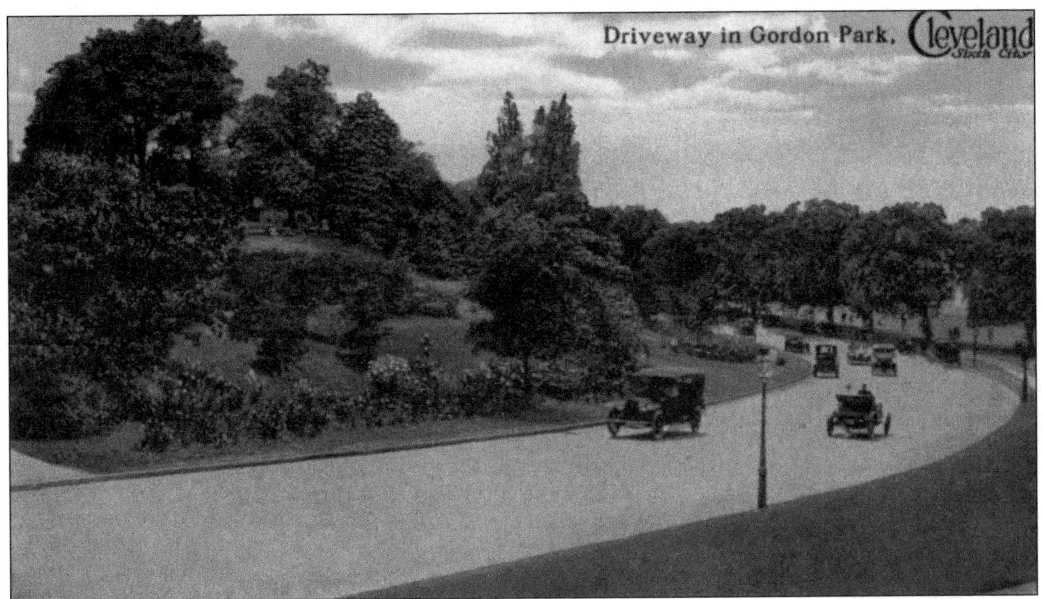

Model Ts and other early automobiles compete for space on Lake Shore Drive in this 1918 view.

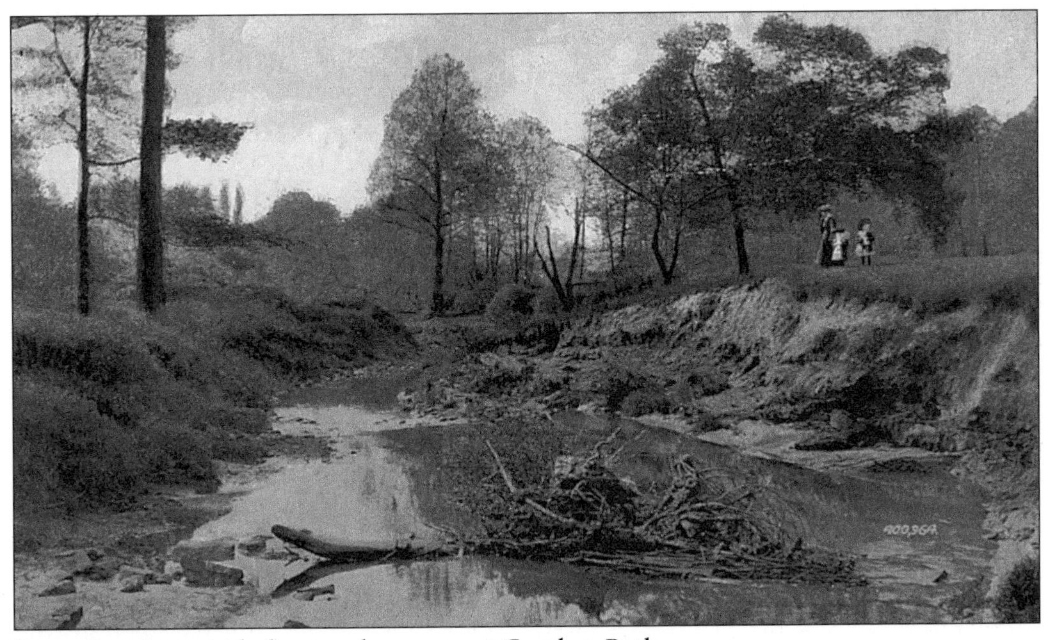
Doan Brook provided natural scenery at Gordon Park.

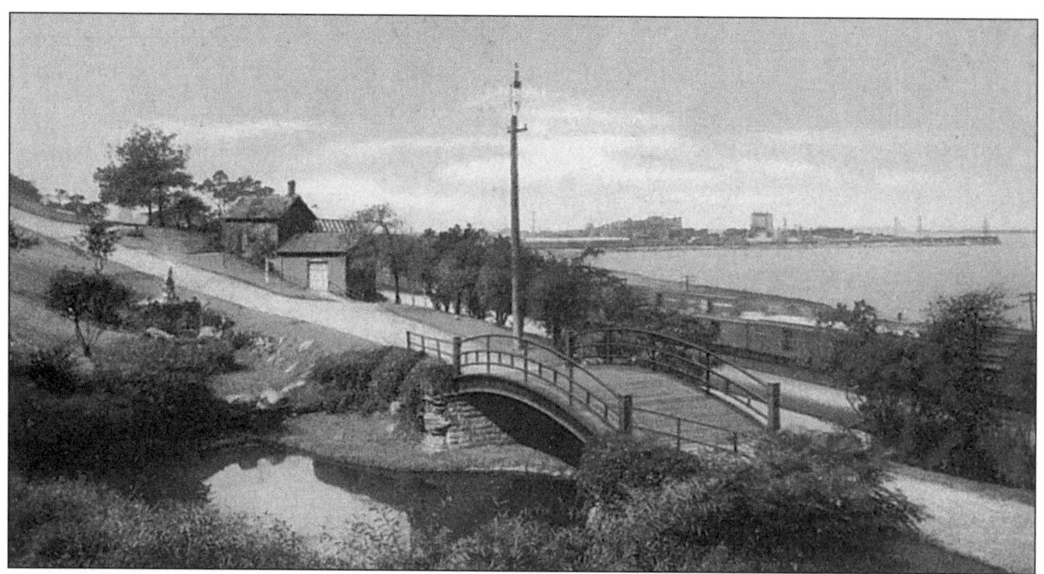

Cleveland's scenic parks have been a source of pride for the city and a welcome relief from urban noise and bustle.

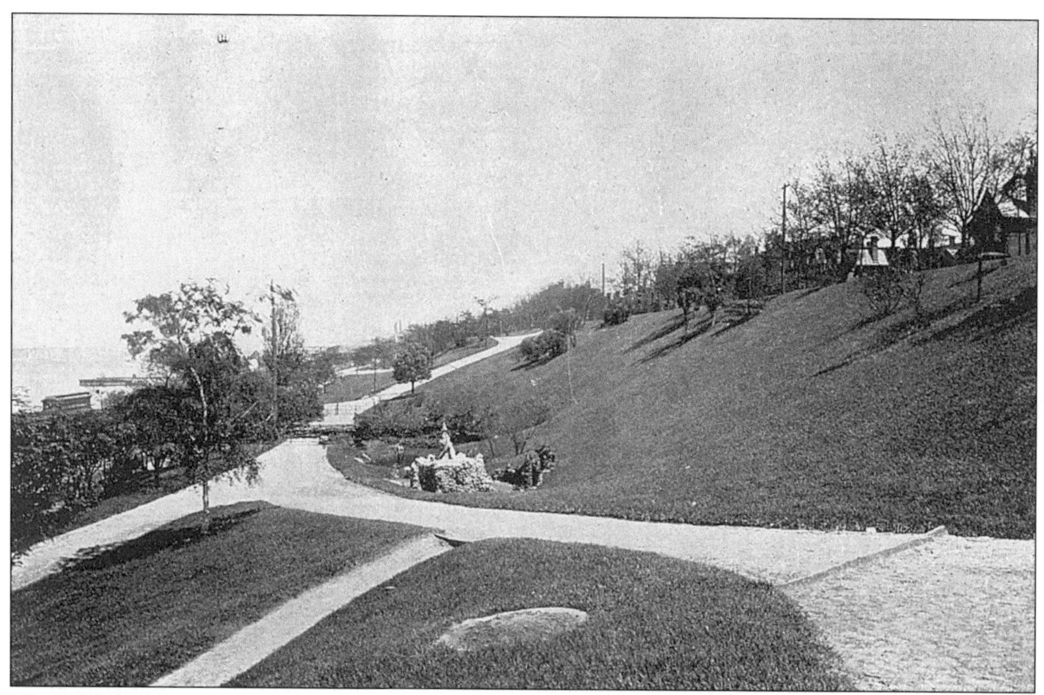

The sloping bank at Lakeview Park, near downtown Cleveland, was an ideal spot for overlooking the Lake Erie shore.

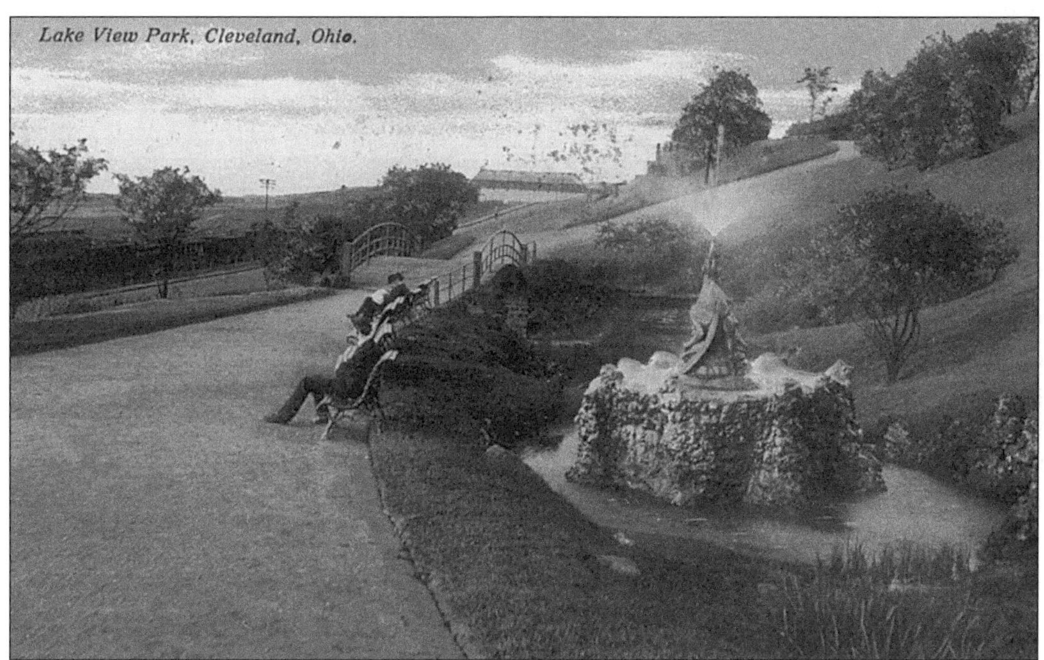

Lakeview Park was a district cluttered with squatter's hovels in 1867, when it became the first park property purchased by the city.

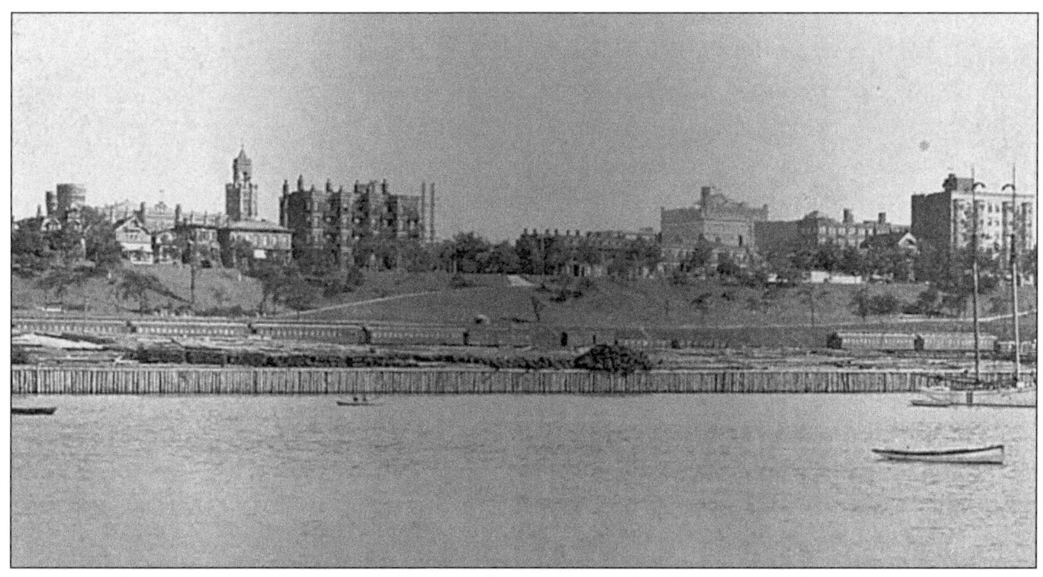

Bridges, fountains, and scenic lake overlooks graced Lakeview Park.

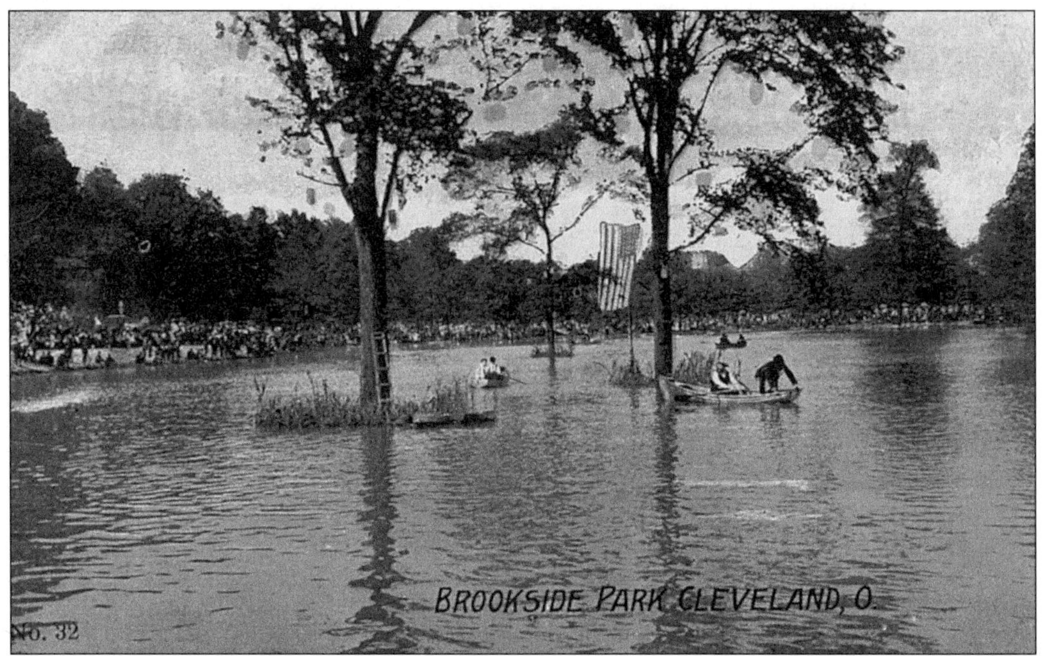

Brookside Park, one of the city's oldest, was created in 1894. It is now home to the Cleveland Metroparks Zoo.

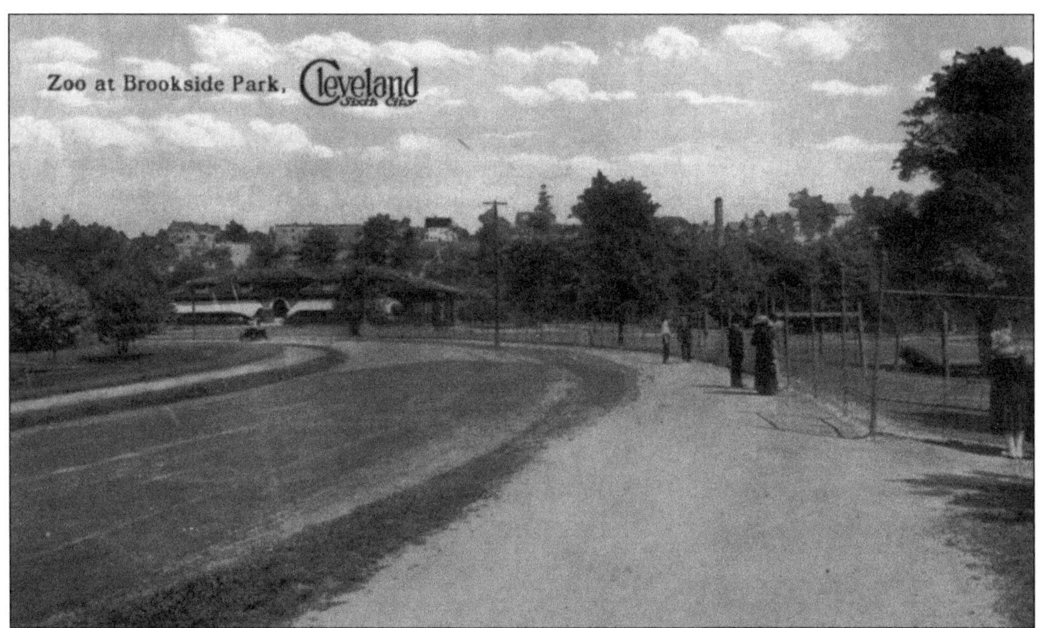

The Cleveland Zoo was established in 1885 in Wade Park (University Circle). It was moved to its current location in Brookside Park in 1907, and has expanded over the years to become the extensive zoological park of today.

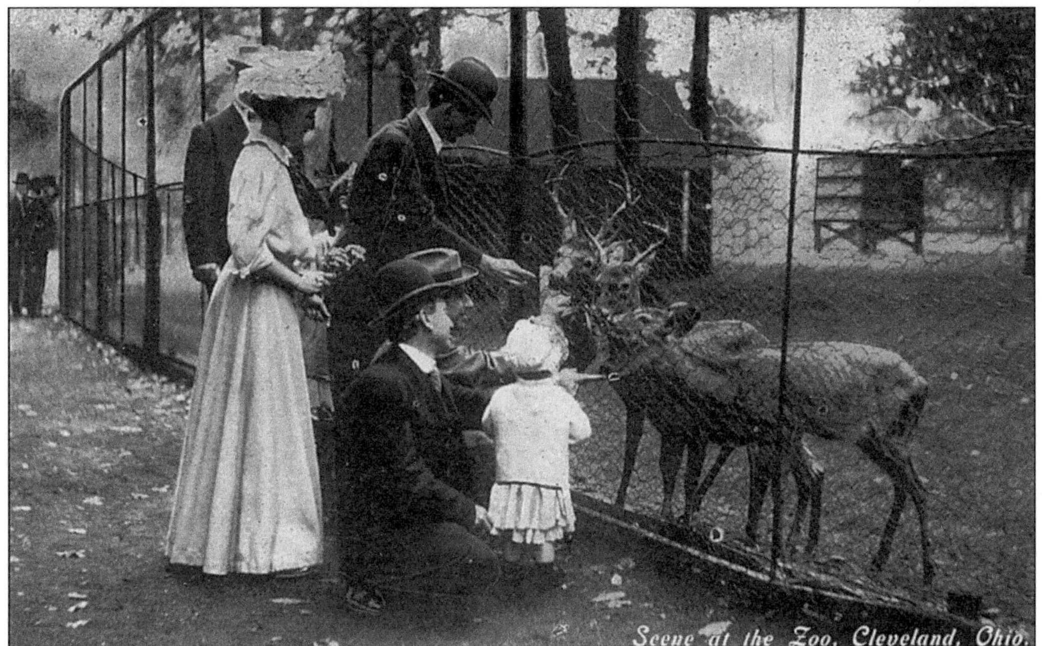

The zoo started with a herd of deer.

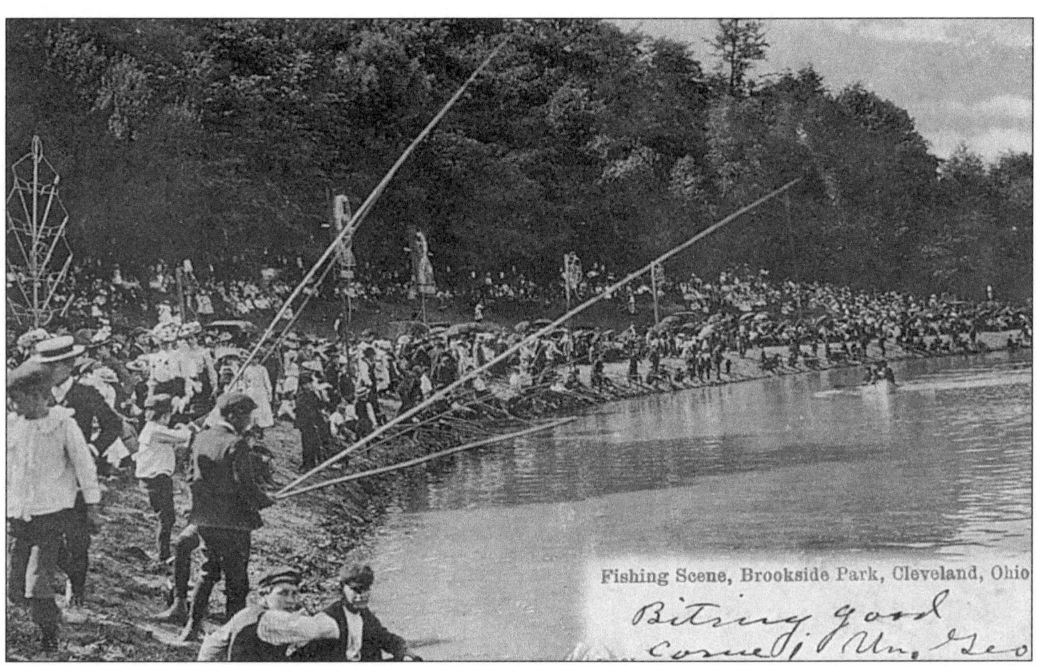

Fishermen line the shore at Brookside Park.

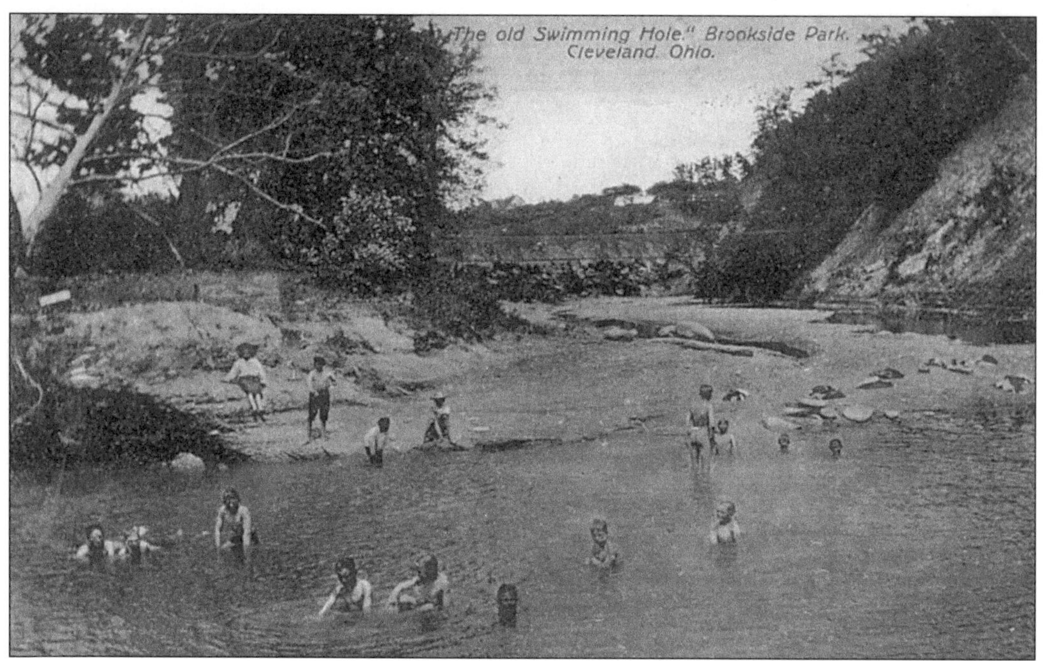

Kids take a dip in "the old swimming hole" at Brookside Park. The skinny-dipper in the center appears to be attracting very little attention.

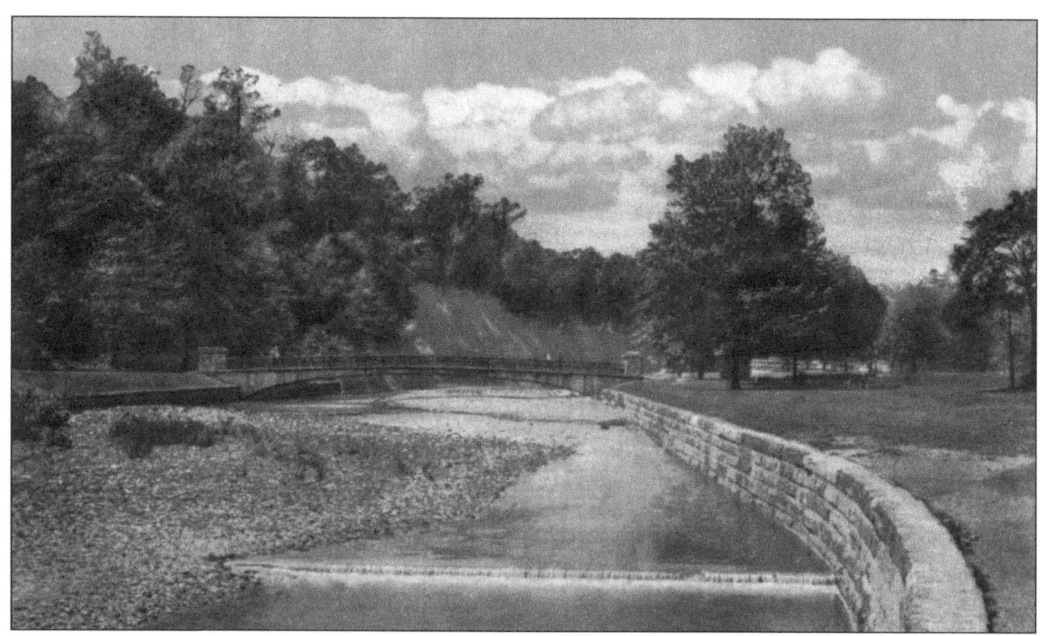

Scenic cliffs and streams were a noted feature of Brookside Park, shown here in pre-zoo days.

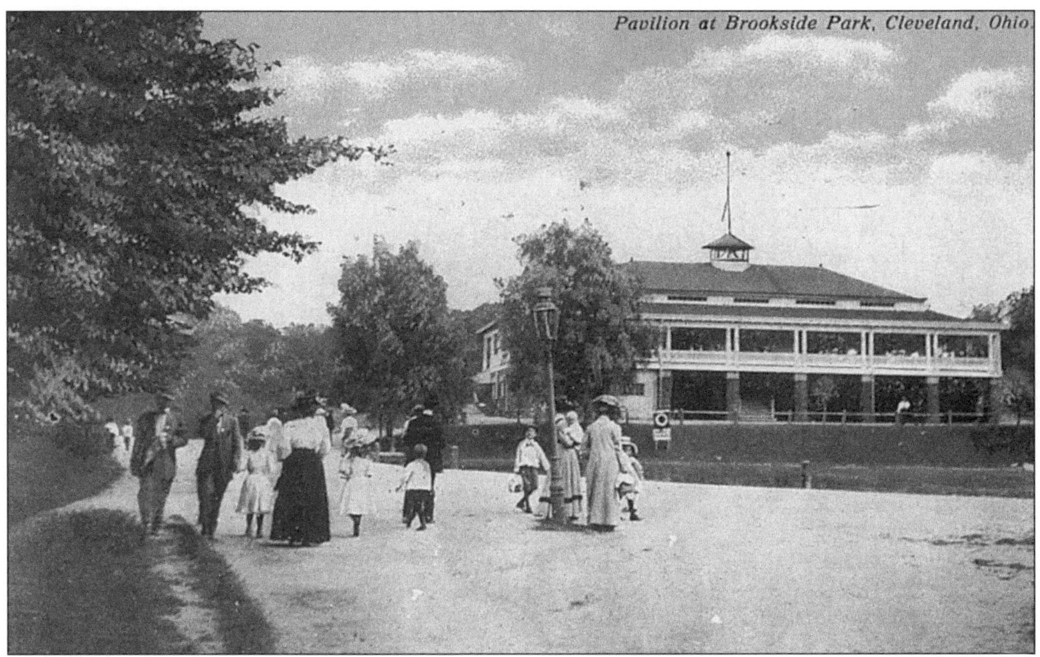

Formally dressed Victorians stroll around the expansive pavilion at Brookside Park in 1912.

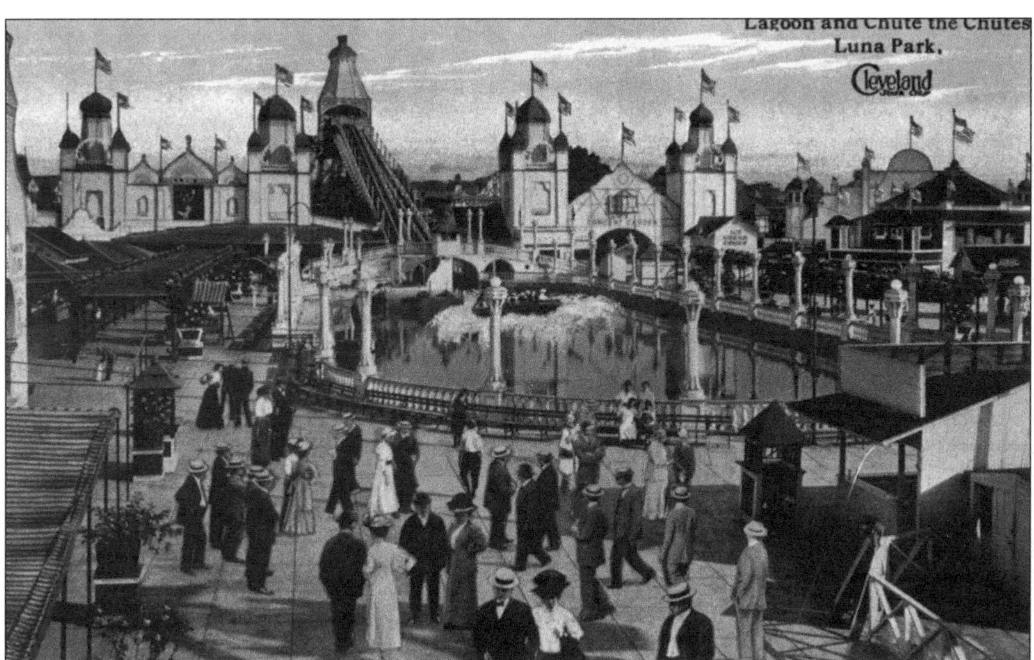

Luna Park was another popular Cleveland amusement park. Established in 1905, Luna was a Coney Island-style entertainment park featuring rides, a roller rink, gardens, and a lake with toboggan slide. At night, the park was ablaze with electric lights.

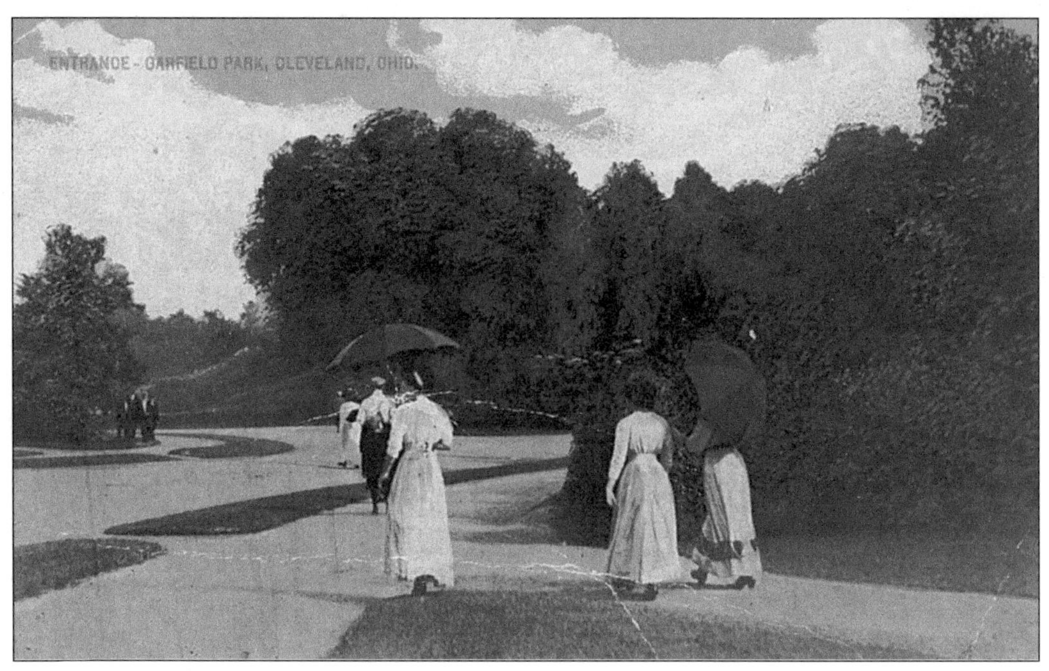

Visitors arrive for a leisurely day at Garfield Park in this postcard dated 1914.

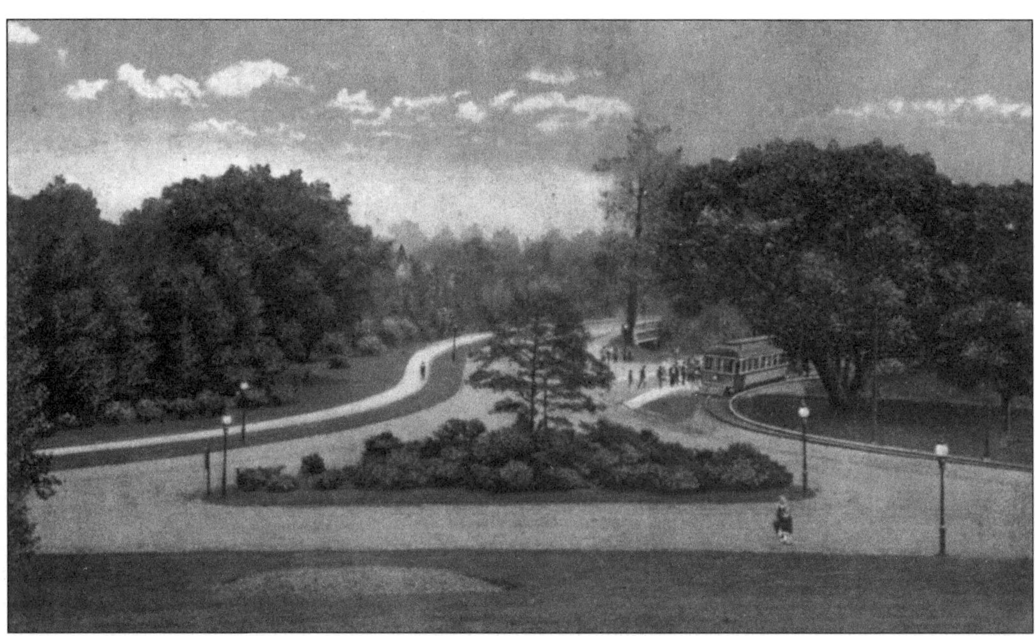

Garfield Park was acquired by Cleveland in 1896 as part of the city's Centennial celebration. It is now part of the Cleveland Metroparks System.

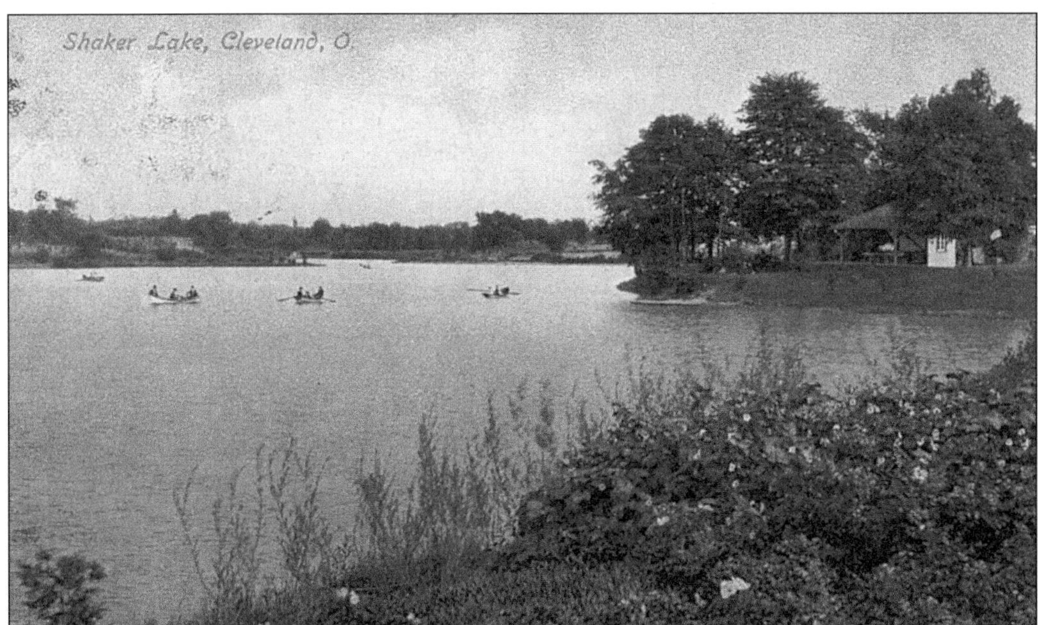

The Shaker Lakes in Shaker Heights were formed when the North Union Shaker colony dammed Doan Brook at two locations, creating the Upper and Lower Lakes. The Shakers used the dam to power their mills. After the colony disbanded in the 1890s, the land became part of residential Shaker Heights, a planned community developed by the Van Sweringen brothers, who also built the Terminal Tower complex on Public Square. This photo was taken after the Shakers left, but before Shaker Heights was fully developed.

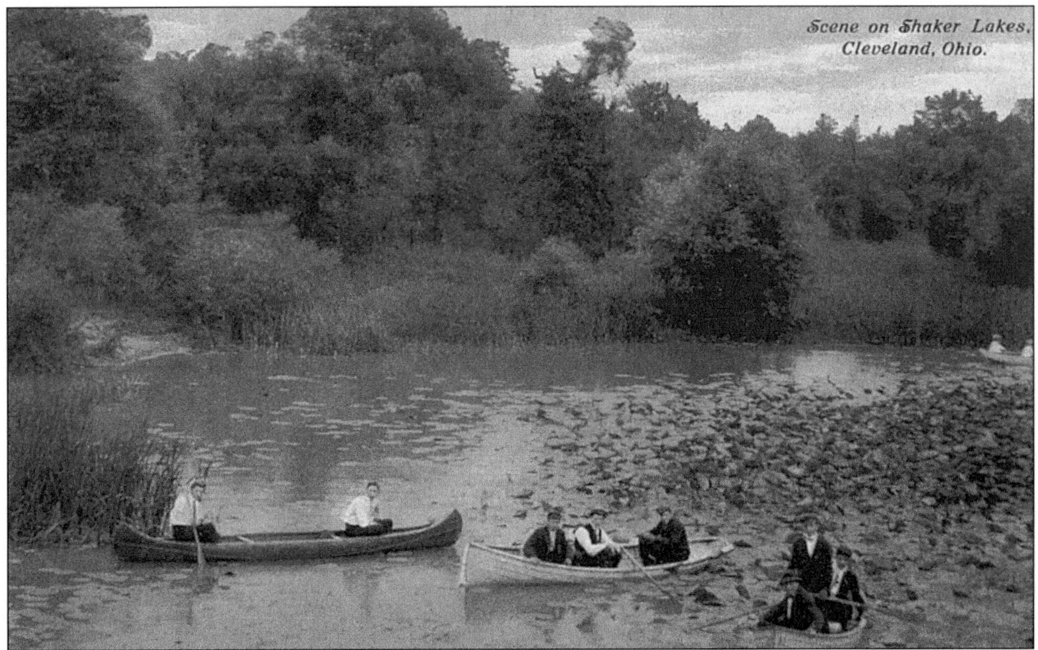

The Shaker Lakes were a popular spot for rowboating and canoeing.

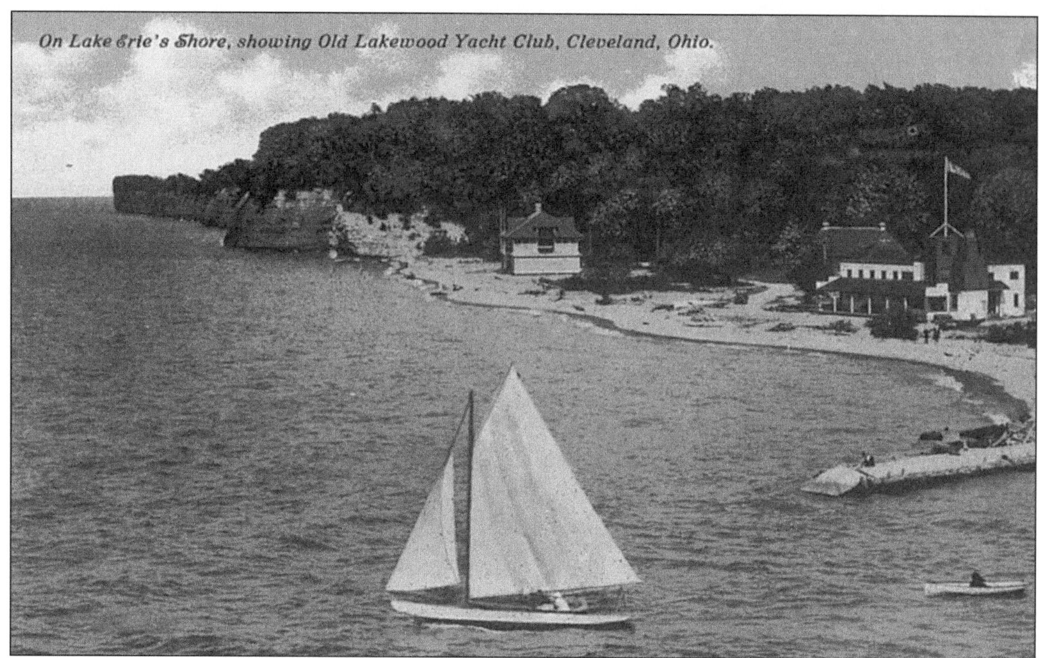

The Rocky River flows into Lake Erie west of Cleveland. Once a popular mill site, the upper river is now part of the picturesque Rocky River Reservation of the Cleveland Metroparks System.

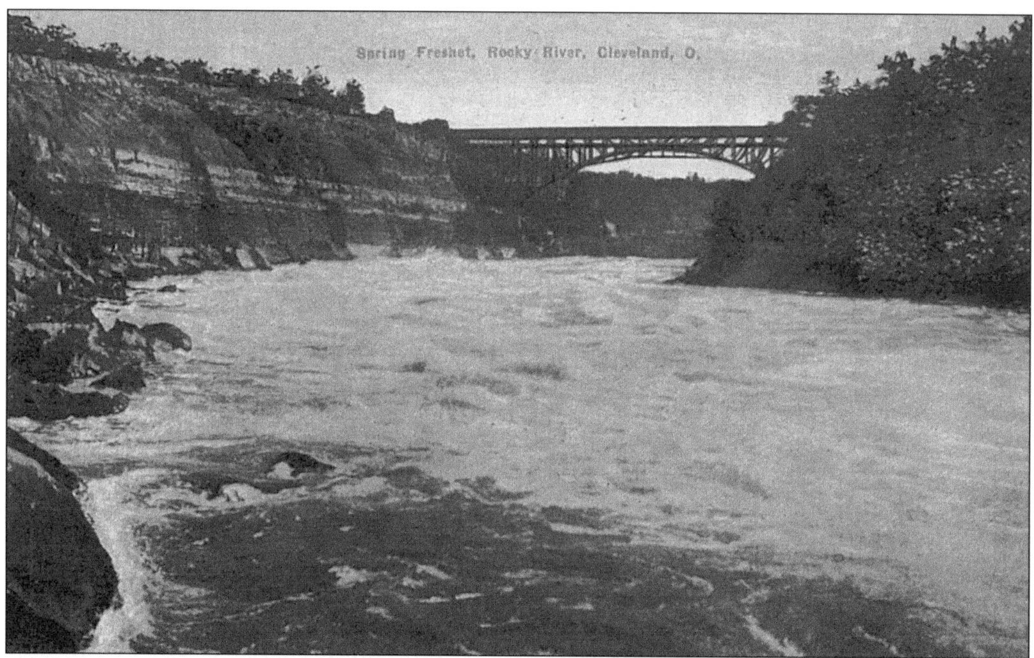

A raging Rocky River scene pre-1910 shows one of the early bridges in the background. The deep gorge was cut by glaciers during the Ice Age.

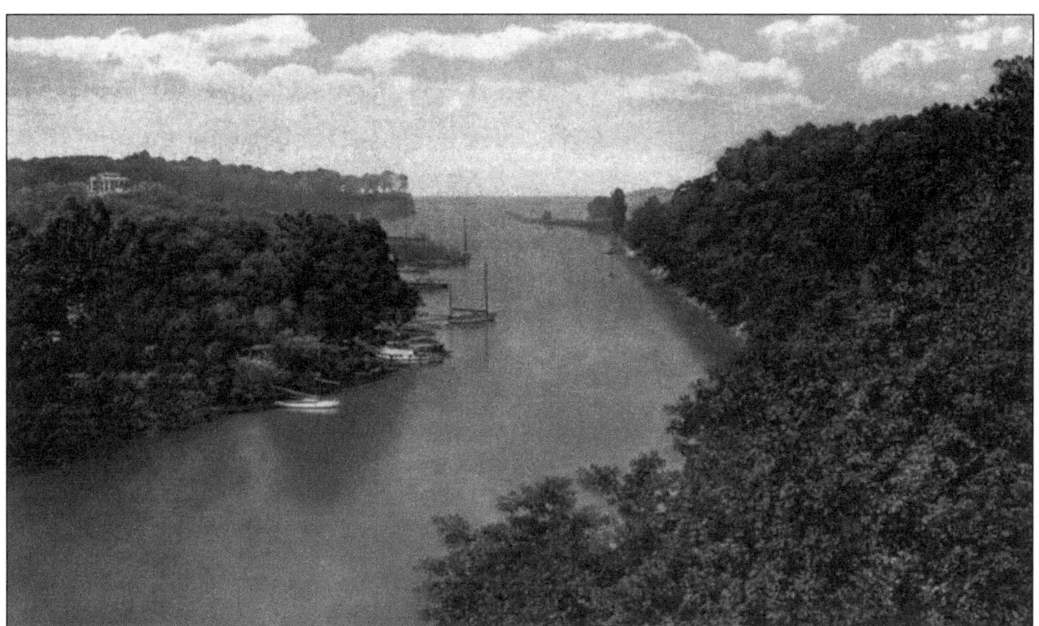

The Cleveland Yacht Club, founded in 1878, is pictured in its new (1914) location on the Rocky River. The club went bankrupt in 1918, but soon reorganized and is today once again flourishing along the Rocky River.

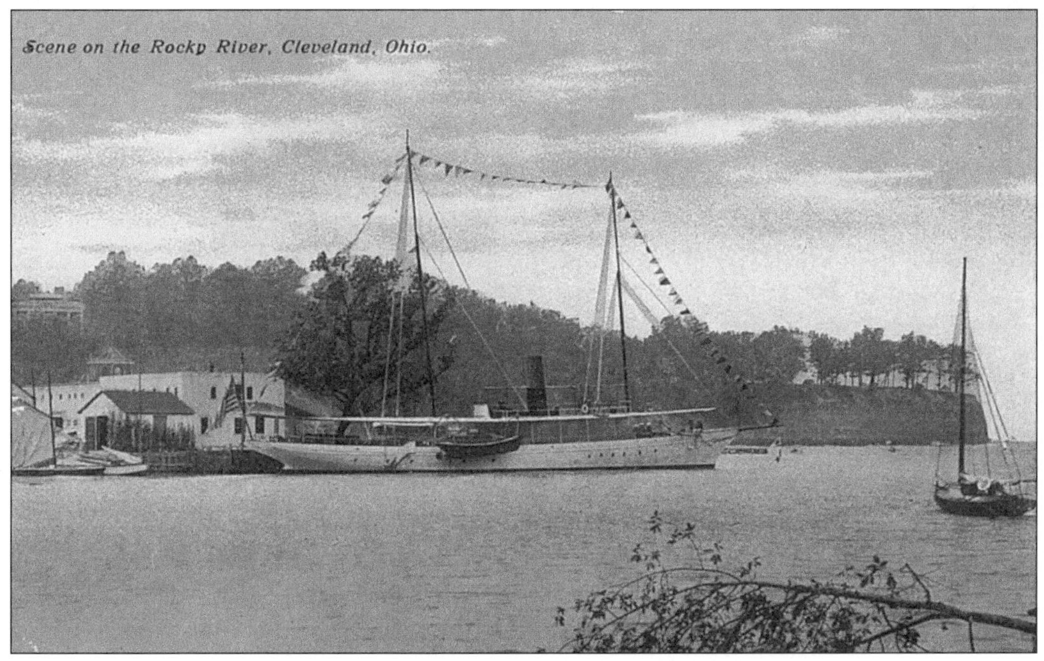

Here, a yacht with a dinghy docks near the mouth of the Rocky River.

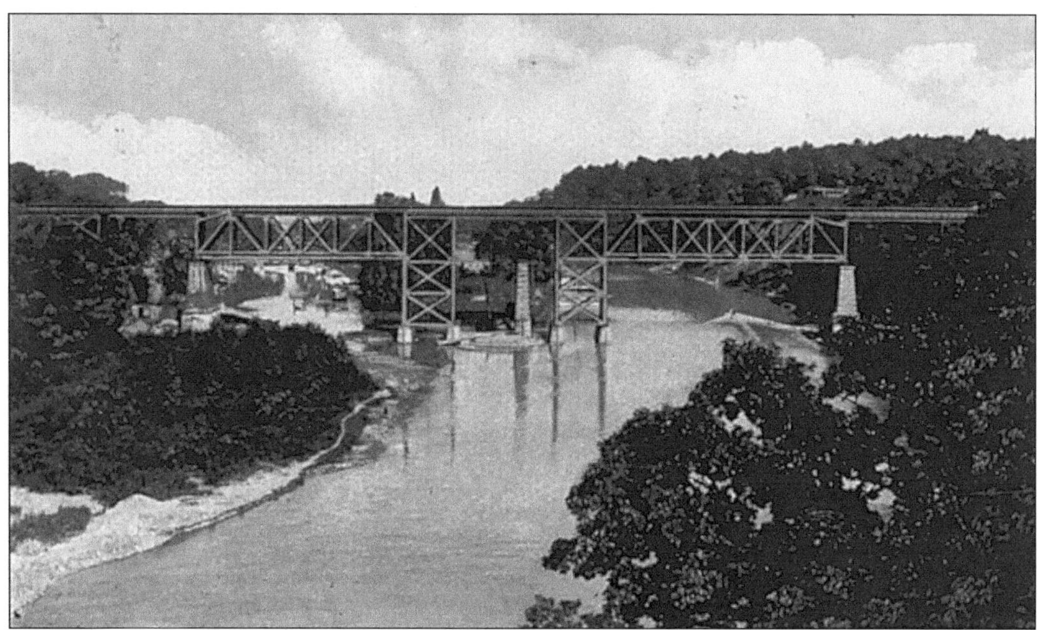

This view of the Rocky River looking north includes the railroad bridge.

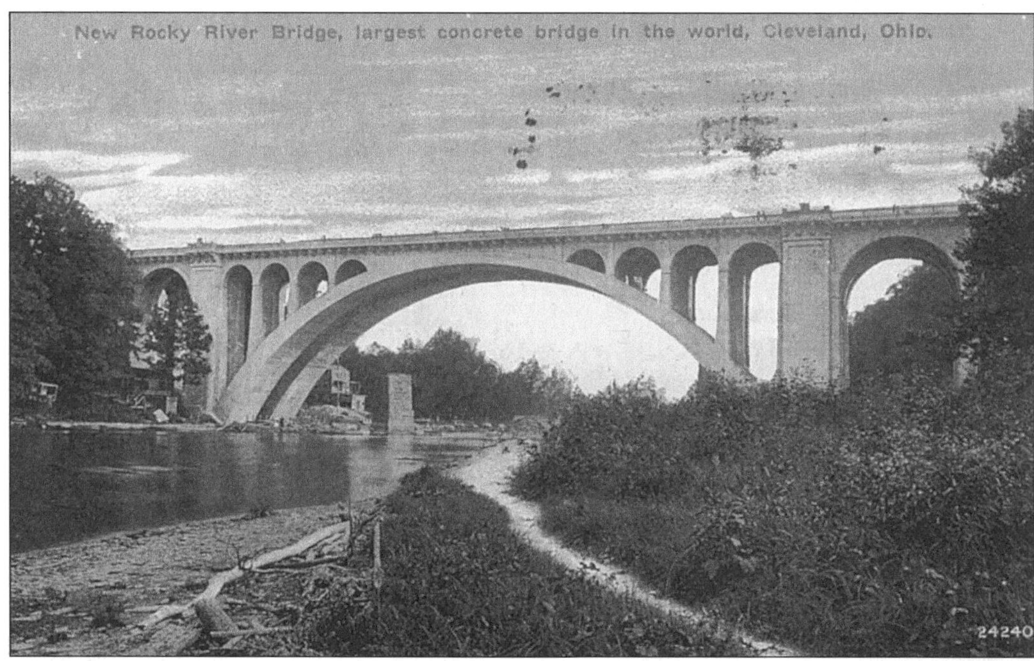

The Detroit–Rocky River Bridge, completed in 1910, had at the time the longest concrete arch in the country. The bridge carried auto traffic across the river until it was demolished in the 1980s and replaced by a new bridge.

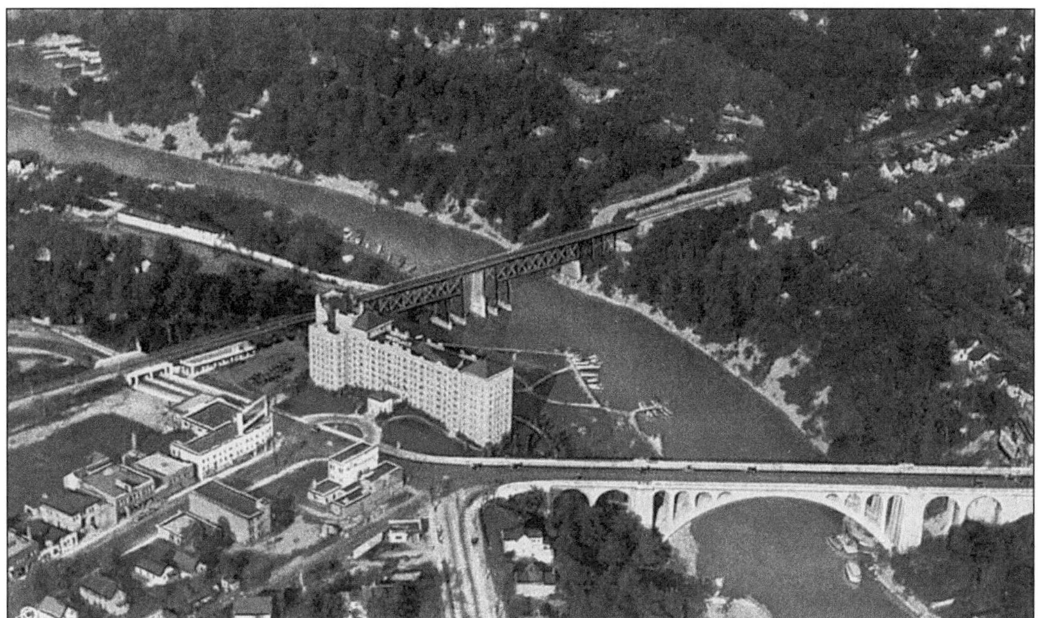

The Hotel Westlake (large building in the foreground) on the Rocky River hosted many famous personages during its heyday in the 1920s and 1930s, including Amelia Earhart and Wiley Post. The structure is now host to the luxury Westlake Condominiums.

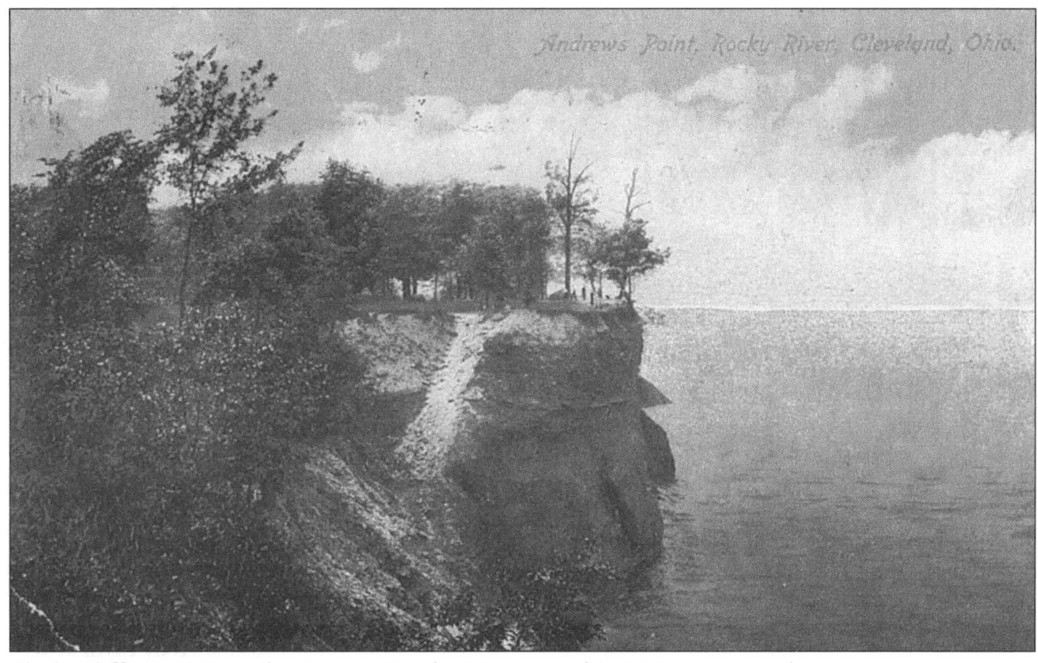

Shale cliffs jut into Lake Erie at Rocky River on this 1910 postcard.

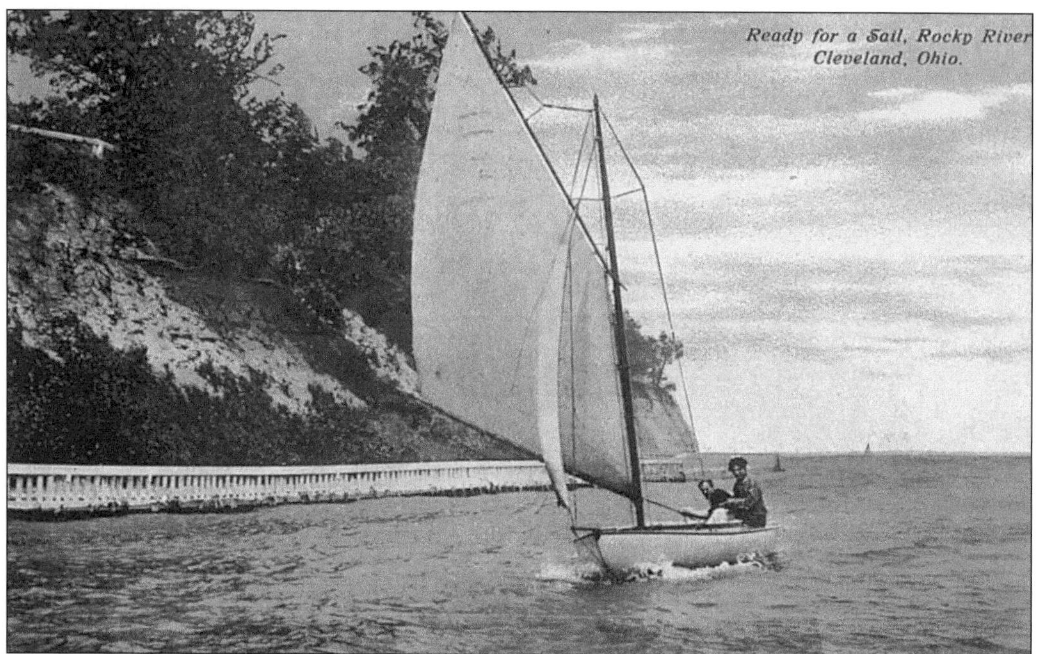

A sailboat is maneuvered into the Rocky River from Lake Erie in this 1912 scene. Sailboats were common pleasure craft in the days before motors, and were especially popular on the windy waters of Lake Erie.

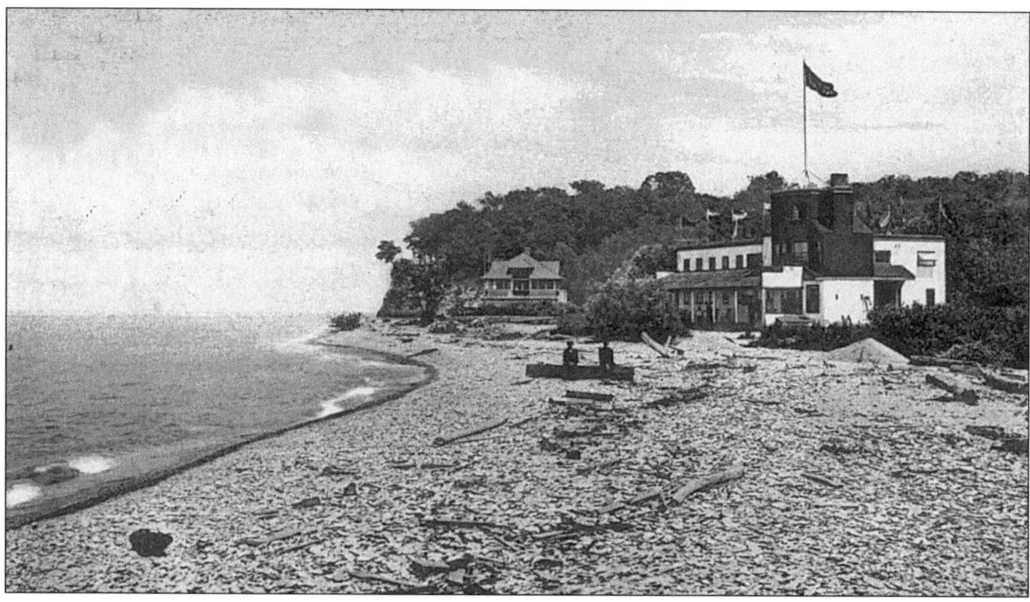

The Lakewood Yacht Club is shown here in this 1909 view. In 1914, the Cleveland Yacht Club clubhouse was towed from the East Ninth Street Pier to the Rocky River and combined with the Lakewood clubhouse, which became its dining room. The two clubs had merged in 1913.

Three

THE FLATS AND HARBOR

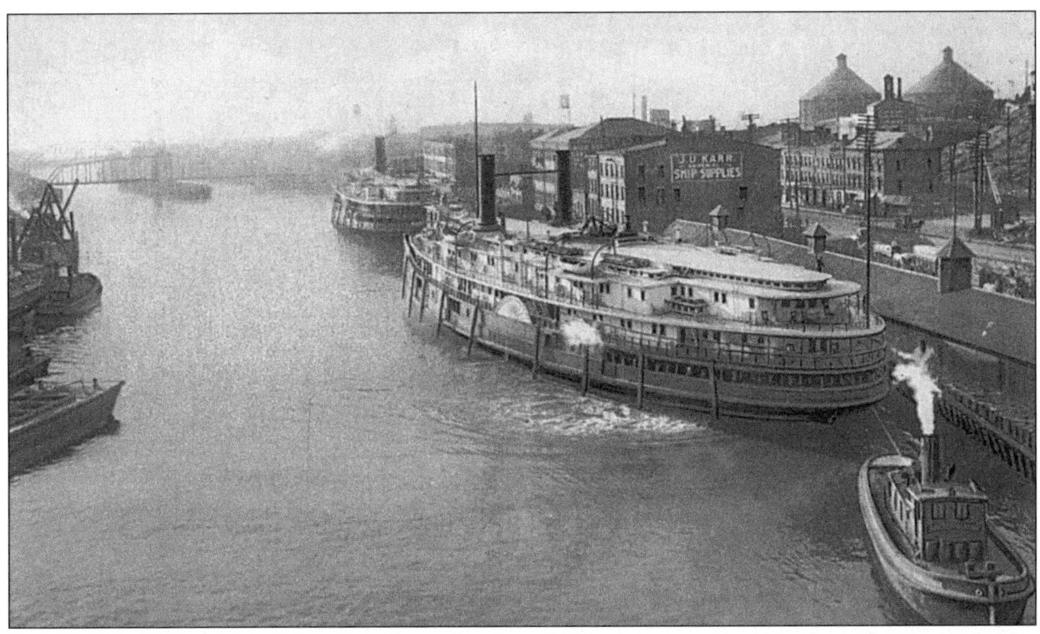

A view of the Flats from Central Viaduct includes steamers at dock and others being towed by tug up the Cuyahoga River. The city originally developed in this area. Long dominated by industry, the Flats is now a popular entertainment district, drawing millions of visitors a year to its eclectic mix of restaurants, bars, and clubs.

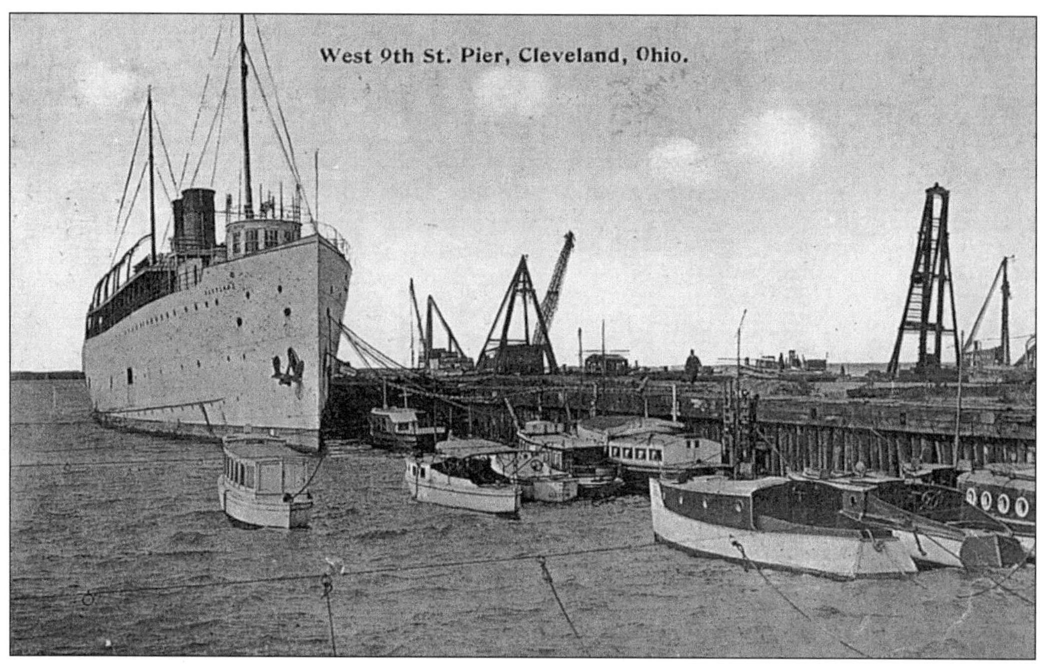

The old West Ninth Street Pier was a busy spot for commercial shipping, as well as pleasure boating. In this image the passenger steamer *Eastland* is at the dock.

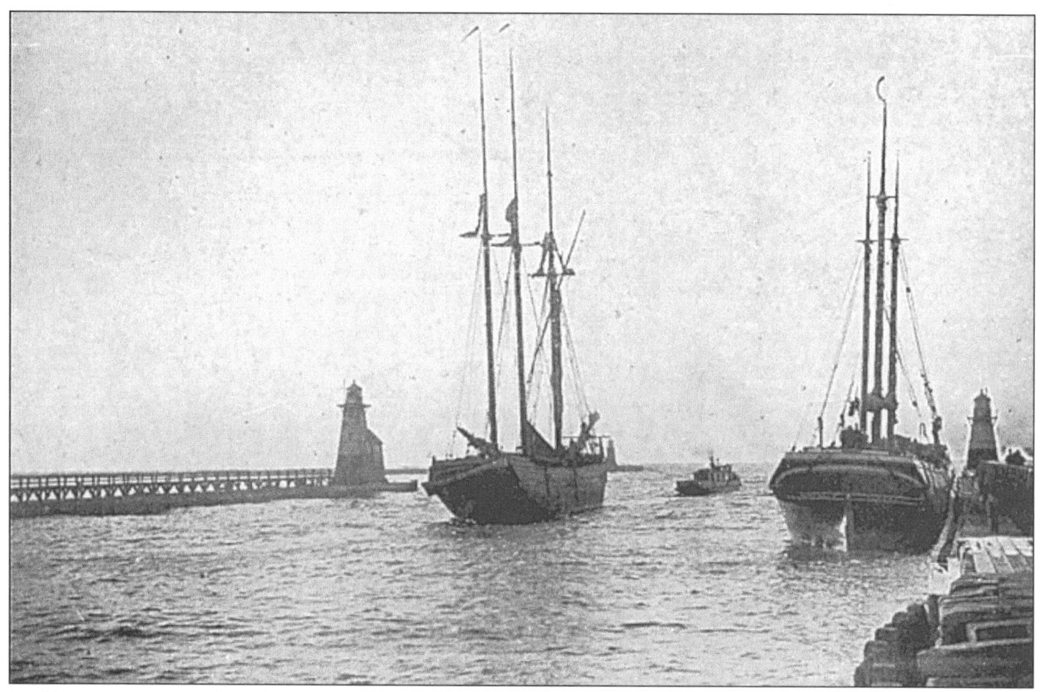

Sailboats enter Cleveland Harbor in the early 1900s, a reminder of the recreational aspect of the river then as now.

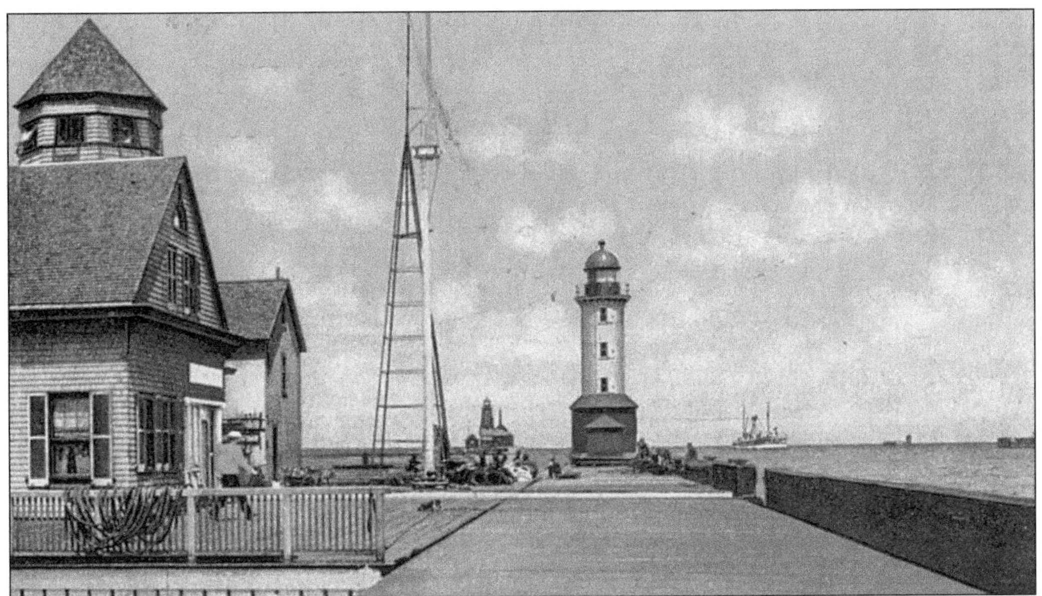

The East Pier light (foreground) and West Pier light (background) guide ships into the Cleveland Harbor entrance in this 1907 scene. These lighthouses pre-date the current Cleveland harbor lights, which were built in 1911.

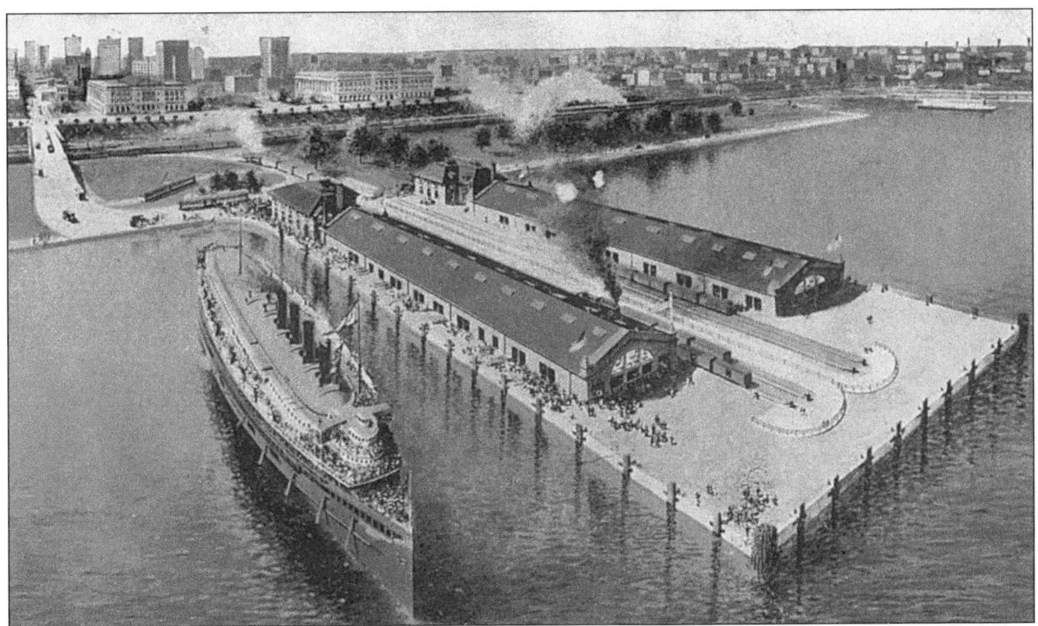

The large terminals of the C & B (Cleveland and Buffalo) and D & C (Detroit and Cleveland) steamship lines, previously located in the Flats, moved to the new East Ninth Street Pier in 1915. Rail lines also had a spur on the pier.

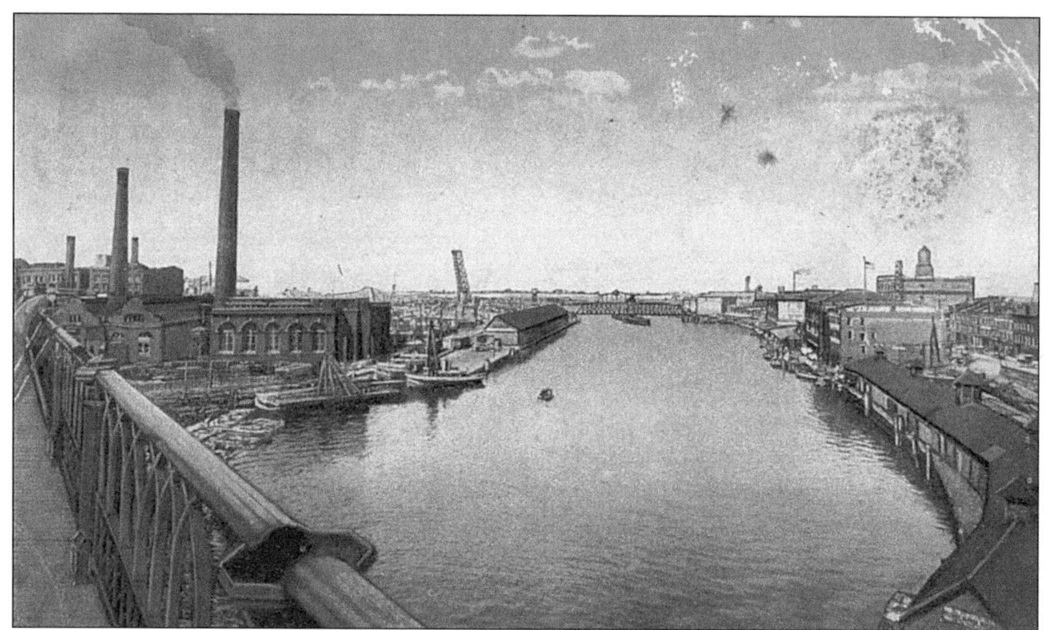

The Powerhouse, at left, was constructed in 1892 by industrialist Mark Hanna to power the streetcars he owned. The predominance of the automobile by the 1920s forced its closing in 1931. Today the landmark structure is the centerpiece of the Nautica entertainment complex in the Flats.

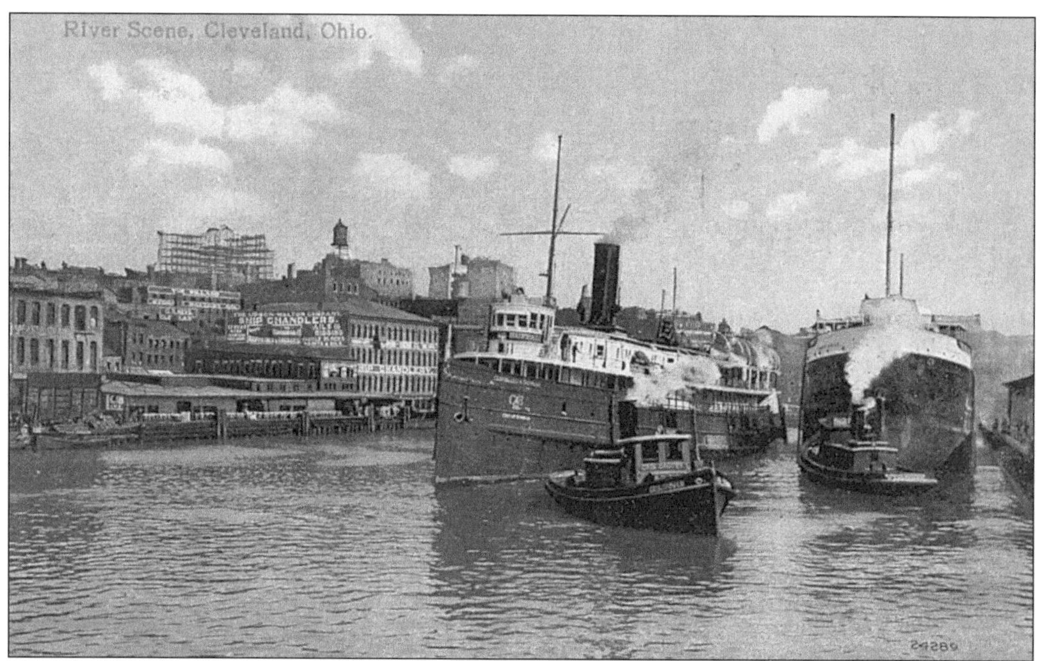

The *City of Buffalo* (at left) is being pulled by a tug in this 1906 postcard. The steamer was part of the popular Cleveland and Buffalo (C & B) transit line, founded in 1885. Destruction of the boat by fire in 1938 helped cause the bankruptcy and liquidation of the C & B line in 1939.

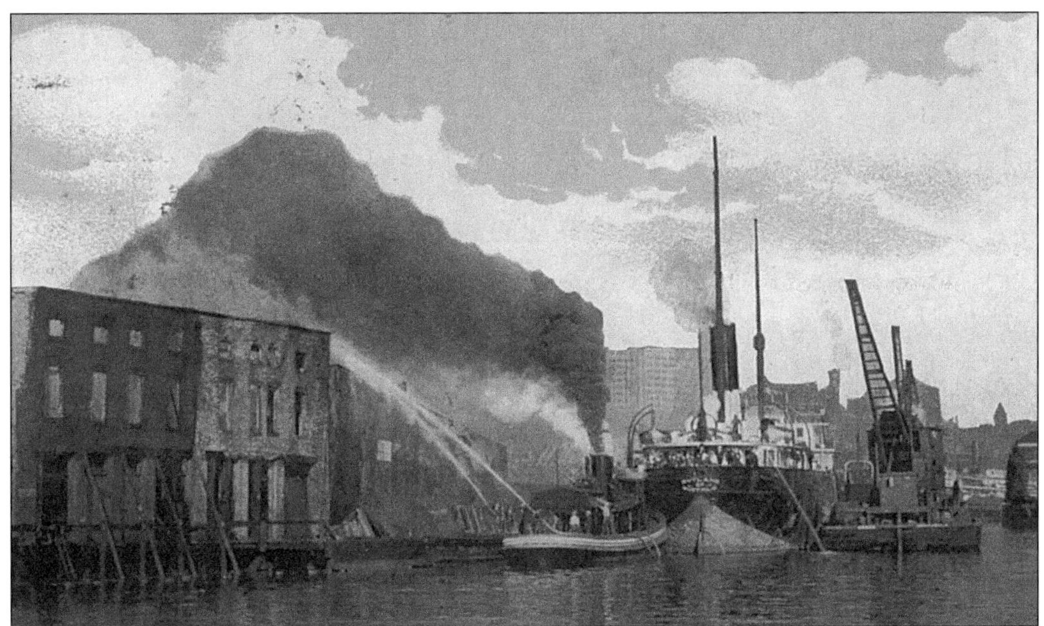

A fireboat squelches a blaze in the Flats. The bulk of the smoke appears to be coming from the boat.

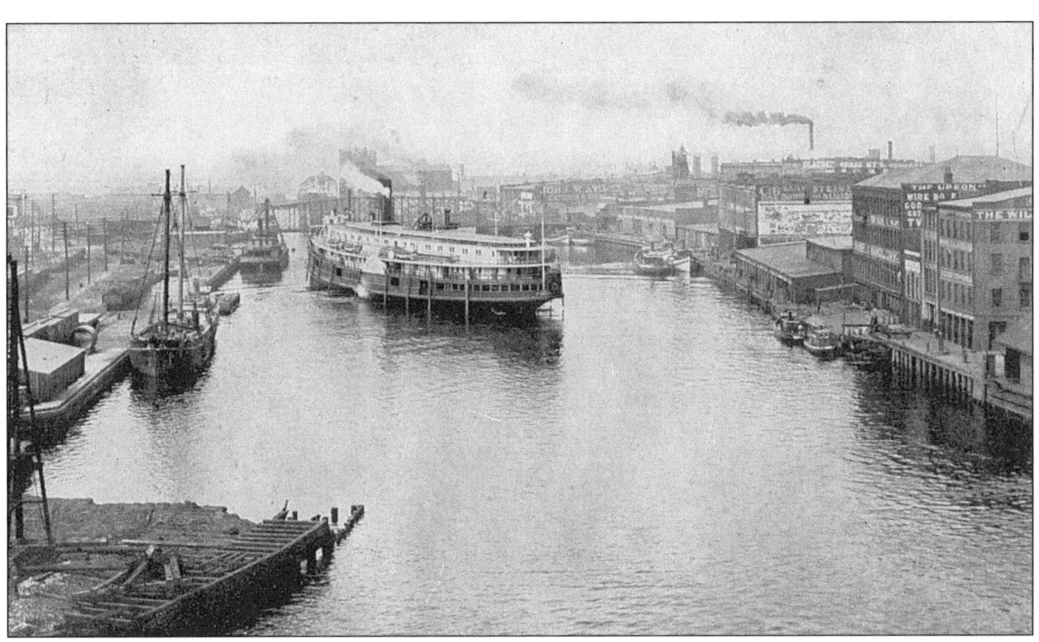

This view of the Flats shows the diversity of shipping and industry in the area. The Flats was home to iron foundries, lumber yards, ship chandlers, flour and rolling mills, metalworking firms, and paint and chemical factories, as well as steamboat and rail facilities. It was a very active place in this photo taken shortly after the turn of the century.

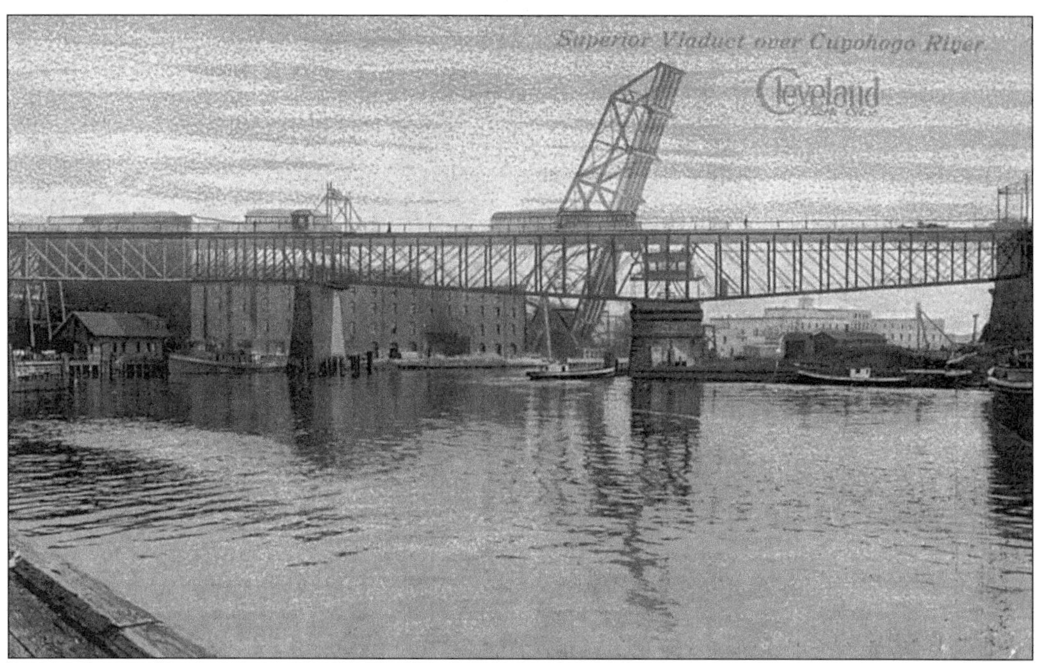

The huge Superior Viaduct, opened in 1878, was Cleveland's first "high level" bridge.

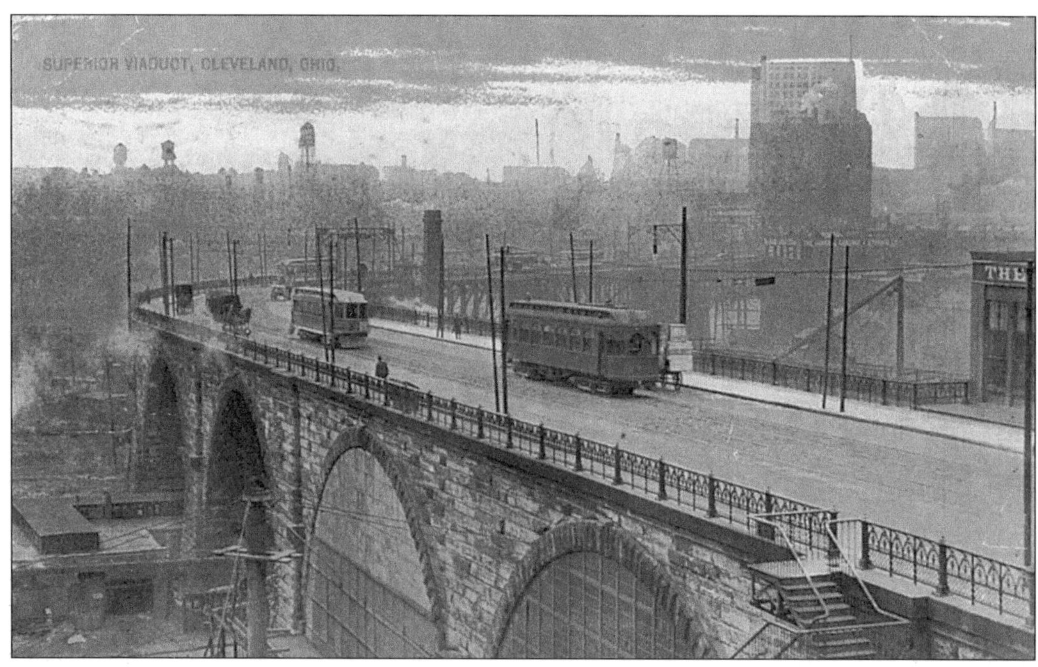

The Superior Viaduct served until 1918, when it was replaced by Veterans Memorial Bridge.

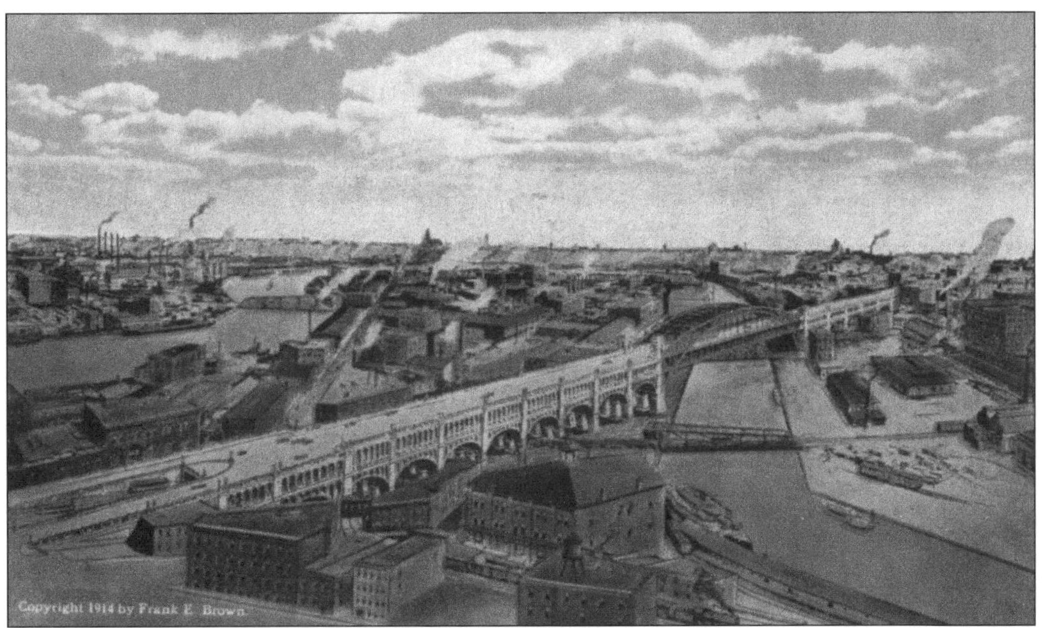

A bird's-eye view of the Flats shows the Cuyahoga River, Ohio Canal, and the Superior Avenue Bridge.

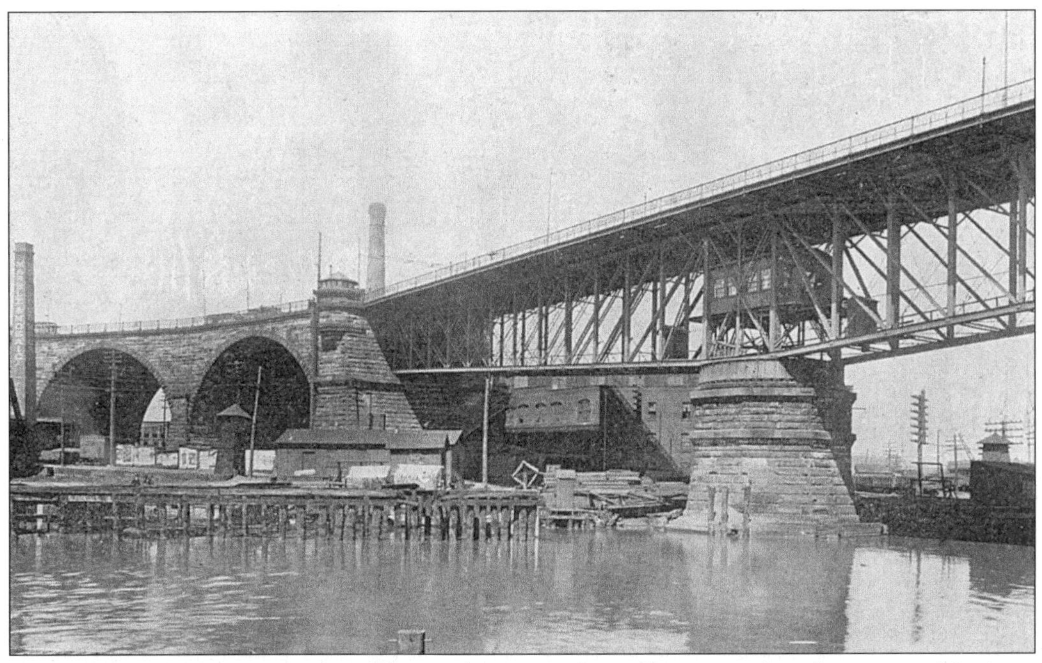

A close-up of the auto viaduct shows the stone foundations and archways, and its iron span. The Central Viaduct bridge was the major artery connecting Cleveland's east and west sides.

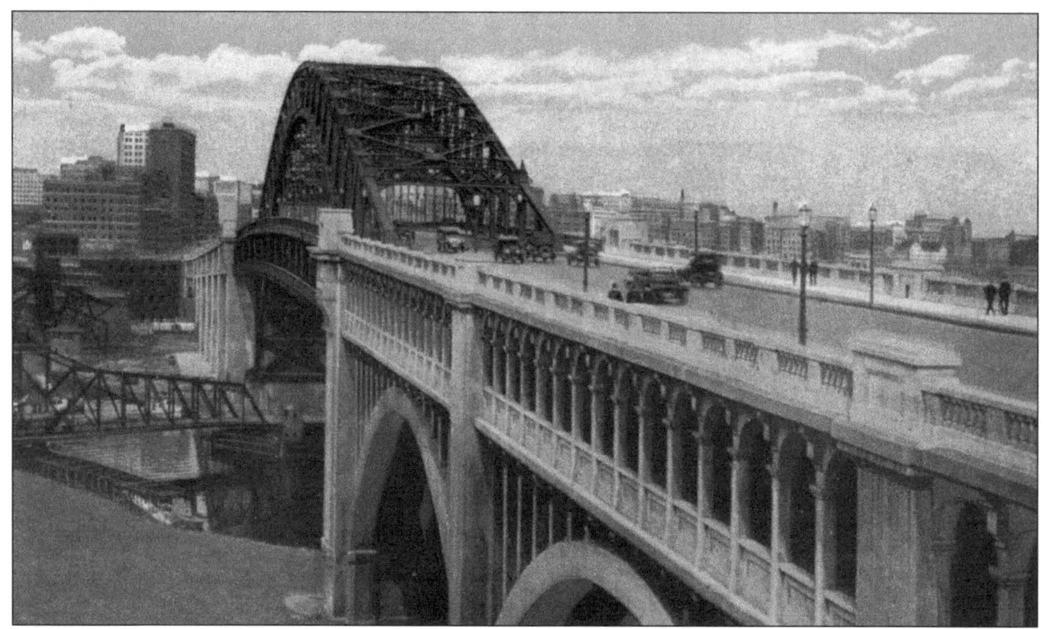

The High Level Bridge, also known as Veteran's Memorial and Detroit–Superior Bridge, opened in 1918, replacing the Superior Viaduct.

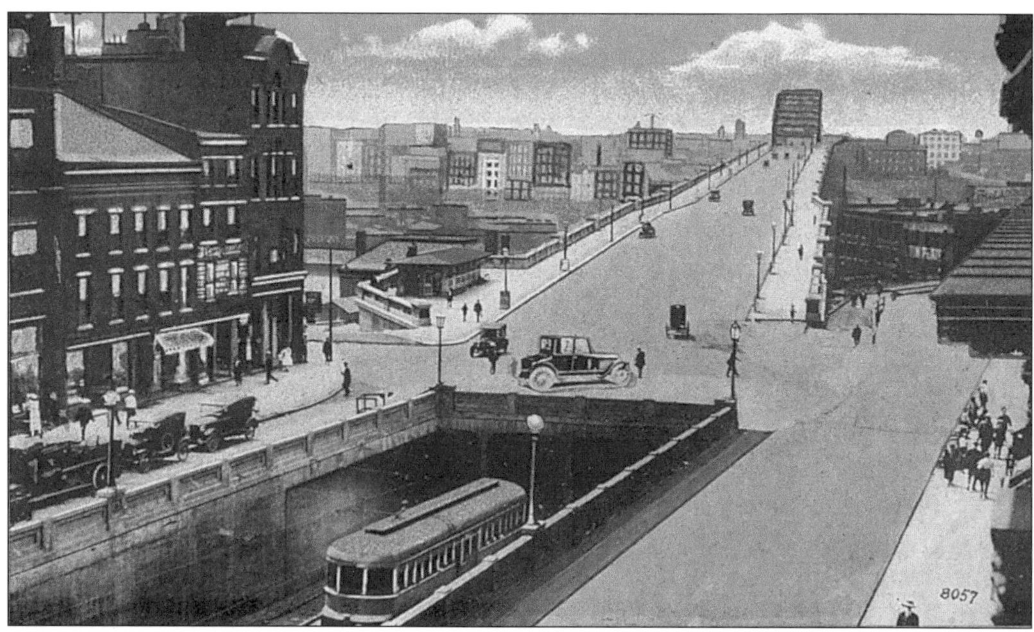

This streetcar "subway" was actually a second bridge underneath the auto bridge.

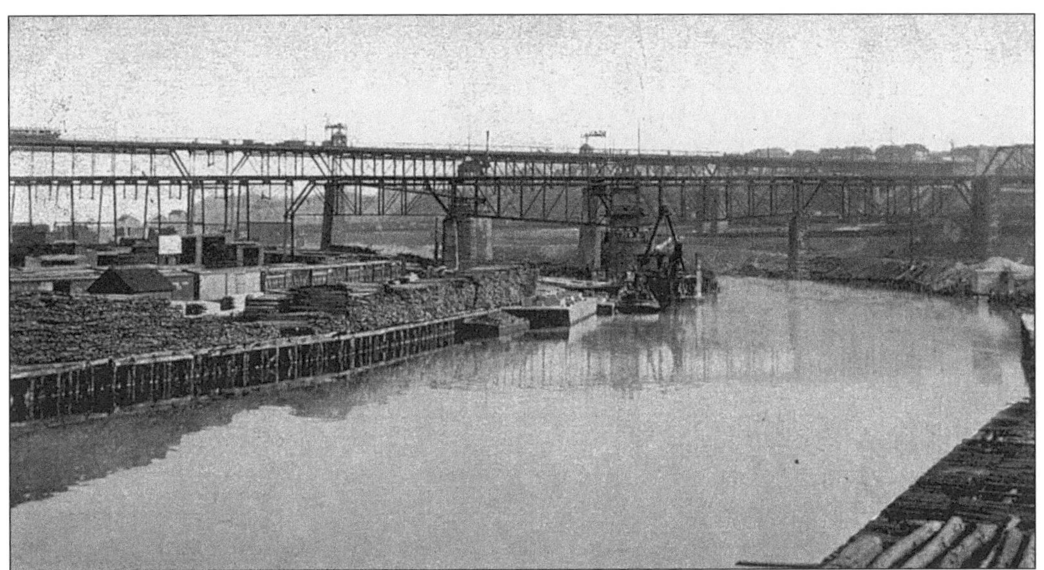

The Central Viaduct, opened in 1888, spanned the Cuyahoga with two steel bridges at the spot of the current Inner Belt (I-90) Bridge. The bridge closed in 1941. This 1903 card asks "Do you recognize this place? I do not."

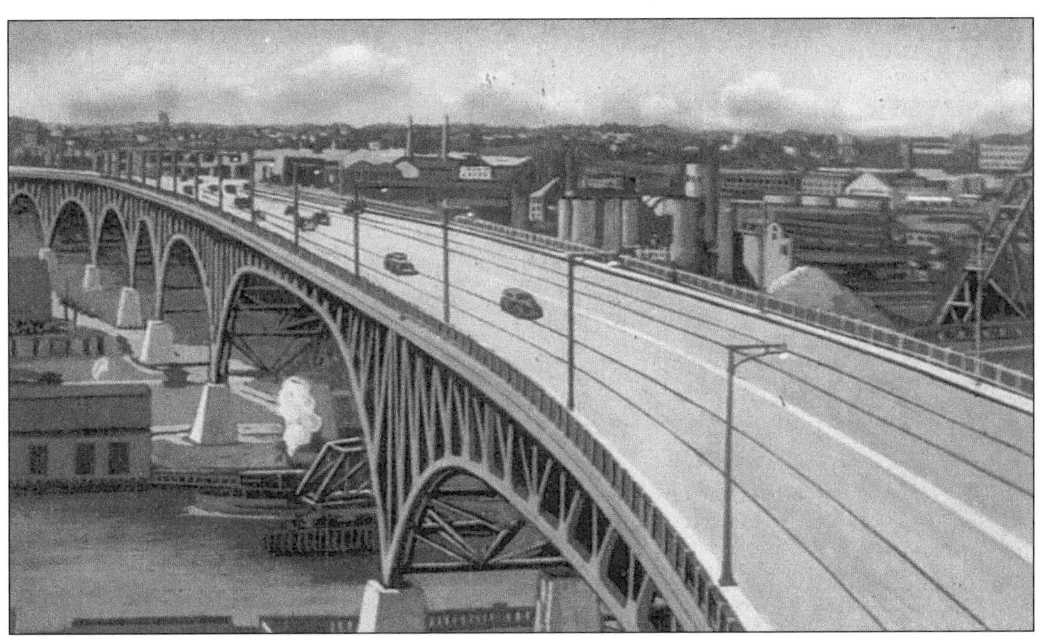

The Main Avenue Bridge, completed in 1939, is a major east-west connector, spanning the Cuyahoga over the Flats.

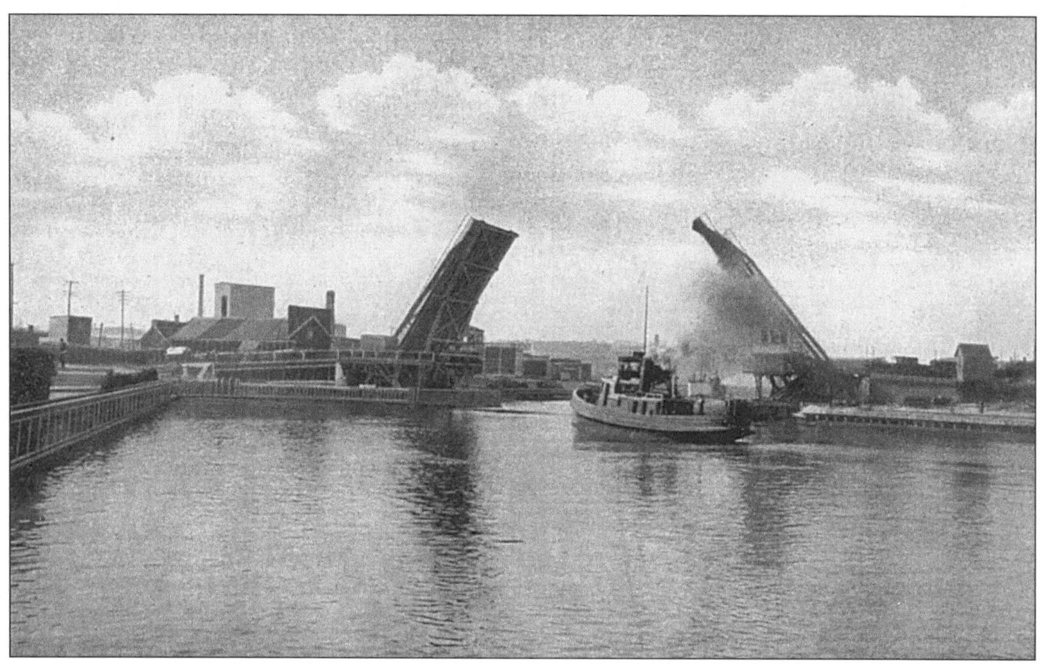

A tug passes through one of Cleveland's famous "jackknife" bridges in this Cuyahoga River scene. The Flats is home to some 16 bridges, eight of which have been beautifully floodlighted by GE as a part of Cleveland's Bicentennial celebration in 1996.

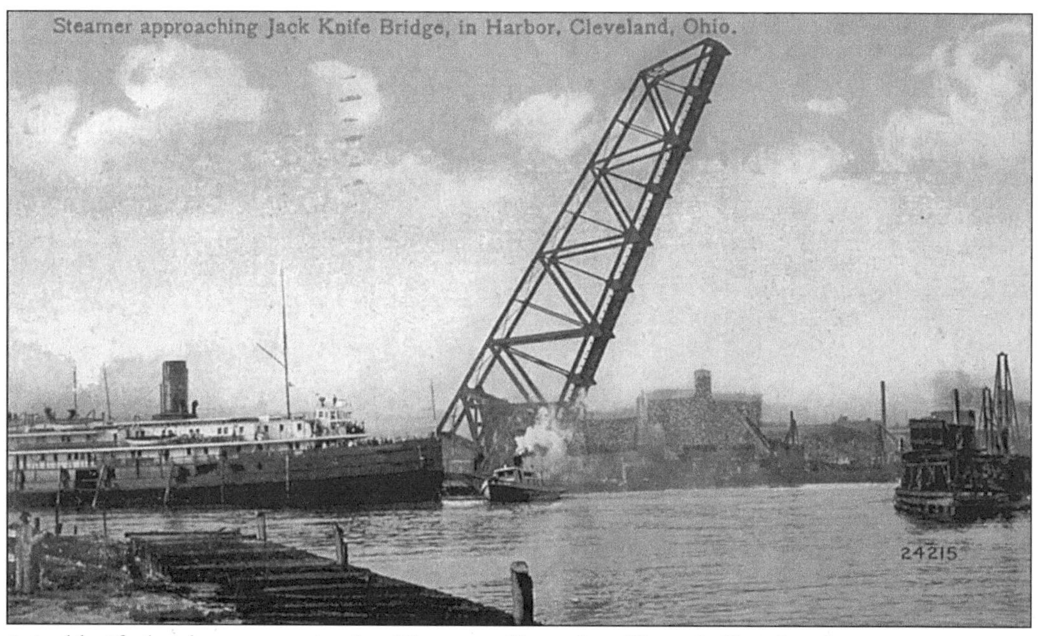

A jackknife bridge opens in the Flats to allow the *City of Cleveland* steamer to pass through.

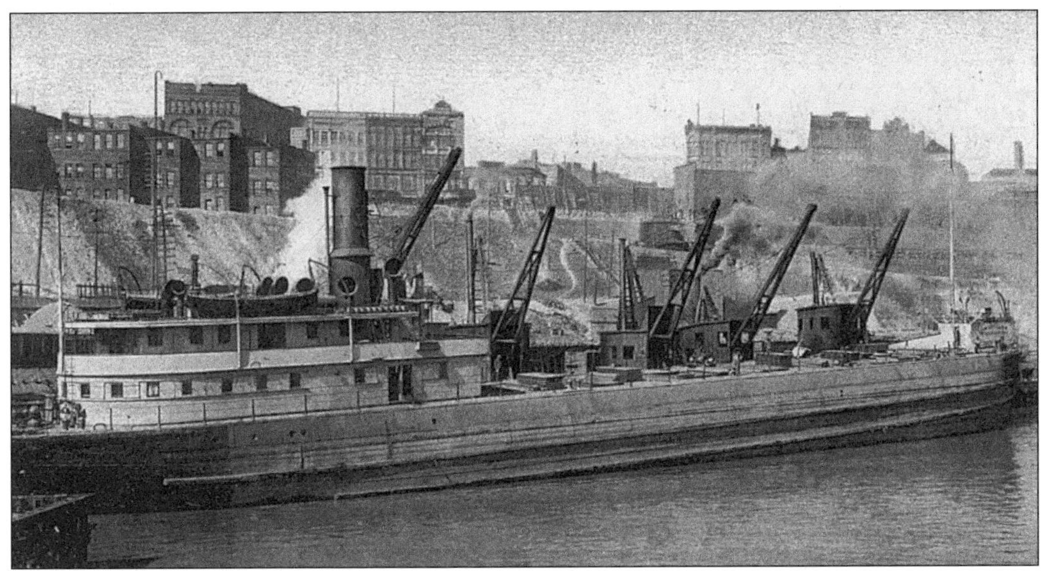

An ore boat unloads its cargo, feeding the metalworking industry on the Cuyahoga River flats in 1907.

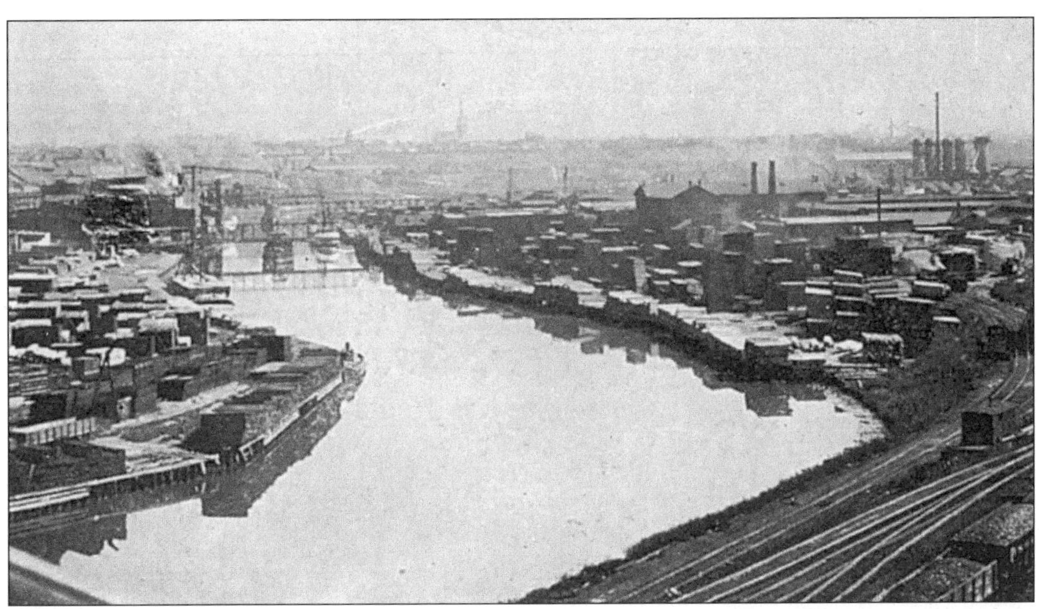

Serving the nation's demand for wood, lumber was a major Cleveland export in the 1800s and early 1900s. An 1852 canal report showed about eight million feet being shipped that year. The 1860 census showed lumber and clothing heading the industrial classifications for Cuyahoga County. In 1911, shipments of lumber and timber products were valued at more than $4 million.

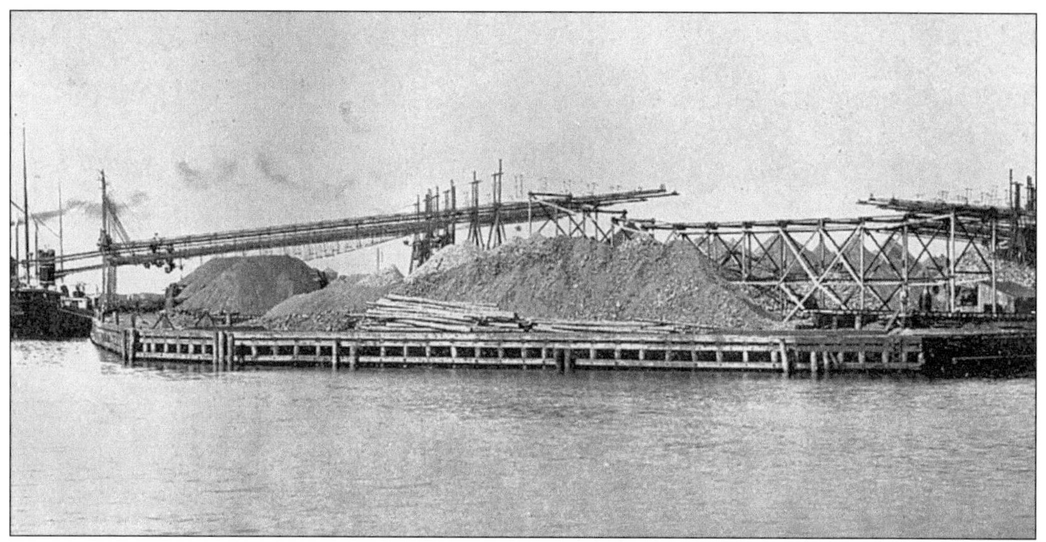

Iron ore, brought by the ore boats from Lake Superior, provided the fuel for Cleveland's iron and steel smelters.

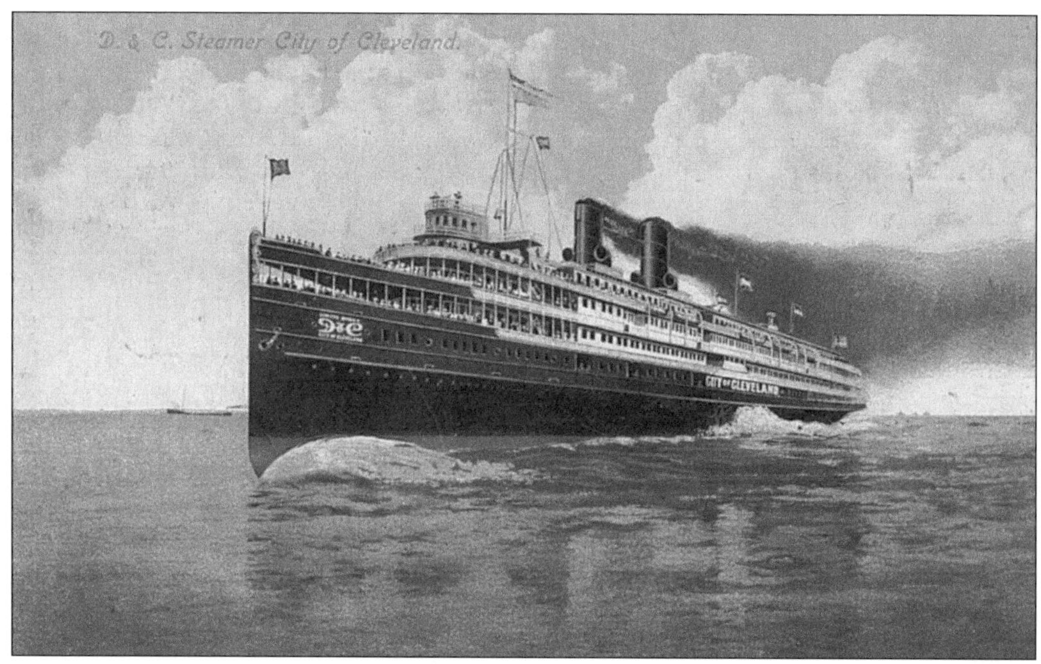

The luxurious *City of Cleveland III* passenger steamer is pictured navigating Lake Erie. It was a popular member of the D & C (Detroit and Cleveland) fleet.

Four

PUBLIC SQUARE

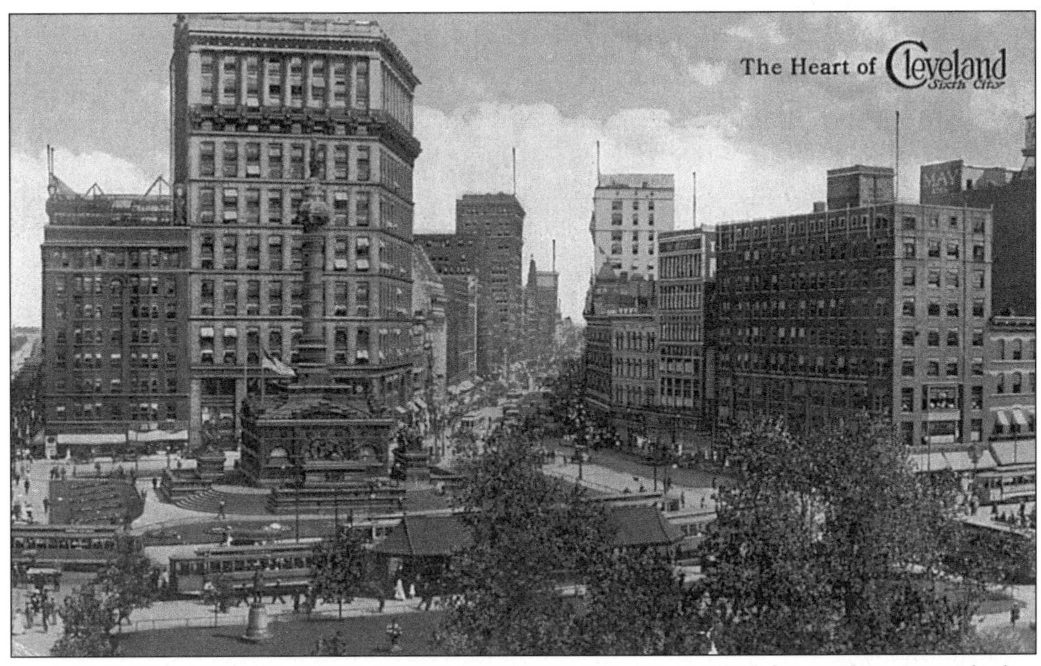

At the center of the city of Cleveland, Public Square was called for in the original plan for the Village of Cleveland in 1796. It was conceived as a place for cattle grazing and public gatherings. Monuments erected in the area resulted in the square being renamed Monument Park for a time in the mid-1800s.

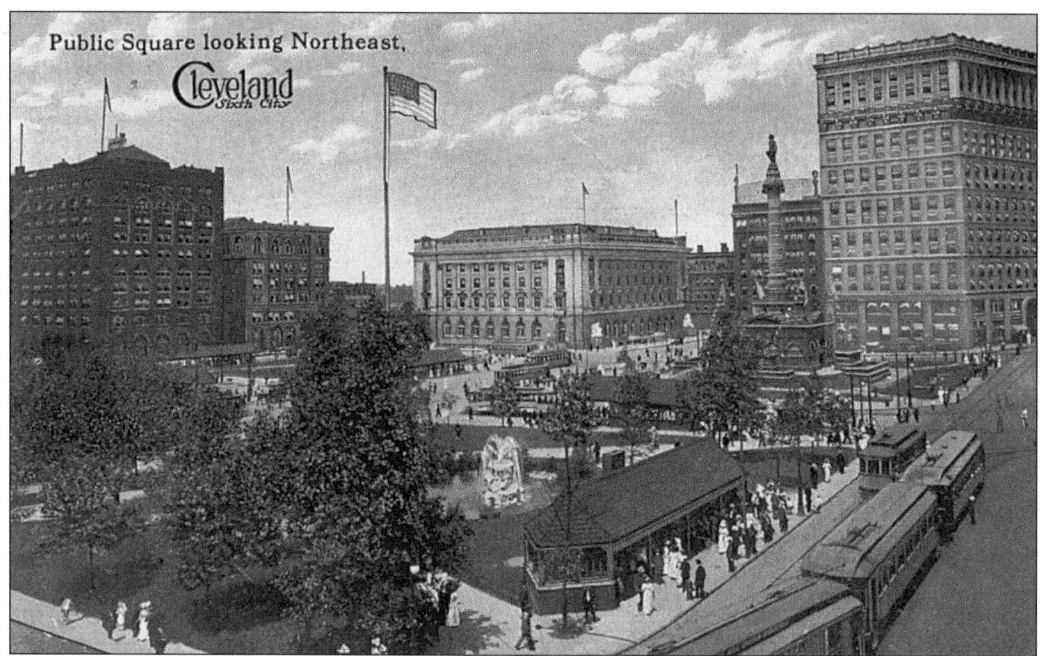

Public Square was the terminus of Superior and Ontario Streets, as well as for Cleveland's streetcar lines. A number of the city's most prominent buildings fronted the Square. Note that Cleveland was already the nation's sixth largest city in 1913.

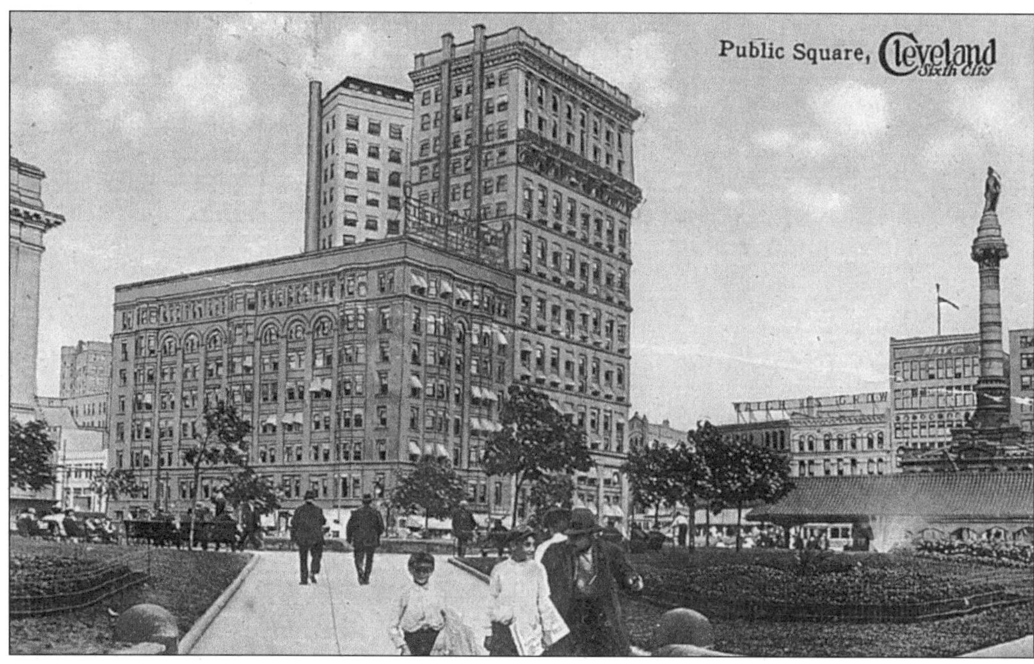

A view of Public Square looking Southeast includes the Williamson Building (Cleveland's tallest building), built in 1900.

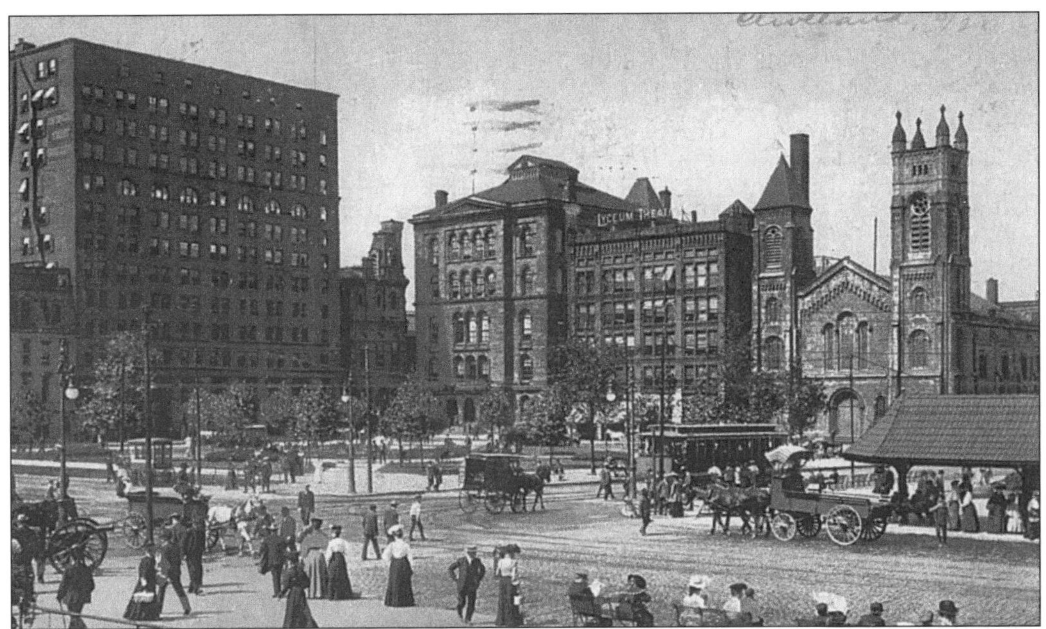

The Old Stone Church (First Presbyterian) at the right, erected in 1853, is the oldest existing structure on Public Square.

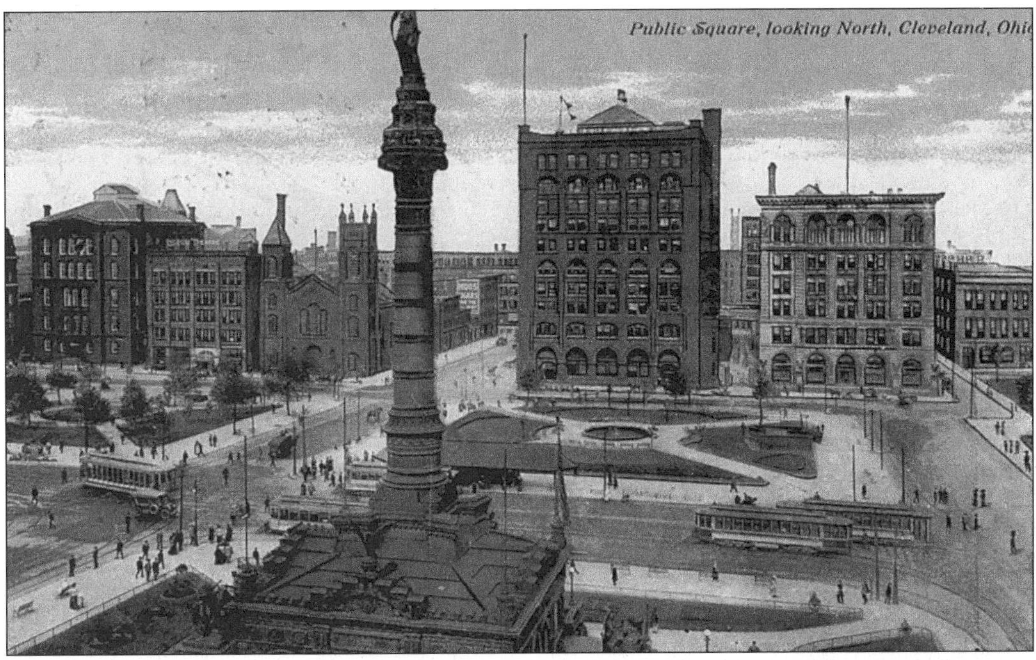

Soldiers and Sailors Monument, honoring Civil War dead, is Public Square's most dominant structure. It has graced the Square since 1894. The monument, as described in *Picturesque Cleveland* (1890s), was "the finest military monument west of New York. It was designed by Cleveland captain Levi T. Scofield, built of Ohio sandstone, and its entire cost was raised by direct taxation."

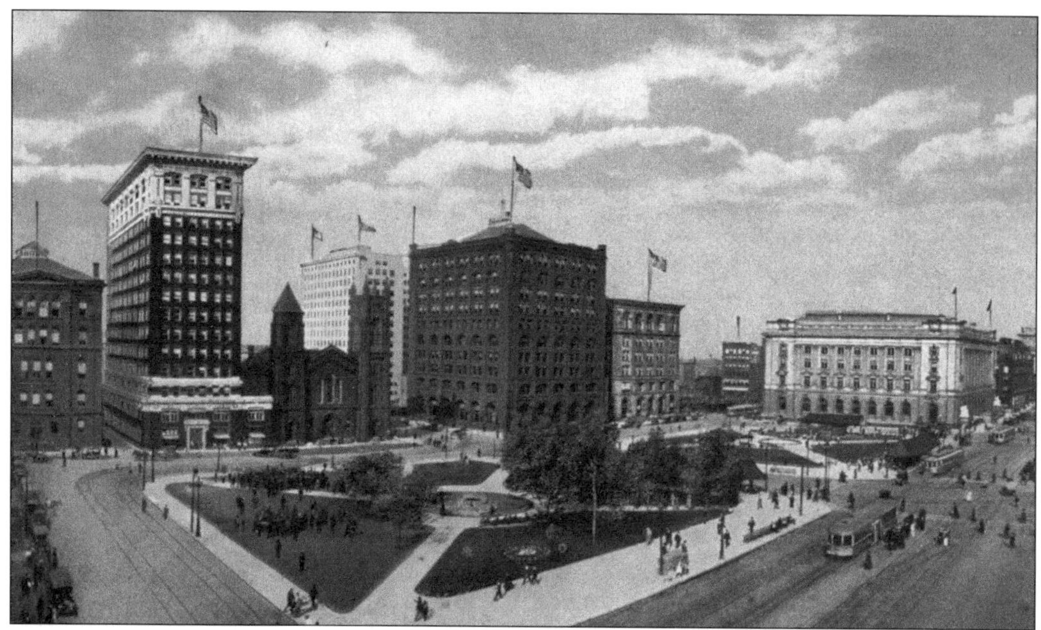

This scene, together with the one on the opposite page, gives a panoramic view of Public Square in 1918. Looking northeast, from left to right, are: the old courthouse, Cleveland Electric Illuminating Company, Old Stone Church, Society for Savings, Chamber of Commerce, and the Post Office.

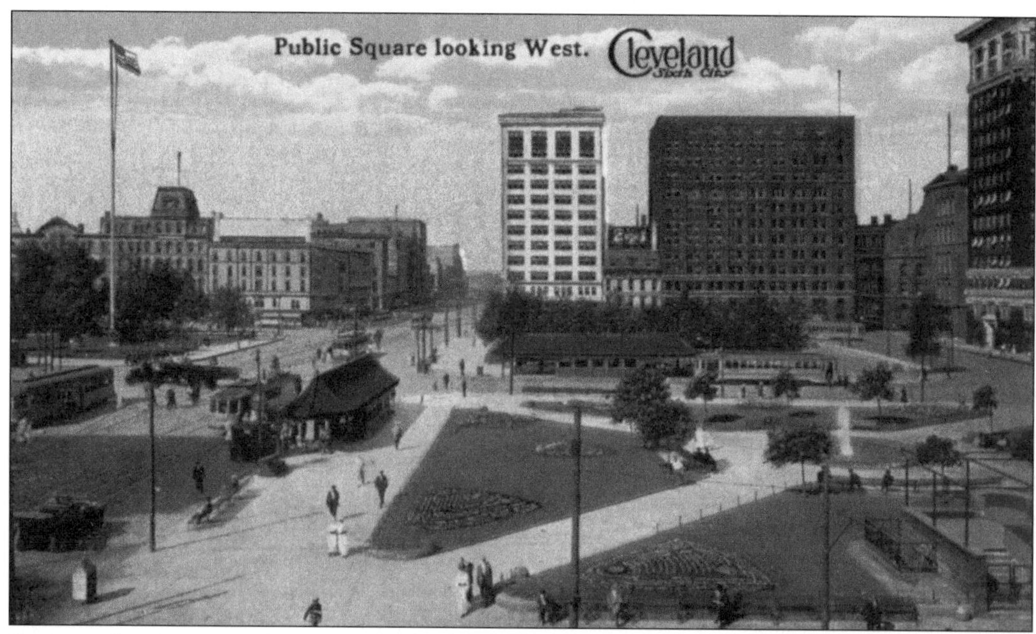

Spring plantings can be seen in this 1914 view looking west. Left to right facing the Square are Forest City House, the Marshall Building, and the American Trust Building.

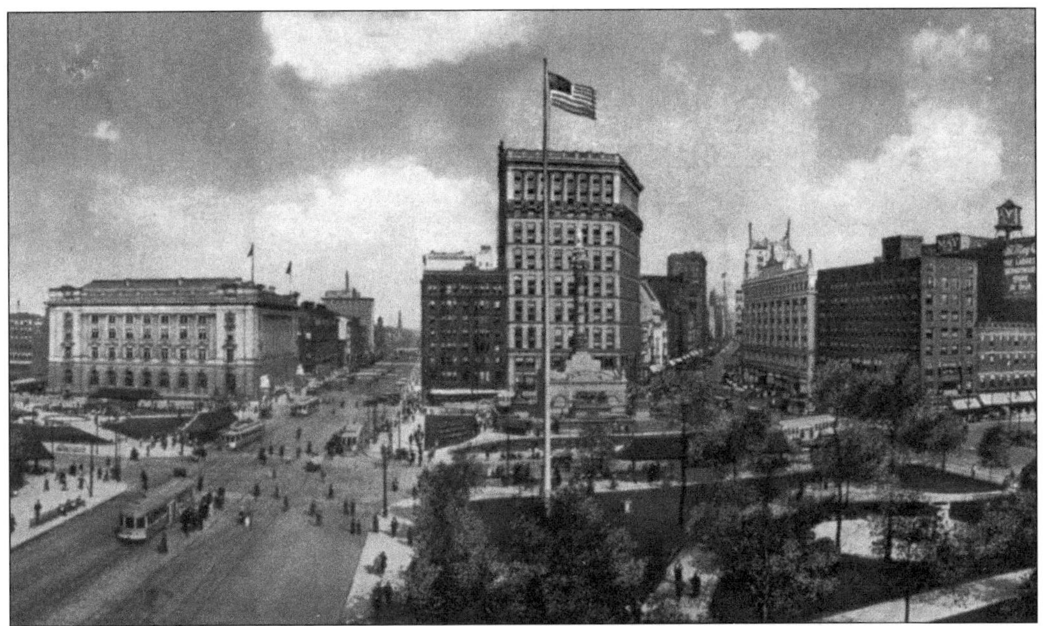

Looking east, this scene includes the Post Office with City Hall behind it, the Cuyahoga Building and Williamson Building in the center, and the May Company and Park Building at the right, facing the Square.

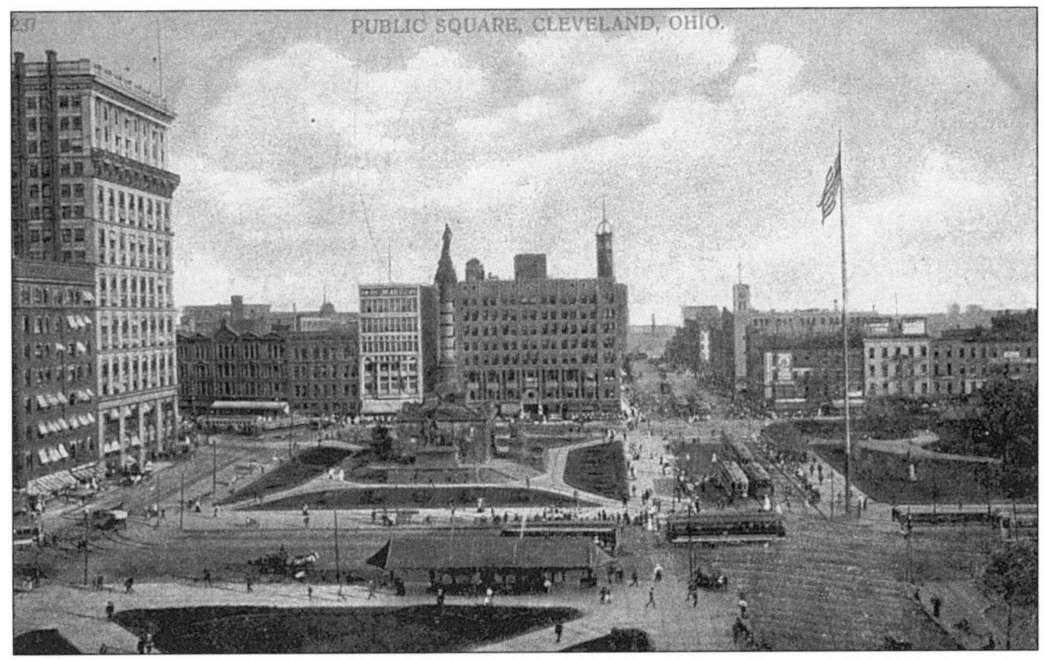

Looking south, the May Company and Park Building can be seen facing the monument. To the right is the spot where Terminal Tower now stands.

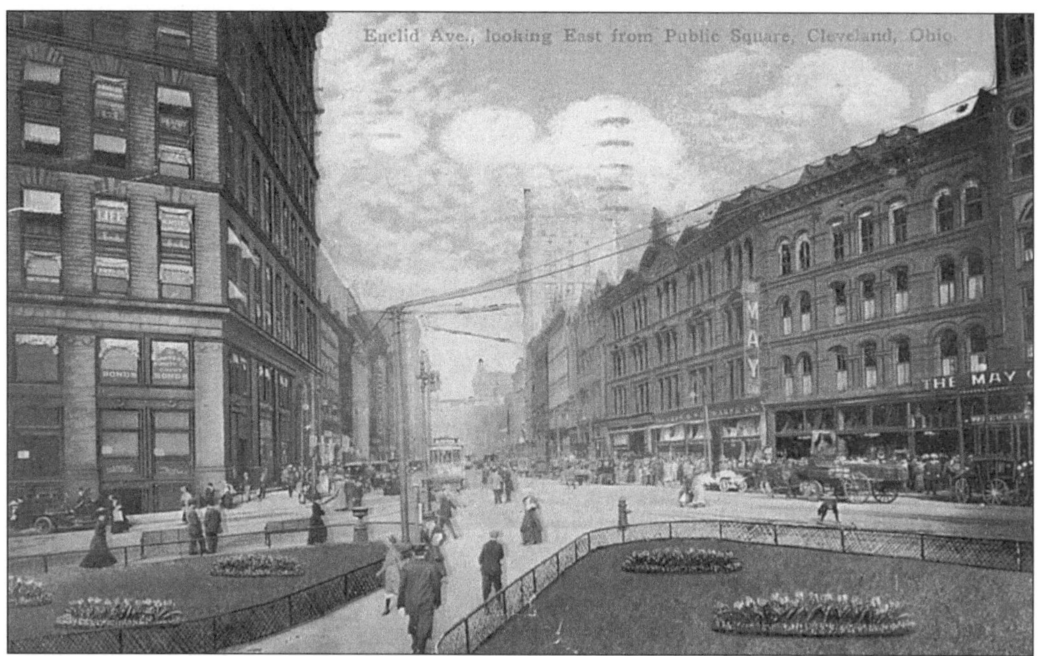

Euclid Avenue originates here, at Public Square. The old May Co. Building can be seen on the right.

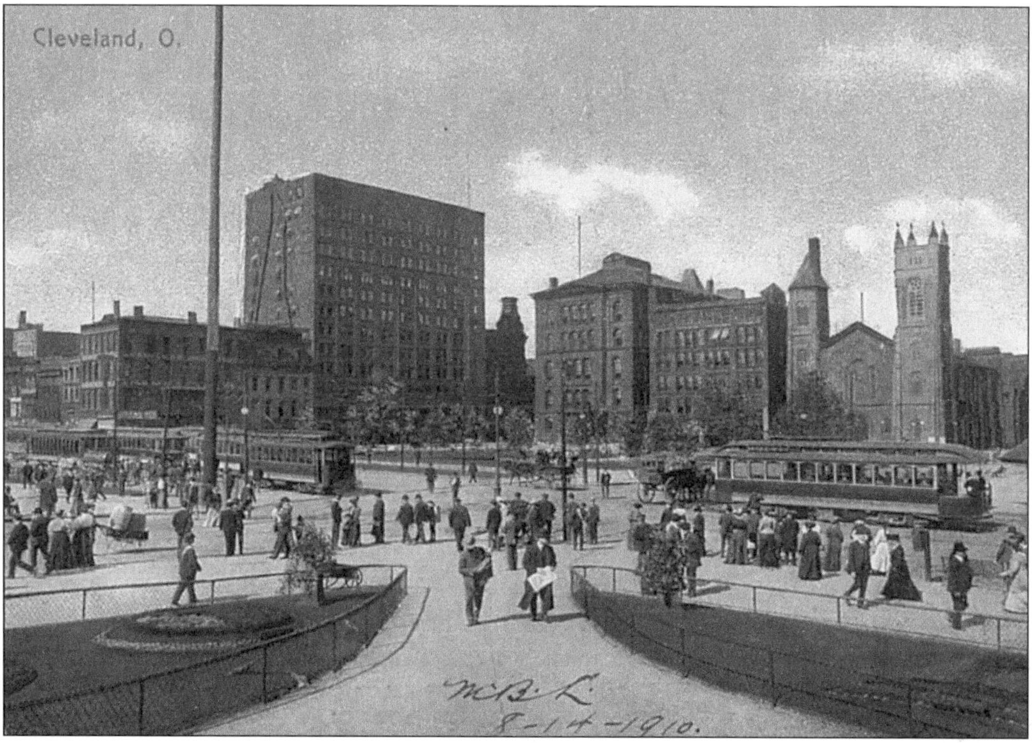

Streetcars and trolleys, as well as horse-drawn carriages, crowd Public Square in this 1910 scene.

Soldiers and Sailors Monument, dedicated July 4, 1894, dominates the Square. The original May Company department store, built in 1899, can be seen in the background.

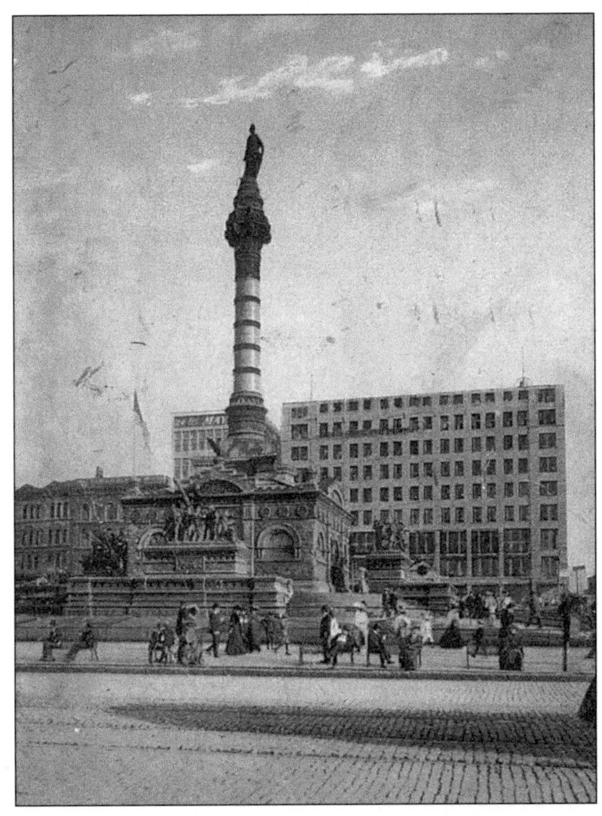

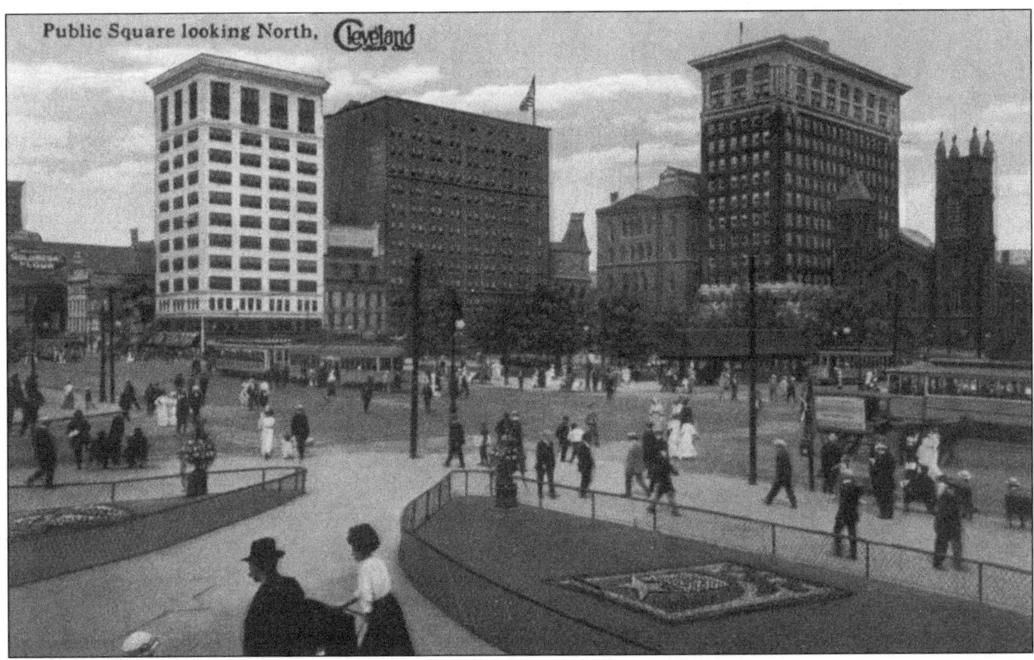

Streetlights can be seen in this view of the Square looking north. Cleveland's Public Square was the scene of the first demonstration of electric streetlighting in 1879.

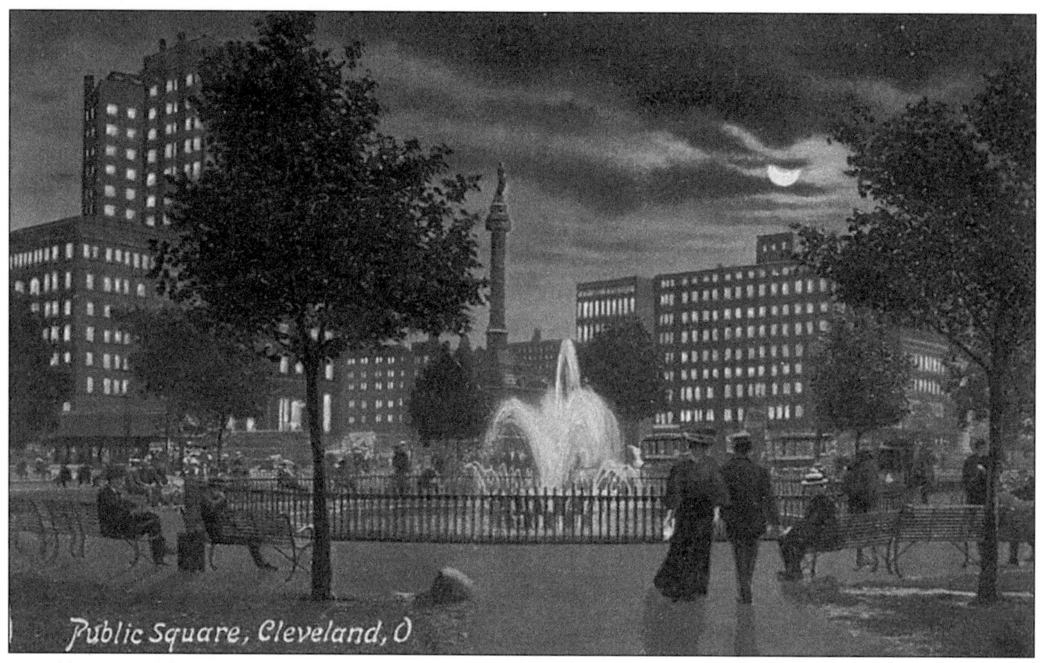

Strollers and loungers enjoy a moonlit summer's night.

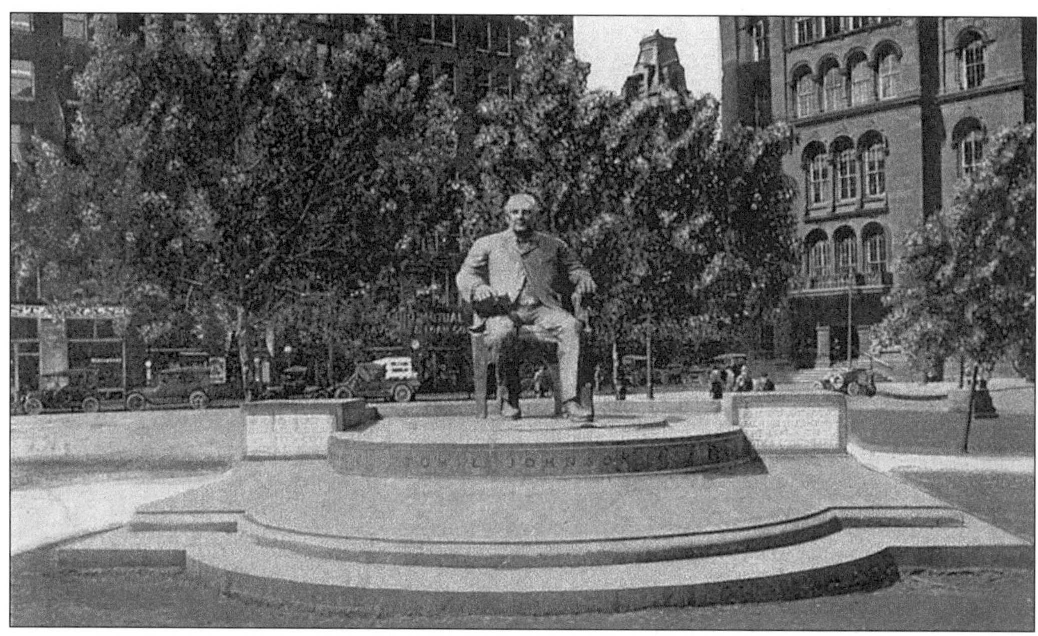

This monument on the Square honors Tom L. Johnson, longtime mayor and influential figure at the turn of the century.

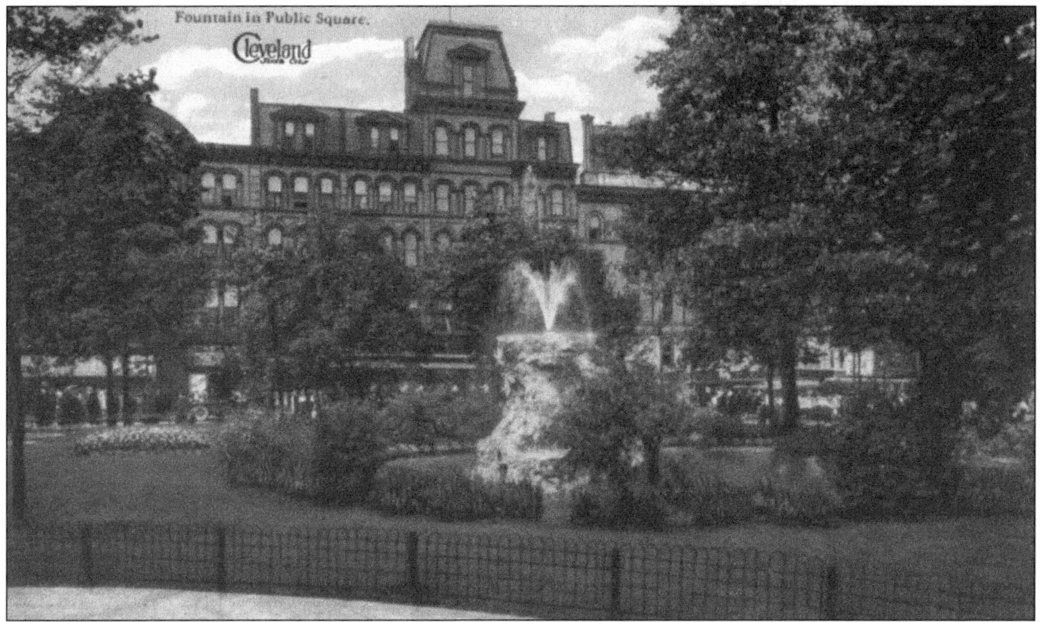

The Forest City House, built in 1855 and one of Cleveland's premier hotels at the turn of the century, rises over a pastoral Public Square.

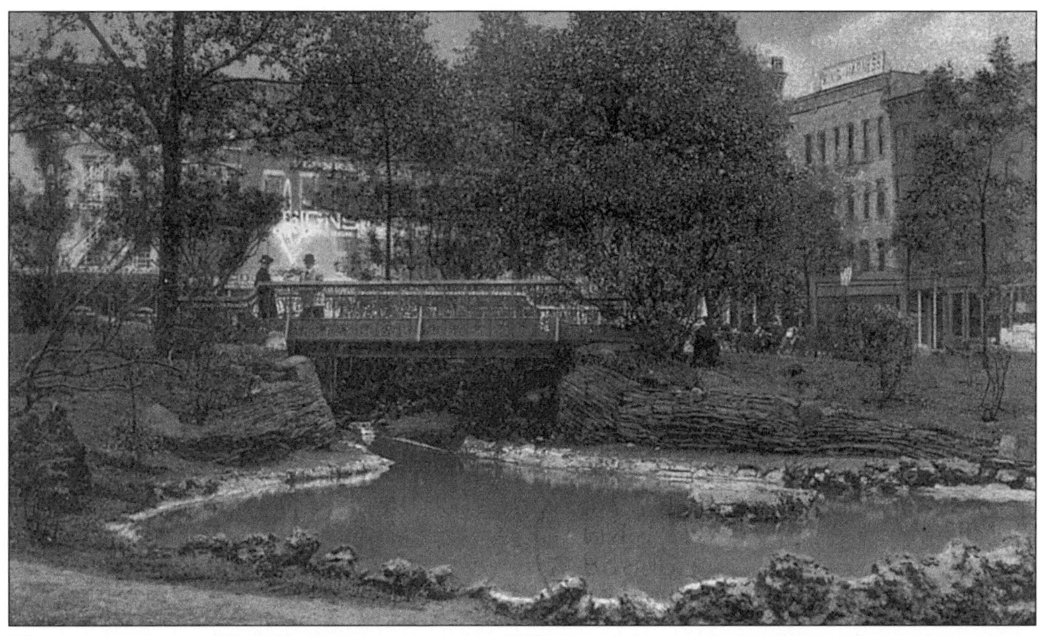

This early view of Public Square is quite different from today, with rock outcroppings and a bridge spanning a creek.

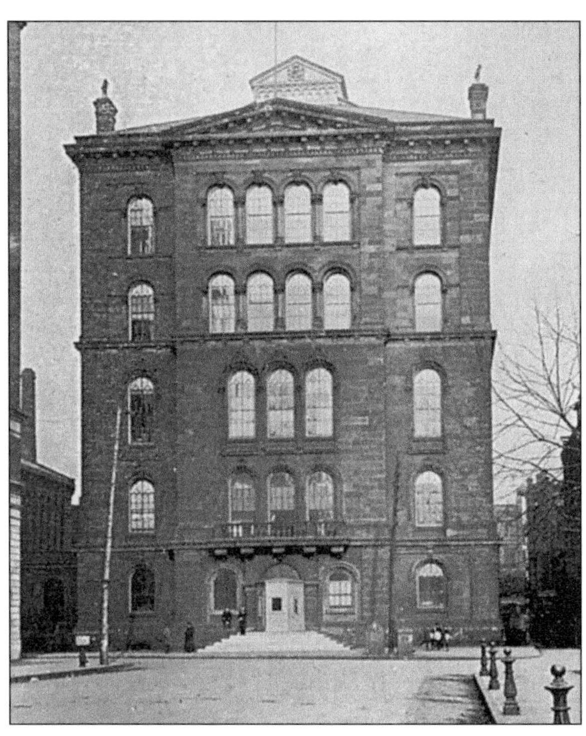

The Old Court House, the third structure erected for that purpose, stood facing Public Square.

The Park Building, on the south side of the Square, was one of the first office buildings in Cleveland to have reinforced concrete floors. The building, constructed in 1904, housed a number of insurance firms. Frank Brothers, on the street level, claimed to be the "world's largest shoe store."

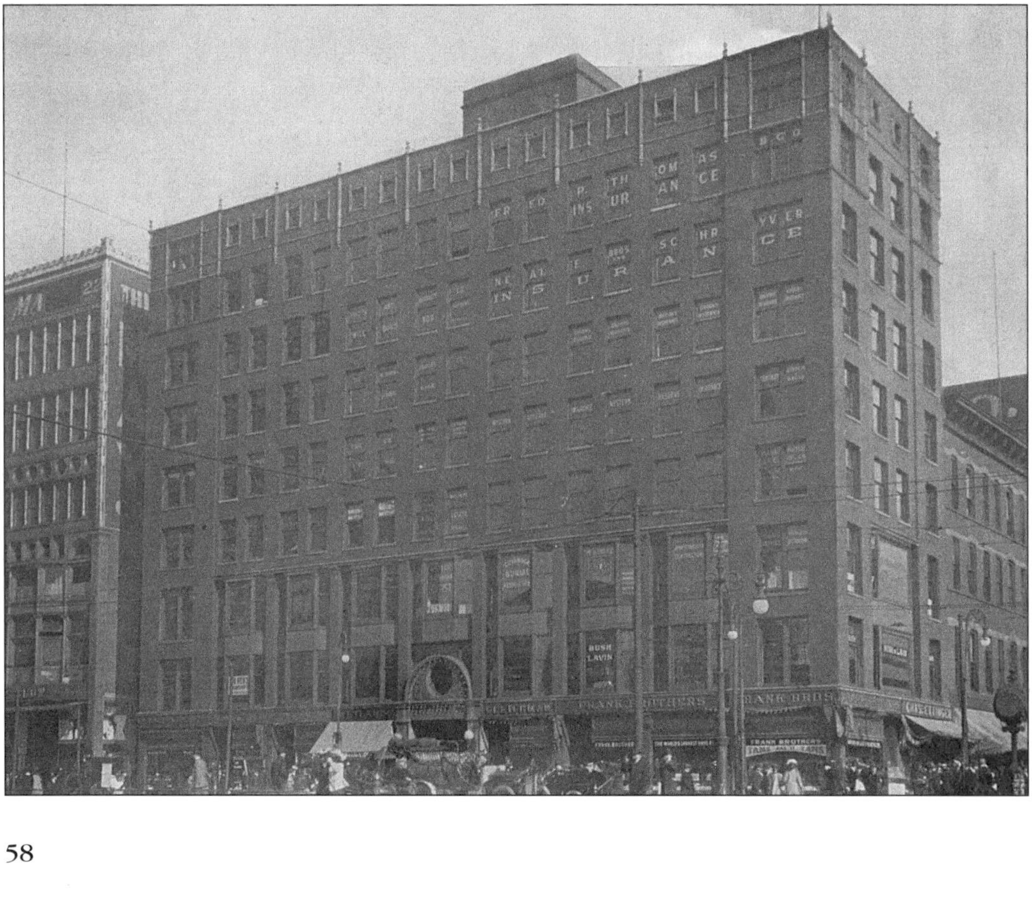

Five

DOWNTOWN

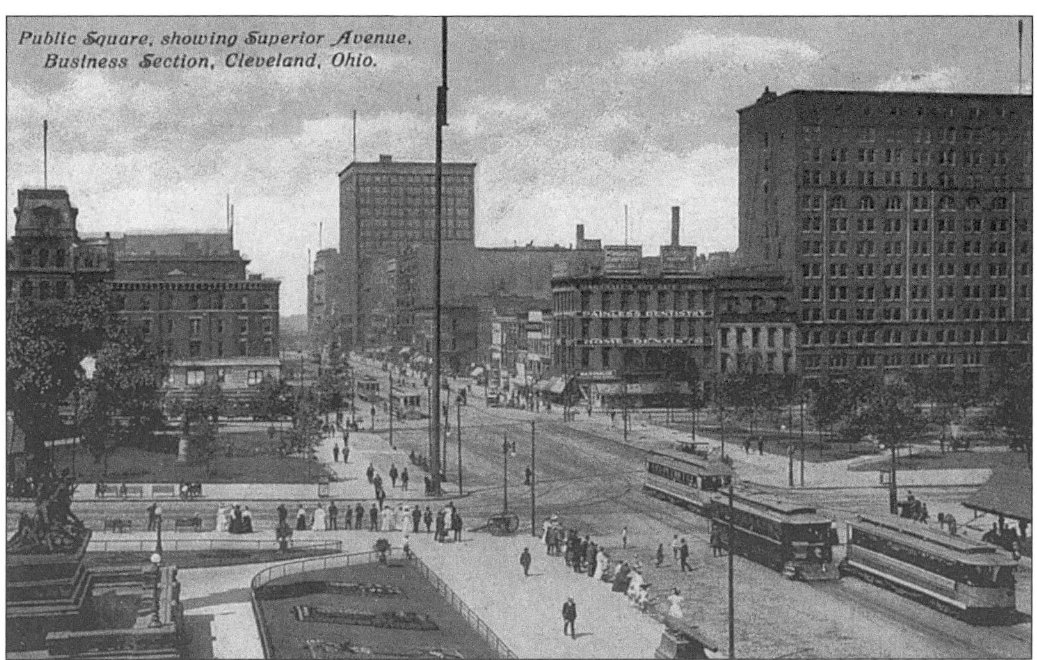

This is the view down Superior Avenue from Public Square in 1911. In the distance are the warehouses that border the Flats. Downtown Cleveland moved "uphill" from the Flats in the mid-1800s, and much of that original downtown still exists as part of Cleveland's Warehouse District, a booming area of restaurants, jazz clubs, offices, and specialty retail shops.

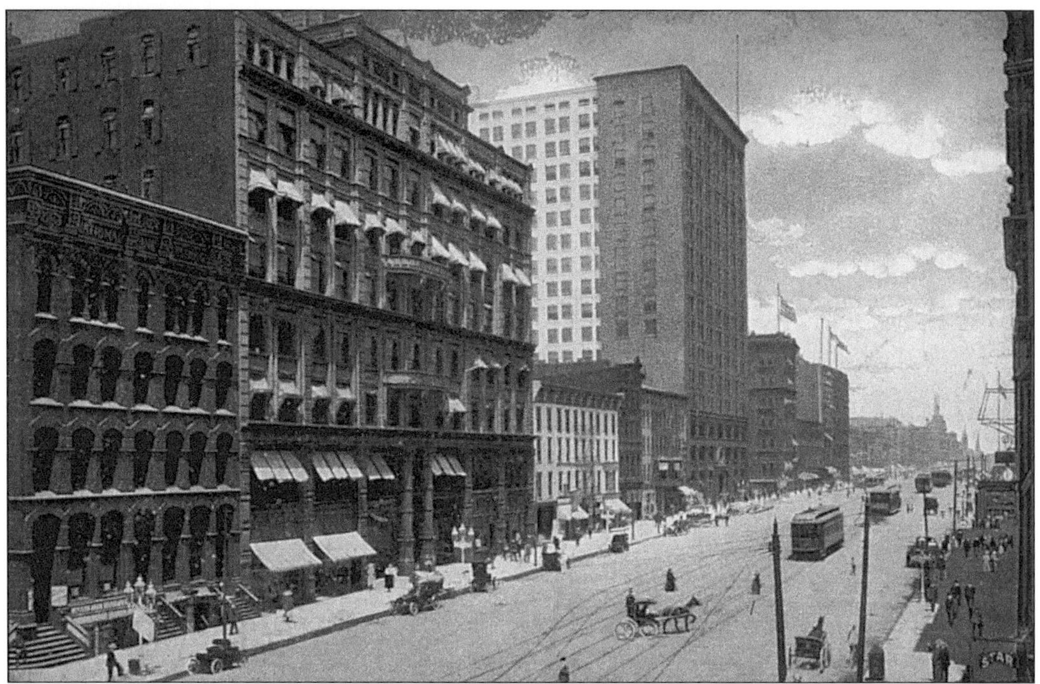

The Rockefeller Building (the tall building at center), on Superior Avenue, was erected by John D. Rockefeller in 1905 and is listed in the National Register of Historic Places. The building was sold in 1925 and the name was changed to the Kirby Building. Rockefeller was so incensed that he bought the building back at three times the selling price and renamed it the Rockefeller Building.

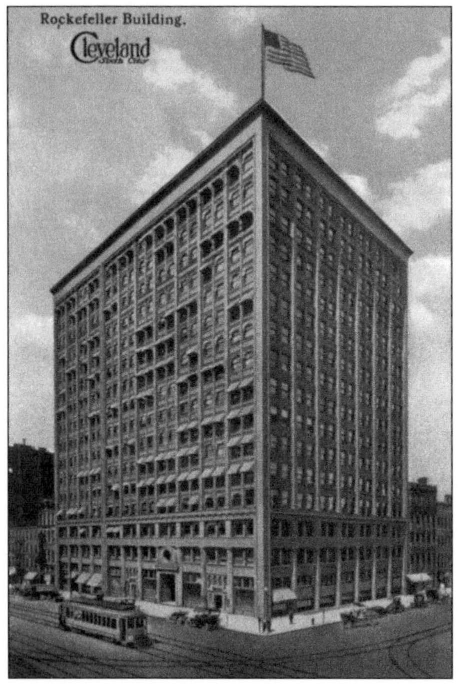

Constructed at a cost of over one million dollars, the Rockefeller Building served as headquarters for Rockefeller's interests, which included iron, coal, and lake shipping. The Weddell House Hotel was partially demolished, over protests, to make way for the structure.

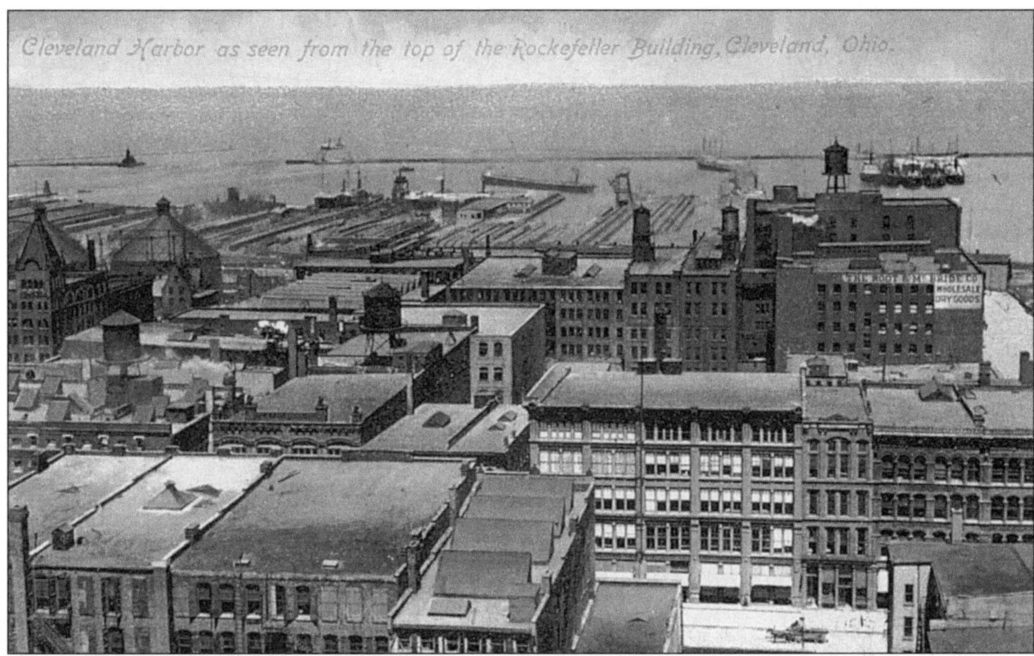

This view of downtown, looking toward Cleveland Harbor, was taken from atop the Rockefeller Building.

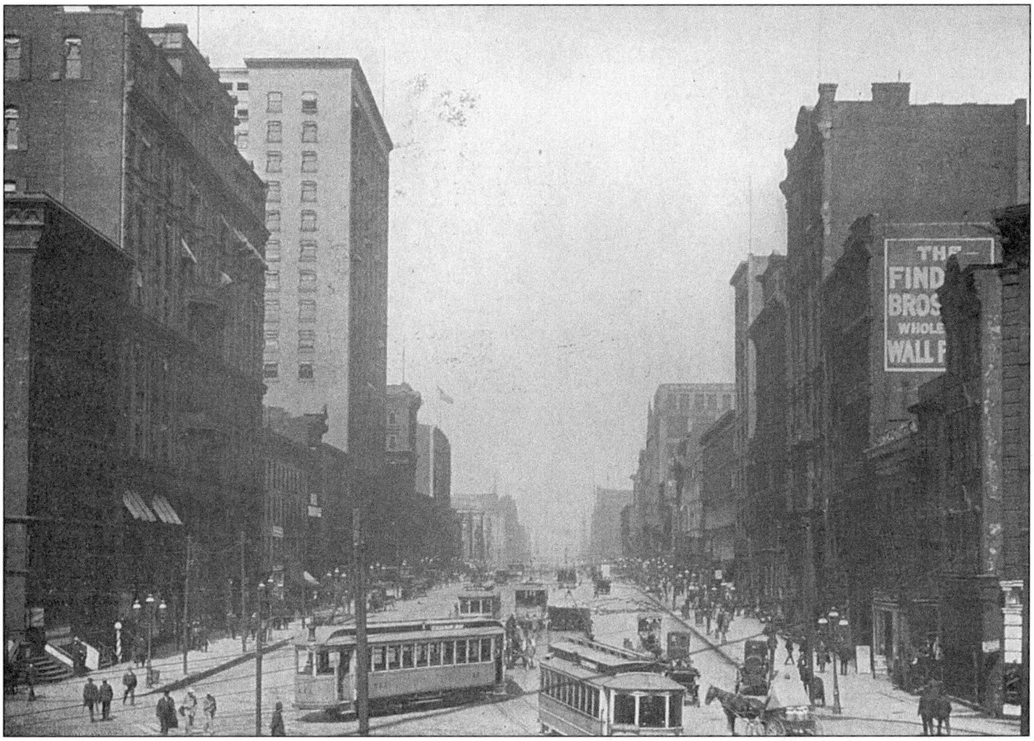

Superior Avenue is shown here looking east from the Superior Viaduct in 1908.

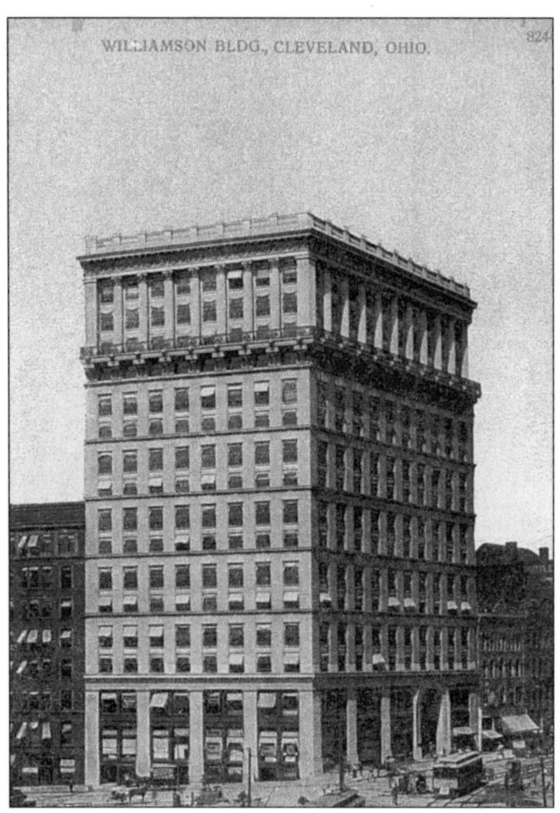

The Williamson Building, erected in 1900, was the second Williamson Building on this site. The location was the site of the original homestead of Samuel Williamson, a noted early Cleveland judge. It was the tallest building in the city when constructed and stood for over 80 years at the corner of Euclid Avenue and Public Square.

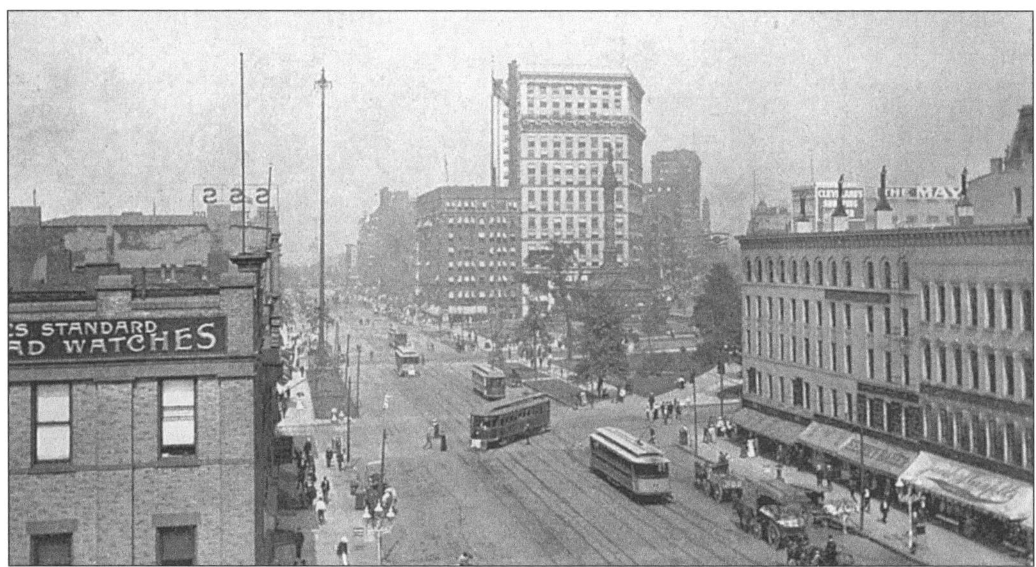

This section of Superior Avenue, looking toward Public Square, is part of the Warehouse District. The Williamson Building is the tall structure in the center.

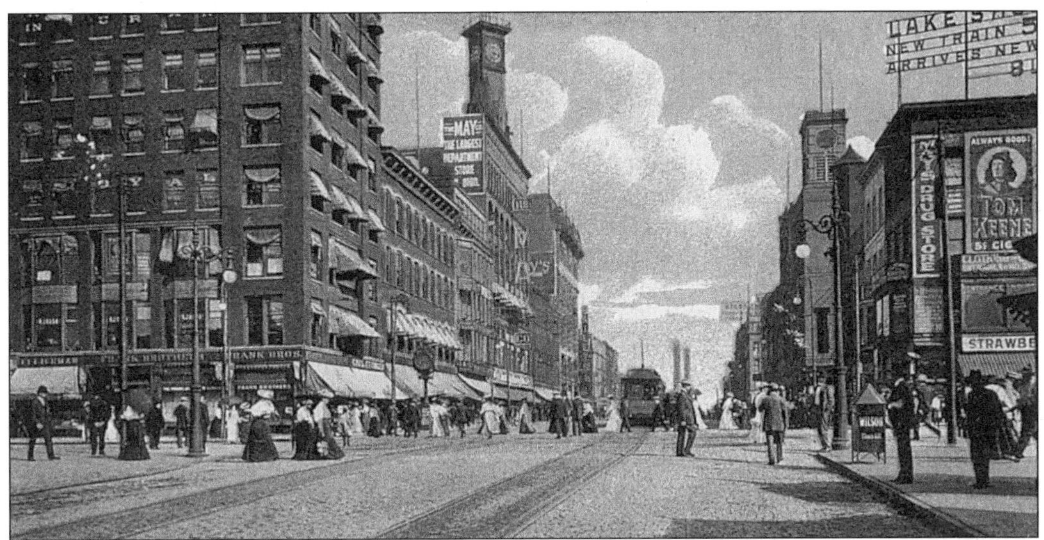

A 1907 view of Ontario Street, looking east from Public Square, shows that the May Company was already "The Largest Department Store in Ohio."

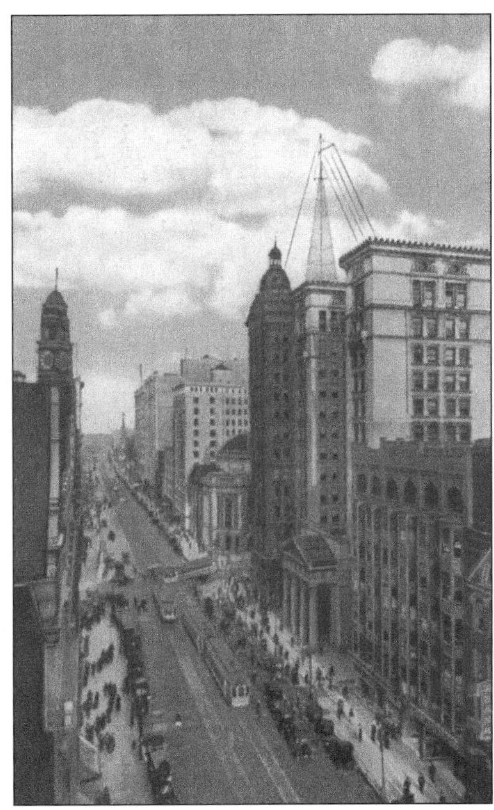

Euclid Avenue was laid out in 1815, and so named because it was the route to the settlement of Euclid to the east. The intersection of East Ninth (then called Erie Street) and Euclid Avenue (in the foreground) is at the center of downtown Cleveland today.

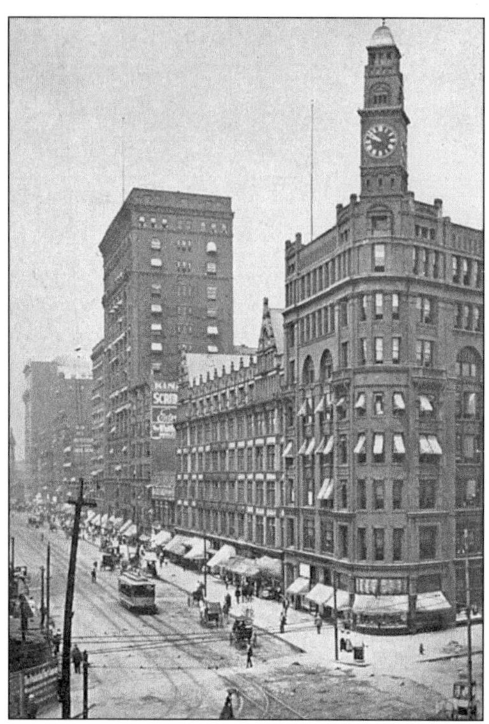

The mammoth Hickox Building dominates the corner in this early view of the north side of Euclid Avenue looking west toward Public Square. The Hickox Building boasted marble walls and mosaic floors. The clock in the tower is from the First Baptist Church, which was demolished in 1890 to make way for the new building.

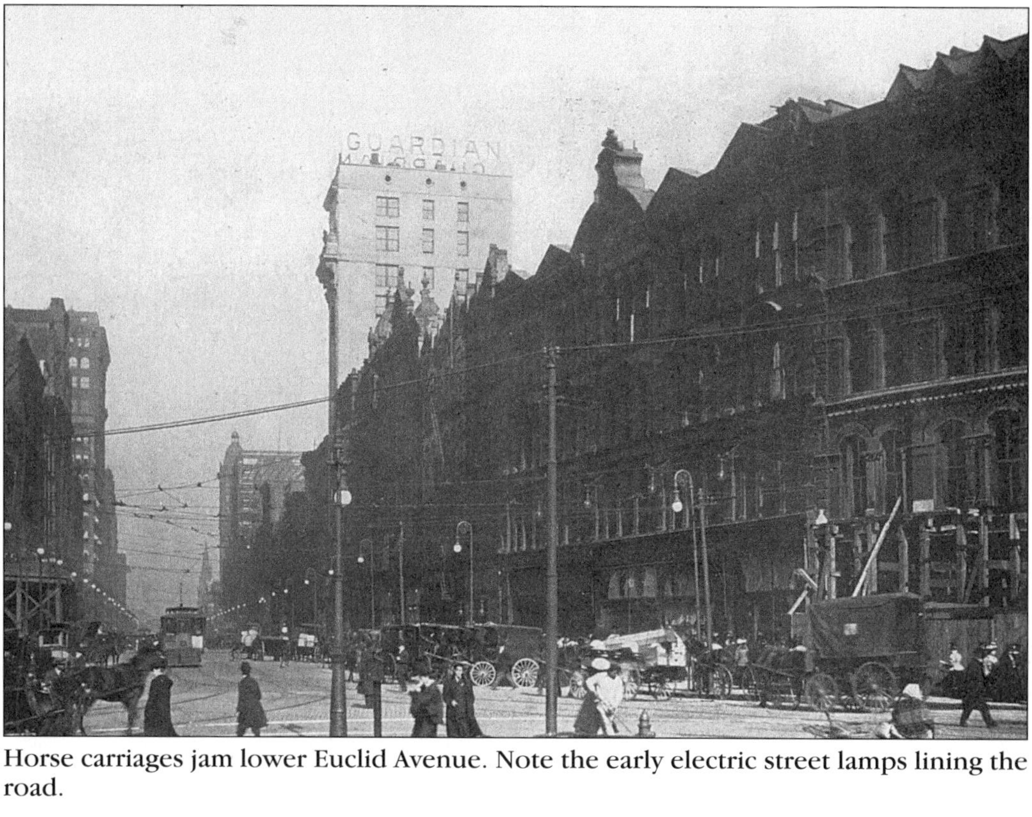

Horse carriages jam lower Euclid Avenue. Note the early electric street lamps lining the road.

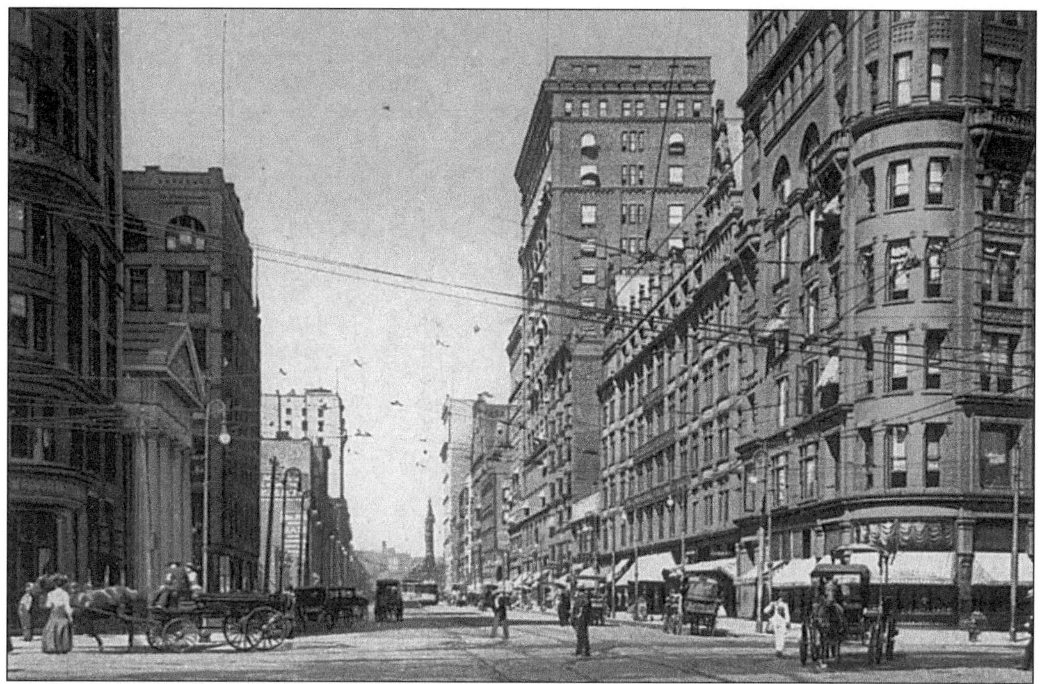

This card shows Euclid Avenue looking toward Public Square from East Ninth Street, the busiest intersection in downtown Cleveland. Ornate Victorian architecture dominates Cleveland's main street in this 1905 view.

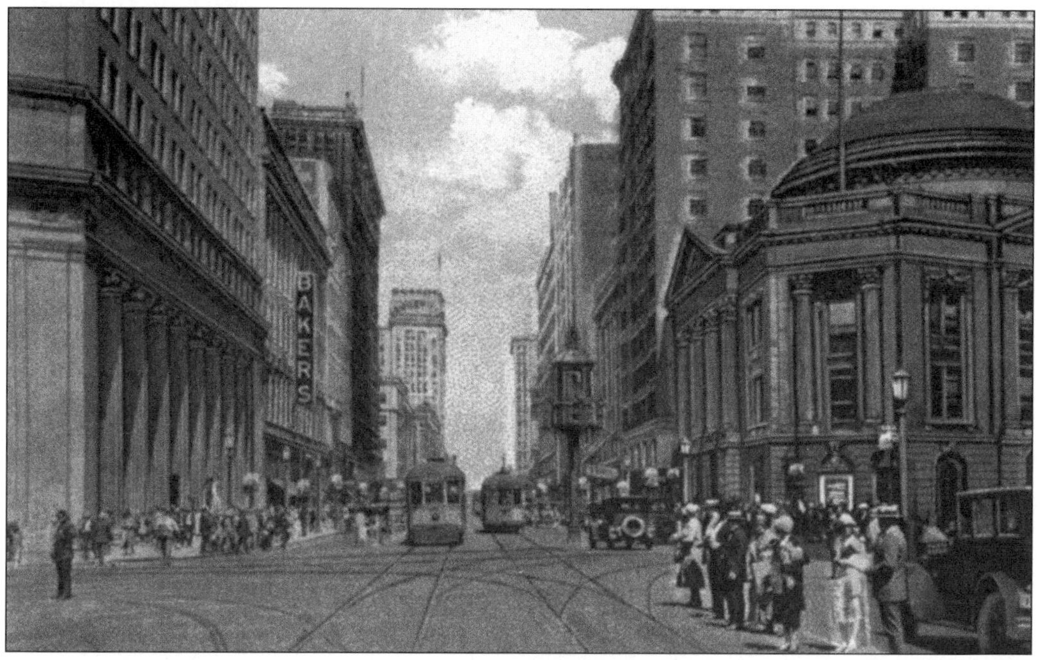

A later scene looks east down Euclid toward Playhouse Square from Euclid and Ninth. The domed building on the right, Cleveland Trust Bank (now part of Key Bank), has anchored the corner since 1908.

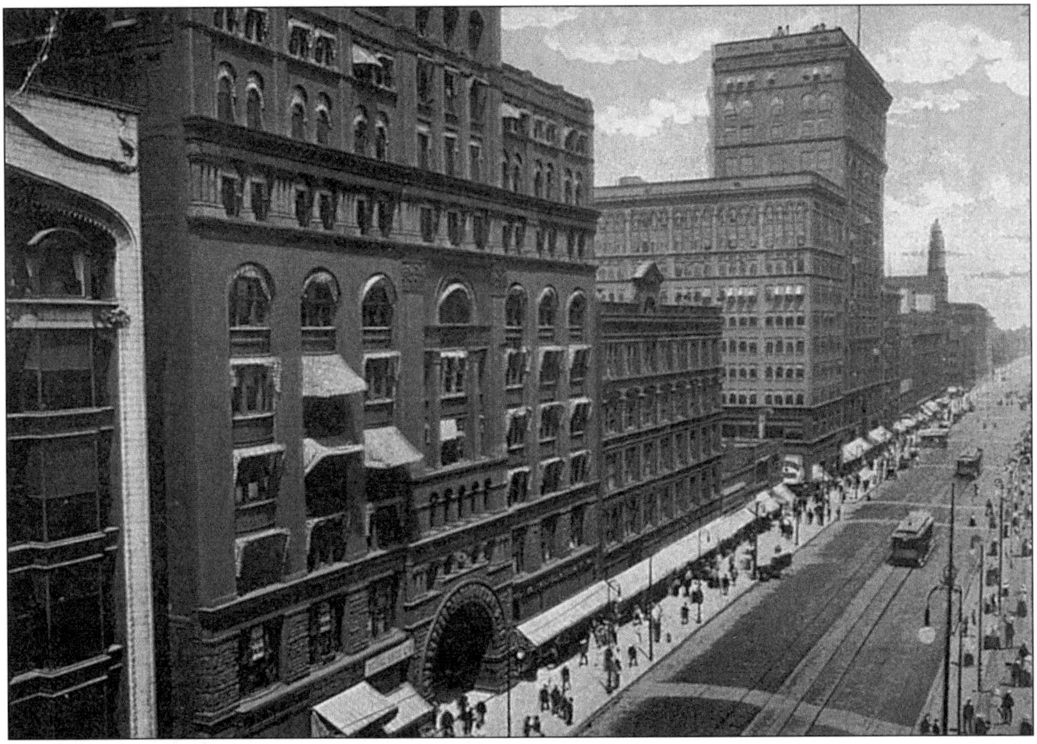

This view of Euclid Avenue shows the Euclid entrance to the Old Arcade at lower left. This 1911 scene shows the common use of awnings to shield pedestrians from the sun.

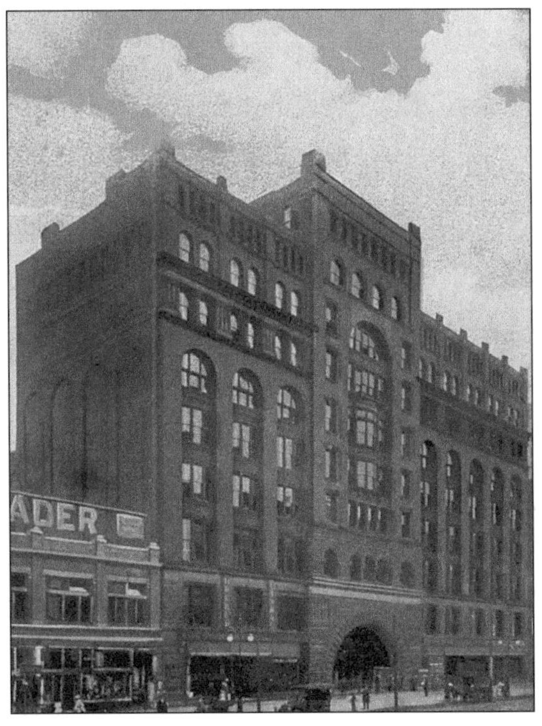

Pictured is the Superior Avenue entrance to the Old Arcade, which is a block-long structure between Euclid and Superior Avenues. The Old Arcade is one of three arcades still existing on Euclid Avenue in downtown Cleveland. In its early days, it was called the Superior Arcade, reflecting that street's importance in early Cleveland.

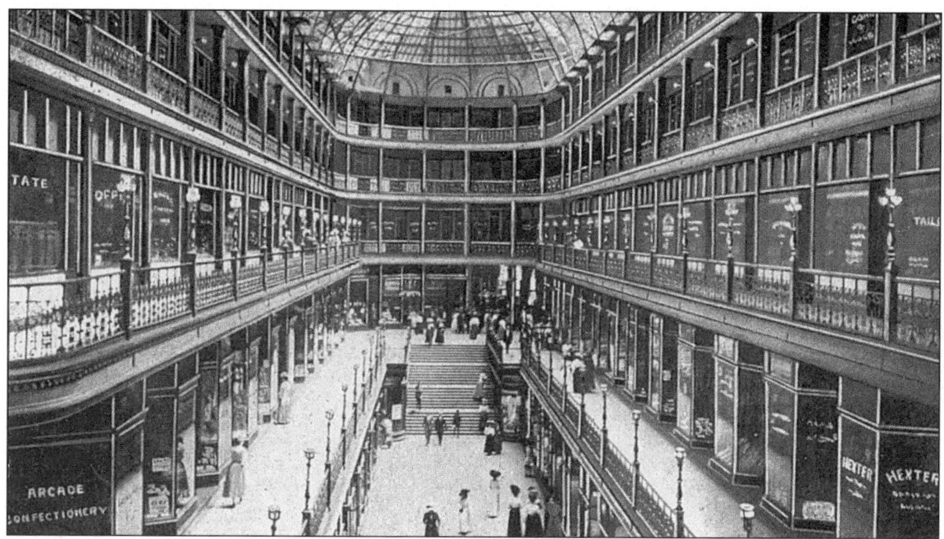

The Arcade was hailed as Cleveland's "crystal palace" when it opened in 1890. Built at a cost of $867,000, it was generally acknowledged to be the world's finest arcade. In the beginning, professionals and real estate companies occupied the first two floors. Later, this space was converted to retail stores. The Arcade has maintained much of its original splendor through the years, and is currently completing a multi-million dollar renovation.

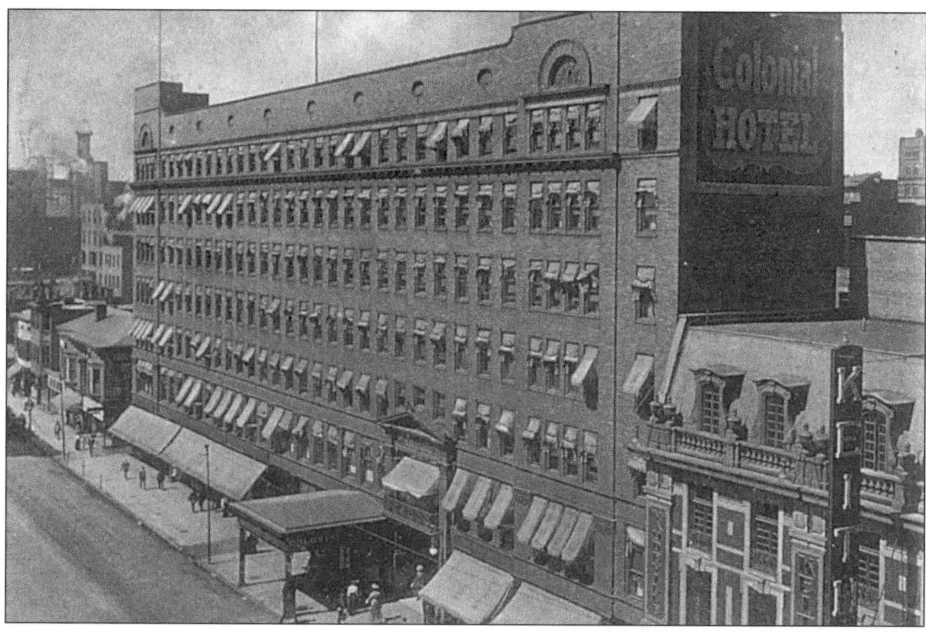

This 1910 view of Prospect Avenue shows the Colonial Hotel and Keith Theater. The hotel building also housed the Colonial Arcade, built in 1893, which, along with the adjacent Euclid Arcade, has undergone an extensive renovation as Colonial Marketplace. The upper floors have been converted back to their original use as a hotel. The Keith Theater opened in 1904 as a vaudeville house. It later became the Hippodrome and served as a movie theater until it was torn down to make way for a parking lot in 1981.

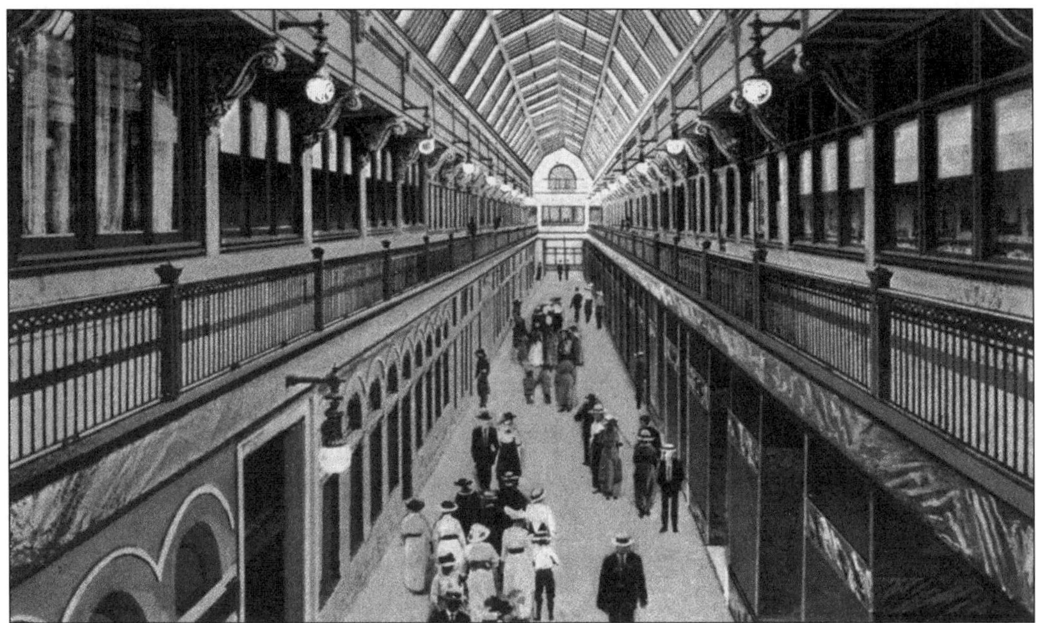

The Colonial Arcade, one of three existing Cleveland arcades fronting Euclid Avenue, runs between Euclid and Prospect. The Colonial was erected in 1893 by John F. Rust, who also built the Euclid Arcade next door.

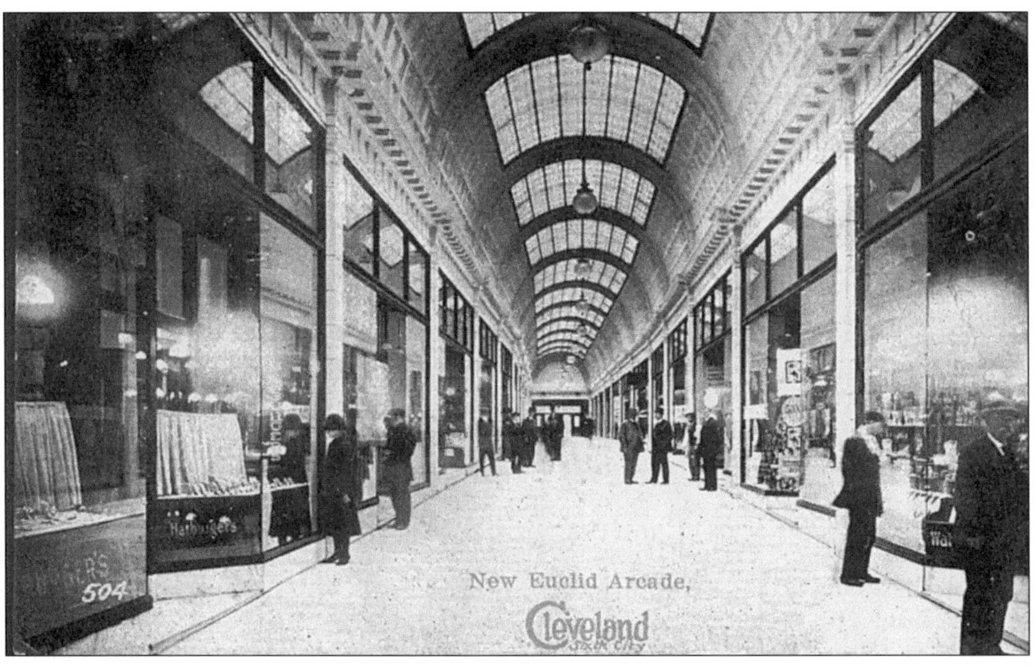

The Euclid Arcade, built in 1892, was the second of four arcades built on Euclid Avenue. This arcade is also part of the Colonial Marketplace development.

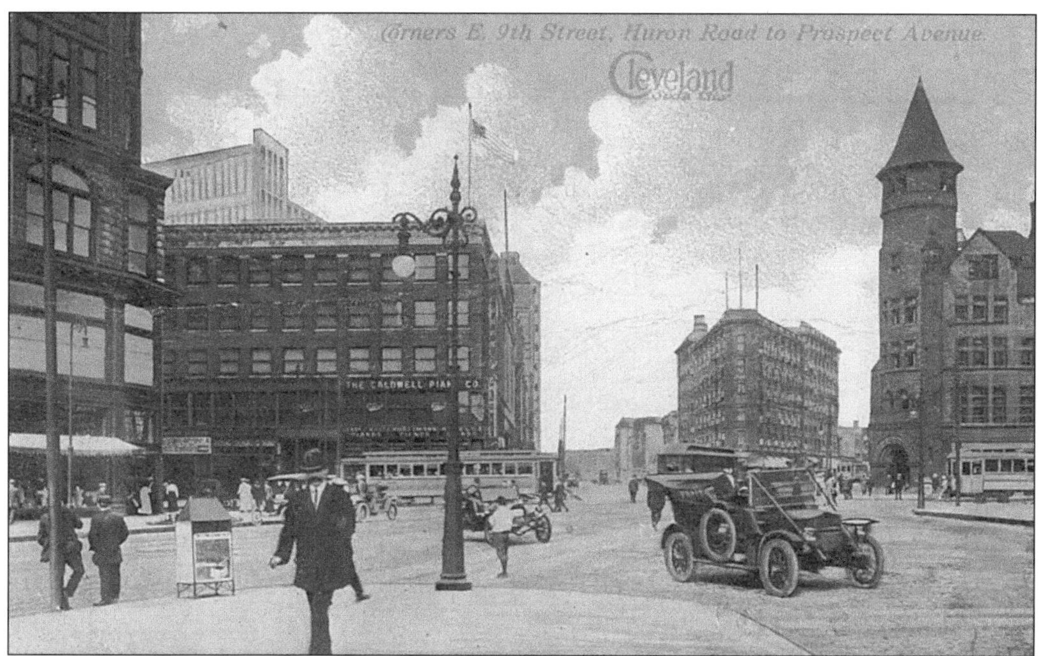

This view looks from East Ninth Street down Huron and Prospect Avenues in "The Sixth City." The Osborne Building (at right center) once housed dentists' offices, and it was said that the windows allowed so much light inside that no artificial lighting was needed. The building is now being renovated into luxury apartments.

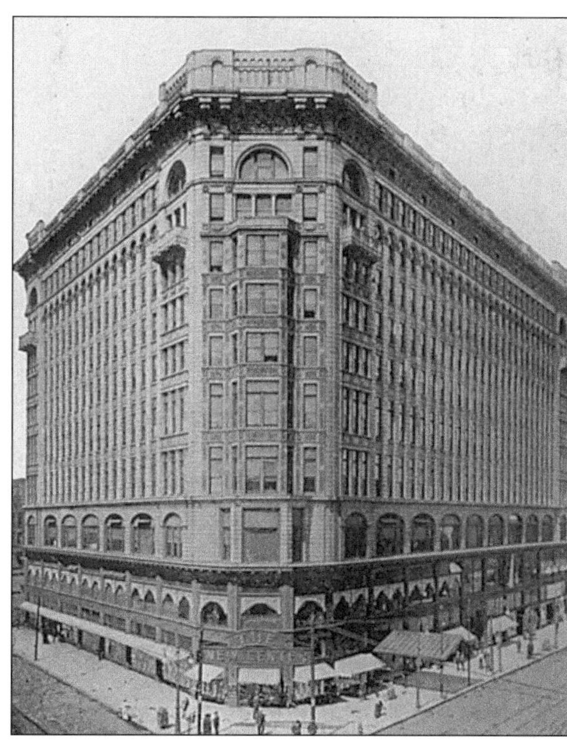

The Rose Building on Erie Street (East Ninth) covered nearly an acre and was the largest building in Ohio when it opened in 1900. Built by Benjamin Rose, philanthropist and owner of the Cleveland Provision Company, the proceeds from this building were dedicated to establish the Benjamin Rose Institute to aid crippled children and older persons.

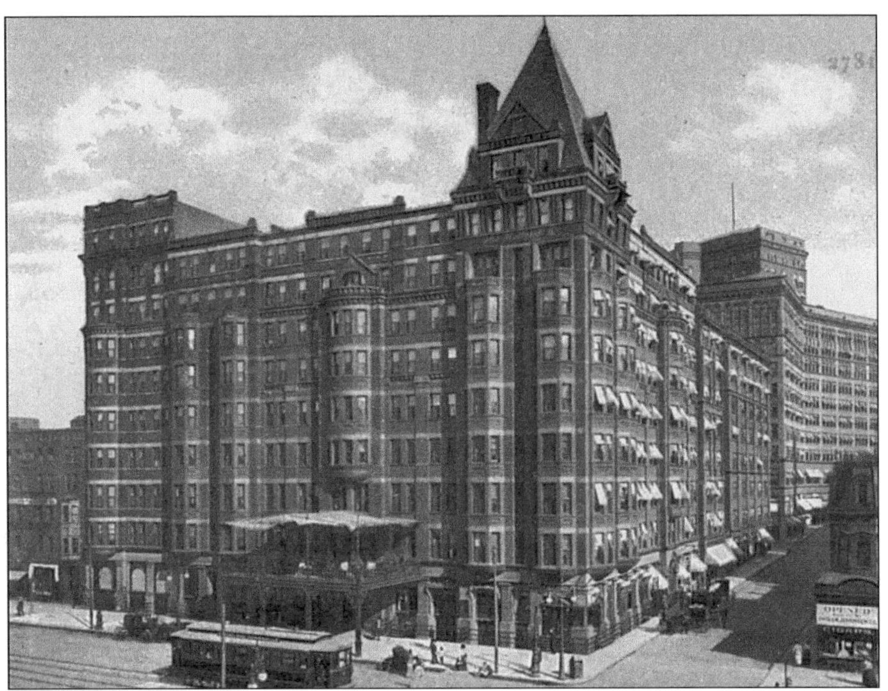

A number of major hotels flourished in downtown Cleveland in the early 1900s to serve the many business travelers and tourists visiting the nation's sixth (later fifth) largest city. The Hollenden House, at East Sixth and Superior, was the first large hotel east of Public Square. The building was replaced by a new Hollenden House in 1965, which was itself demolished in 1989, bringing the Hollenden era to an end in Cleveland.

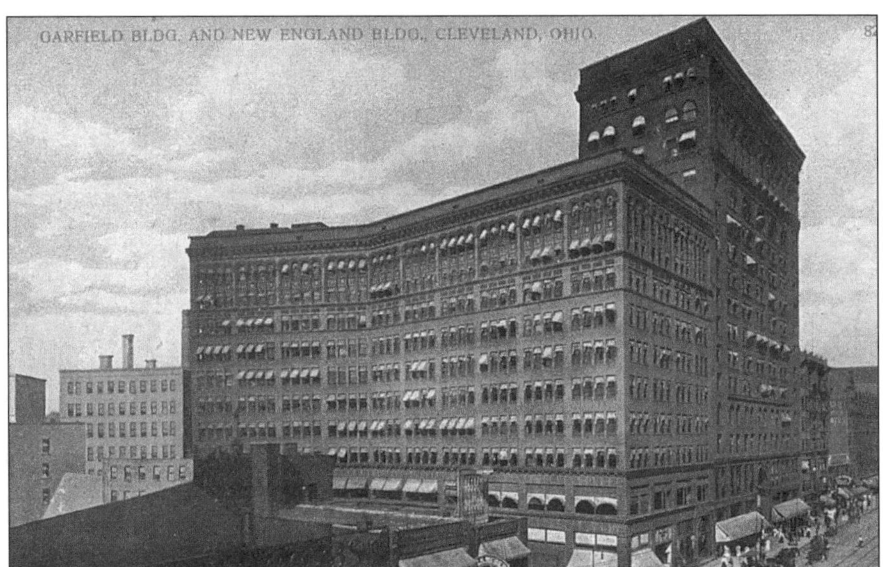

The Garfield Building was erected in 1893 by Harry A. and James R. Garfield, sons of the late president. The building was the first steel-framed office building on Euclid Avenue, and still stands at East Sixth and Euclid. Weber's Restaurant, at the bottom, was a famous Cleveland eatery from 1900 until 1960.

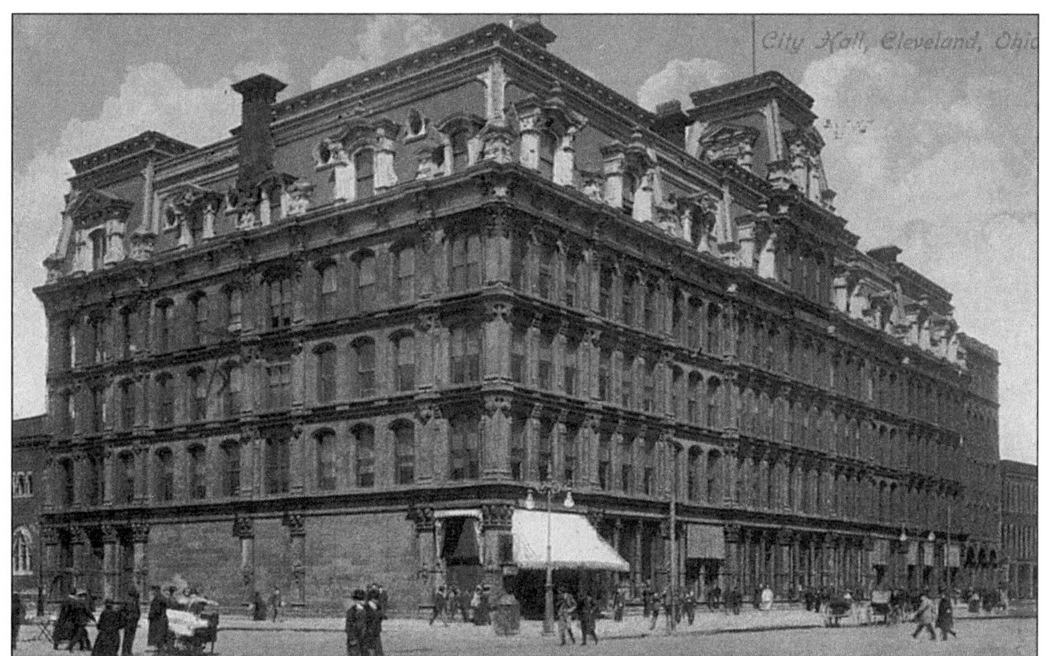

Cleveland City Hall is shown in the early 1900s, before the Group Plan for public buildings was implemented. This building, at Superior and East Third, was leased by the city for its public offices.

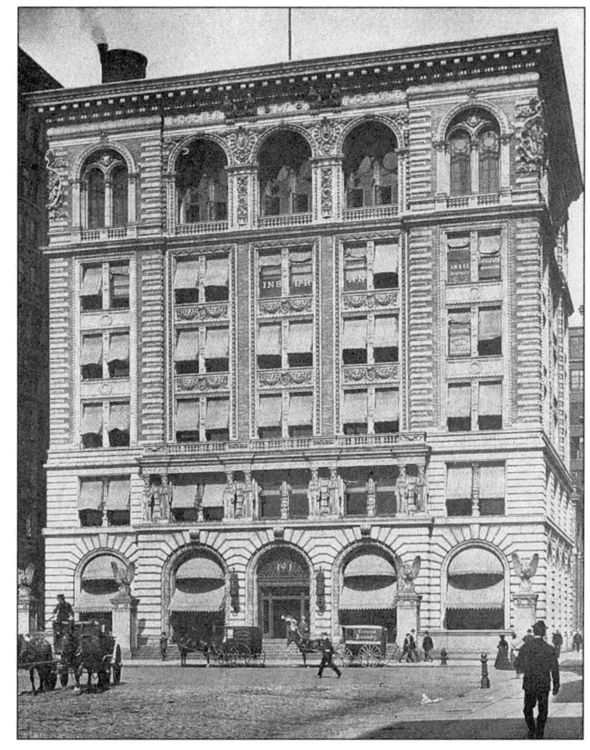

Built just before the turn of the century, the Cleveland Chamber of Commerce building fronted the northeast corner of the Square where the Marriott is today. A number of major functions were held in its impressive auditorium.

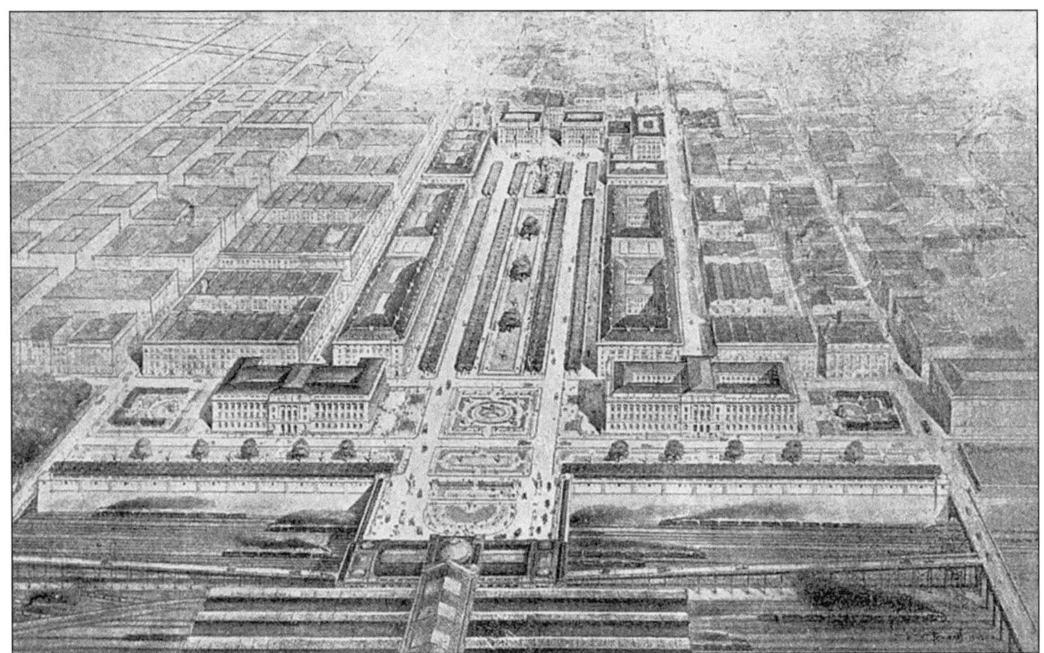

The Group Plan, which includes seven public buildings and the Mall, was unveiled in 1903 and was hailed as the most comprehensive civic building plan in the nation outside of Washington. The classically-styled buildings and statuesque Mall grace downtown Cleveland today and are a testament to the planning and foresight of early Cleveland leaders. Prominent engineers, architects, and financiers worked together to bring about this monumental achievement.

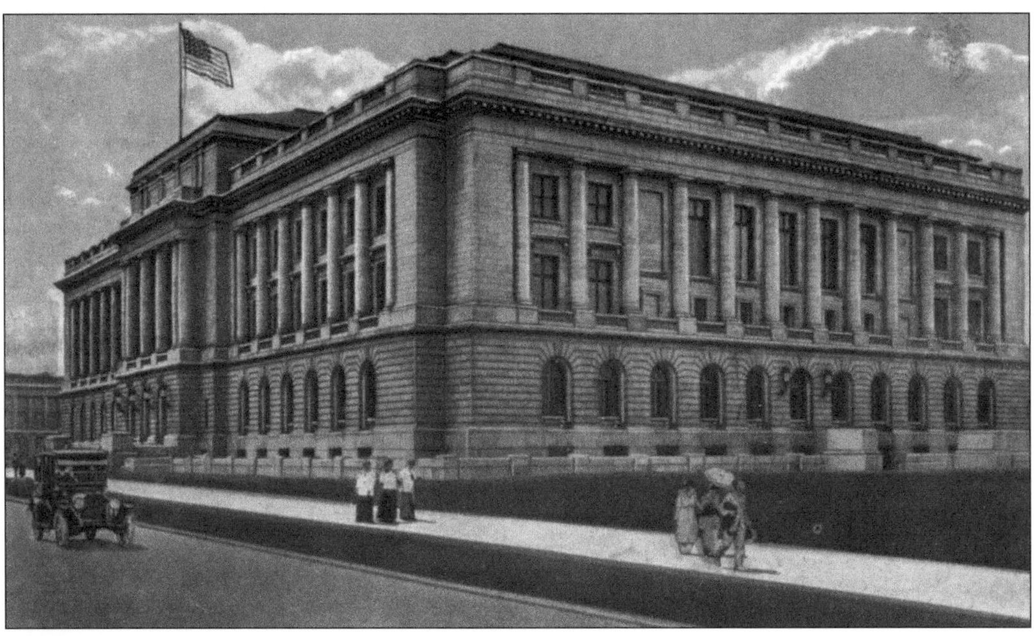

Dedicated on July 4, 1916, Cleveland City Hall was built in symmetry with the Cuyahoga County Court House. It is located at the north end of the Mall.

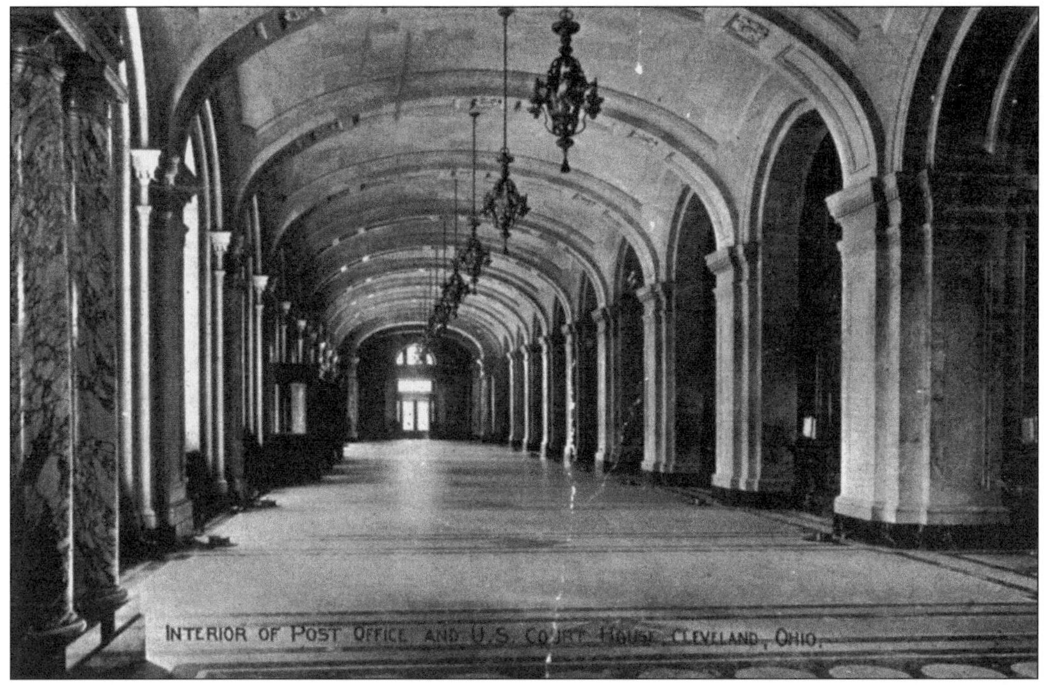

The interior of the Post Office and Court House Building shows off the splendid marble interior and spacious corridors.

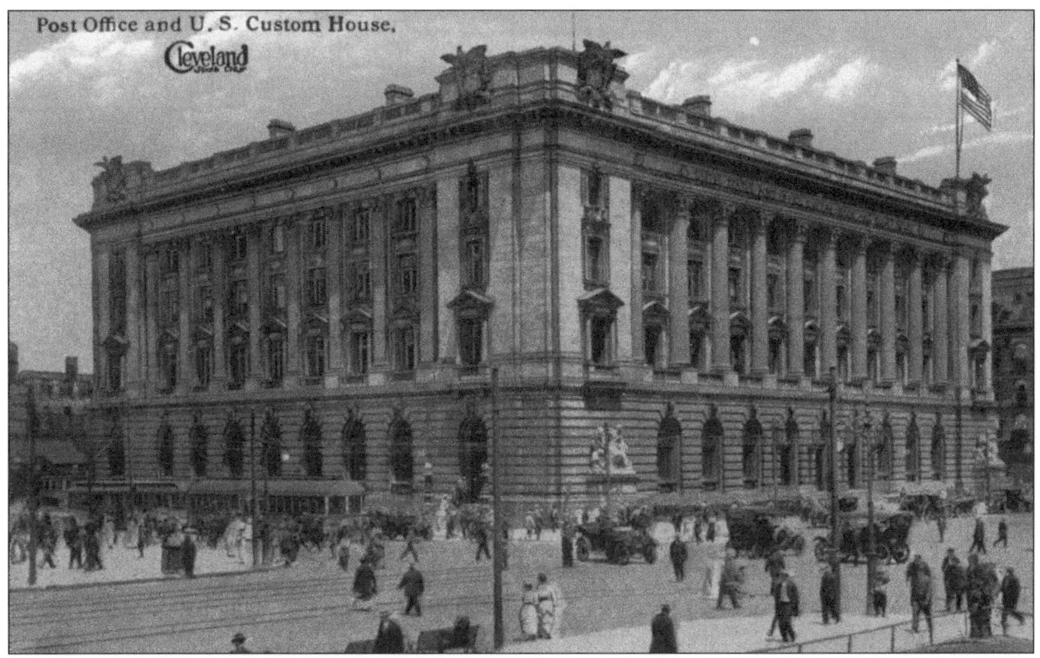

This Group Plan structure was built to serve as Post Office, Custom House, and Court House. It anchors the south end of the mall.

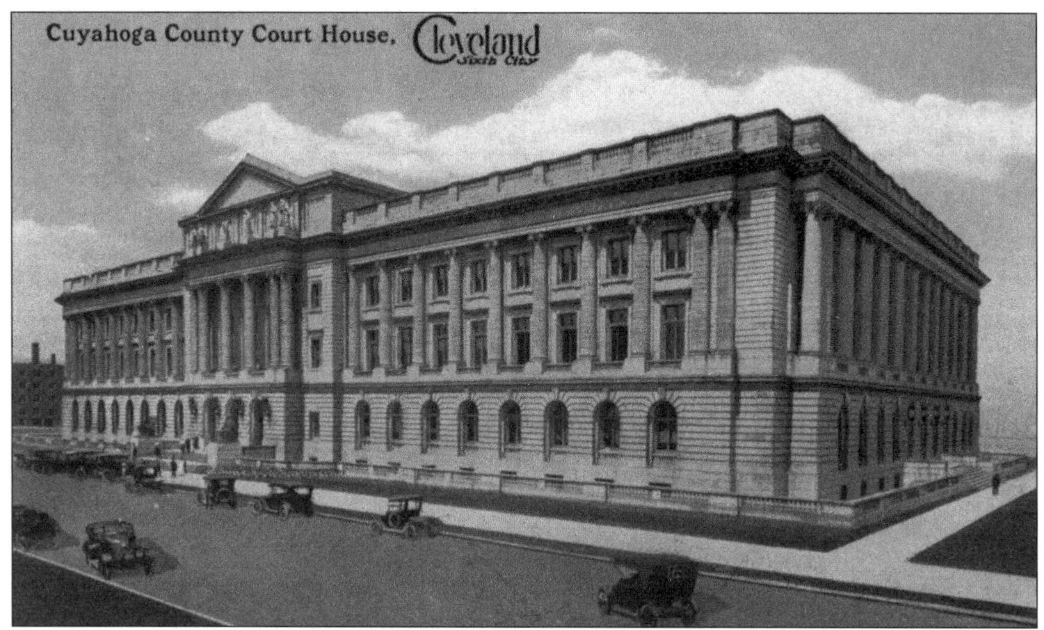

Cuyahoga County Courthouse, part of the Group Plan, was recognized as one of the finest in the country. It opened on January 1, 1912. All of the Group Plan buildings feature noteworthy statuary on the exterior and mural paintings in the interior, the works of famous sculptors and artists.

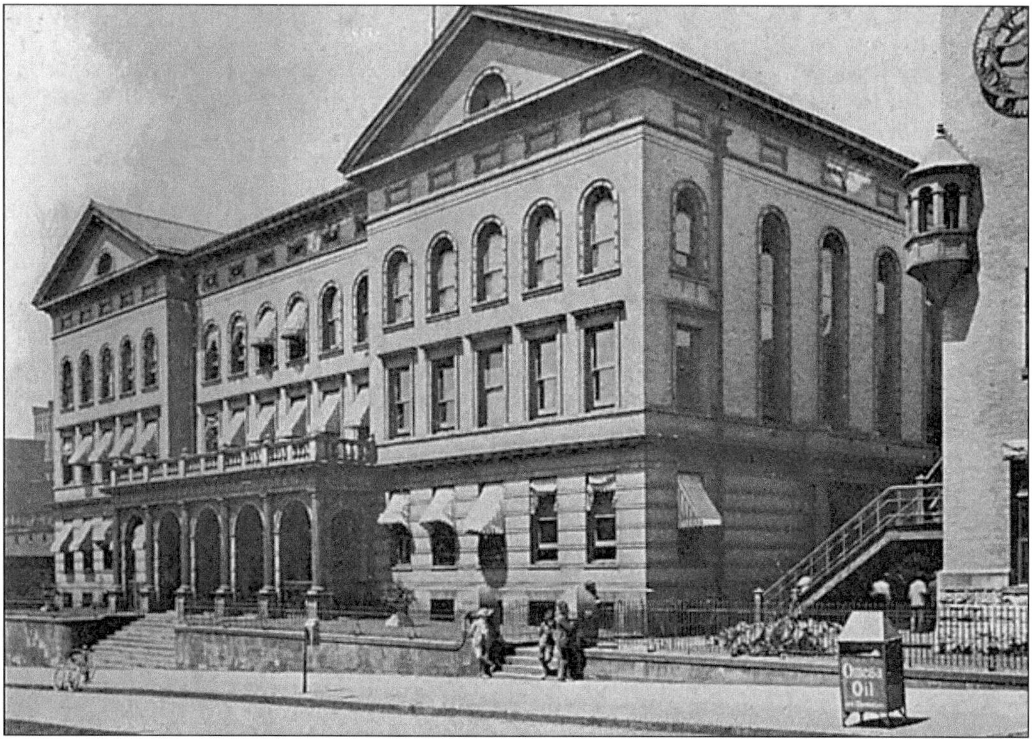

Central Police Station was the headquarters of "Cleveland's finest" in 1890.

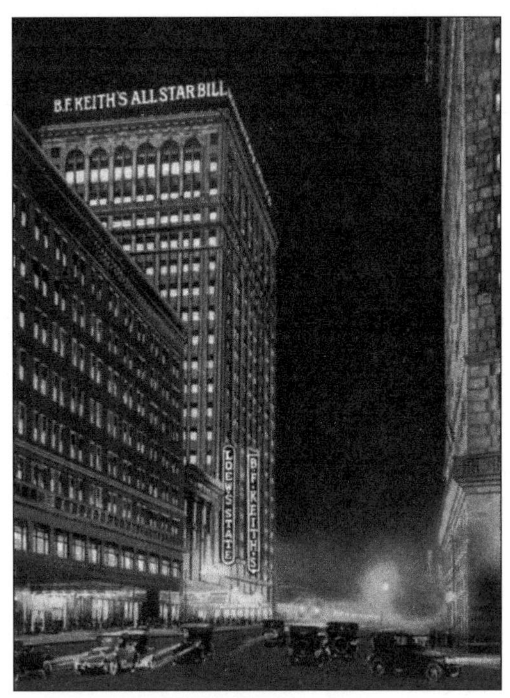

Playhouse Square, Cleveland's Theater District, includes five theaters—the State, Ohio, Palace, Allen, and Hanna—built in the 1910s through the 1920s. They featured plays, vaudeville shows, and movies. Today, the theaters have been meticulously restored and are home to Cleveland theater companies and Broadway shows. The Playhouse Square complex is the largest theater restoration in America after Lincoln Center.

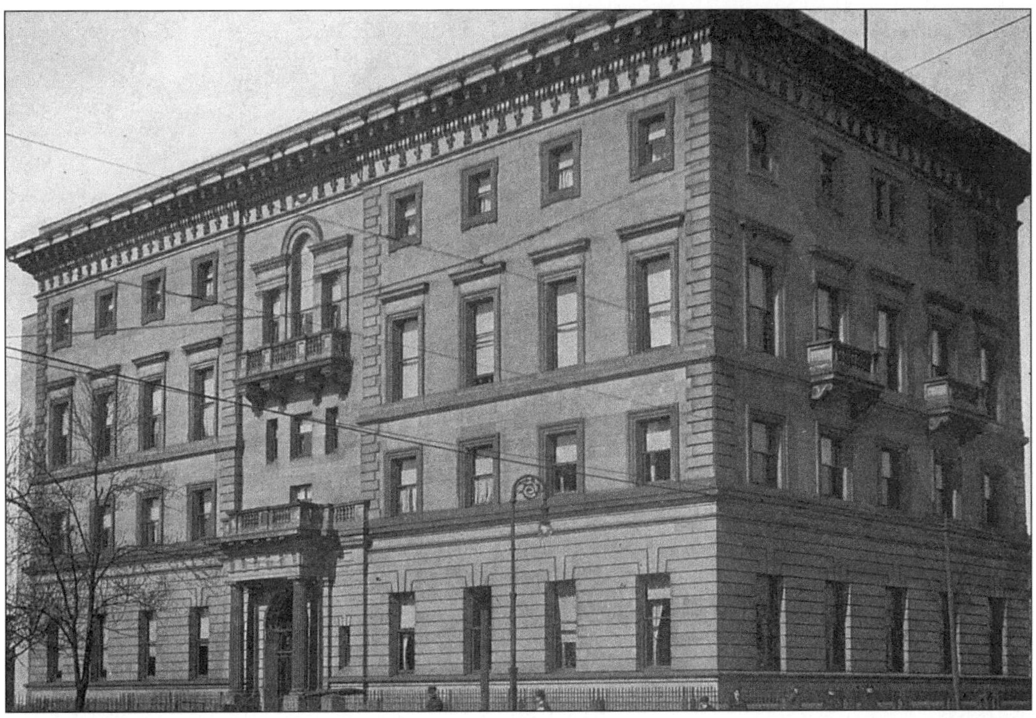

The Union Club was founded in the 1870s with an elite membership that included national leaders. By 1900, the club was so popular that prospective members could expect to wait as long as ten years for admittance. The club is located (still) at East 12th and Euclid.

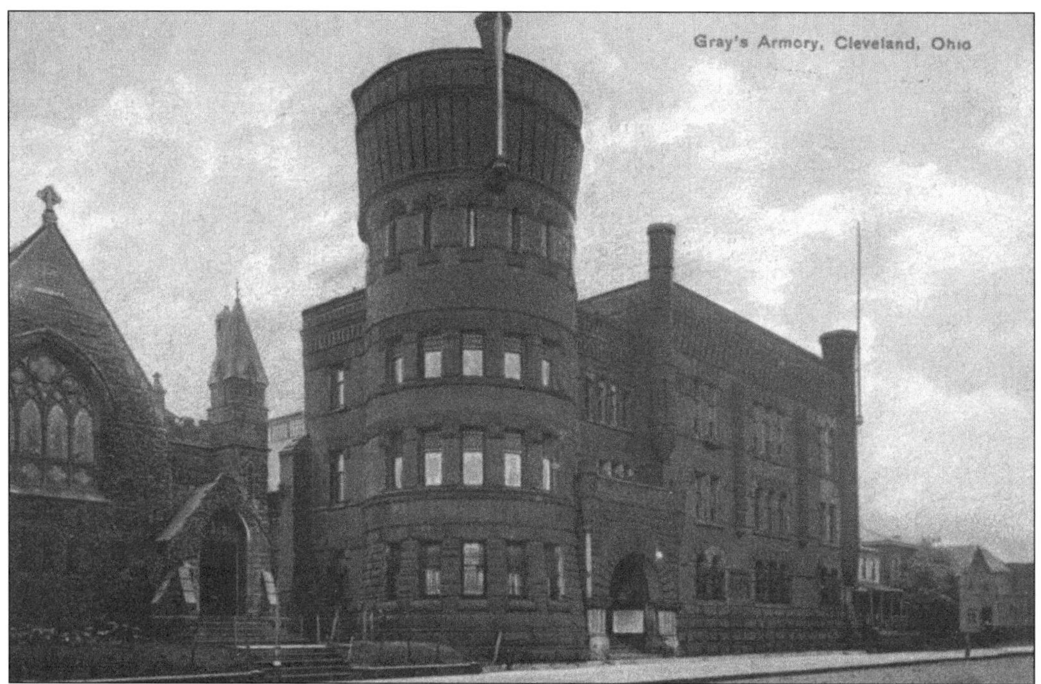

Built in 1893, Gray's Armory was home to the Cleveland Grays, and also hosted civic and cultural events. The Cleveland Orchestra gave its first concert at Gray's in 1918. The Grays were a private military company founded in 1838 to provide trained men for military service. The building is still in use today.

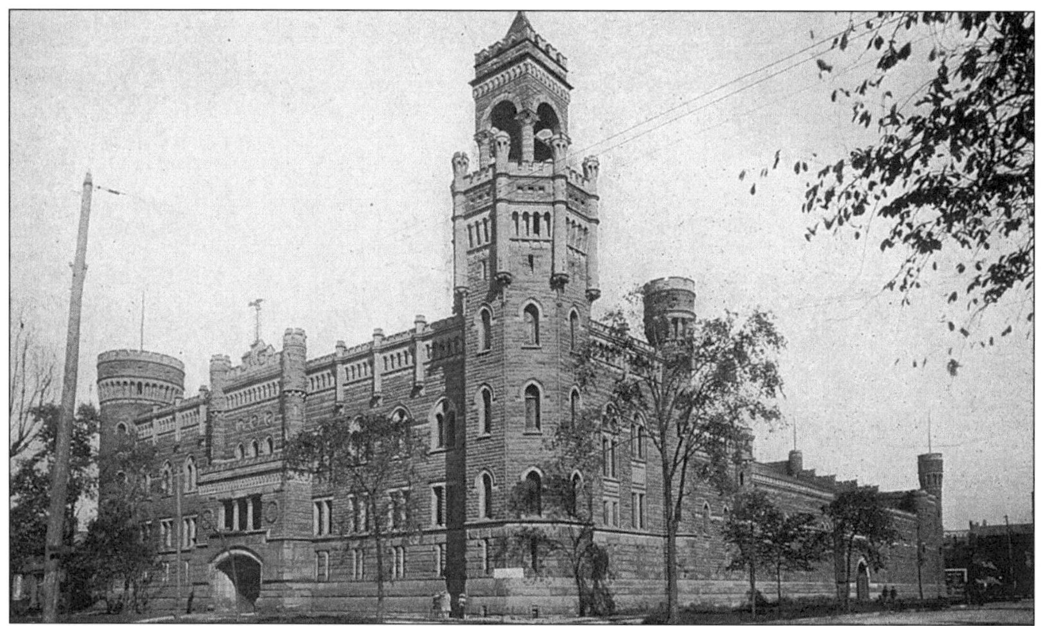

Central Armory, built in 1893 at Lake Avenue (now Lakeside Avenue) and East Sixth, was one of two armories (along with Gray's) erected that year for military purposes. It was torn down in 1965 to make way for the Celebreeze Office Building.

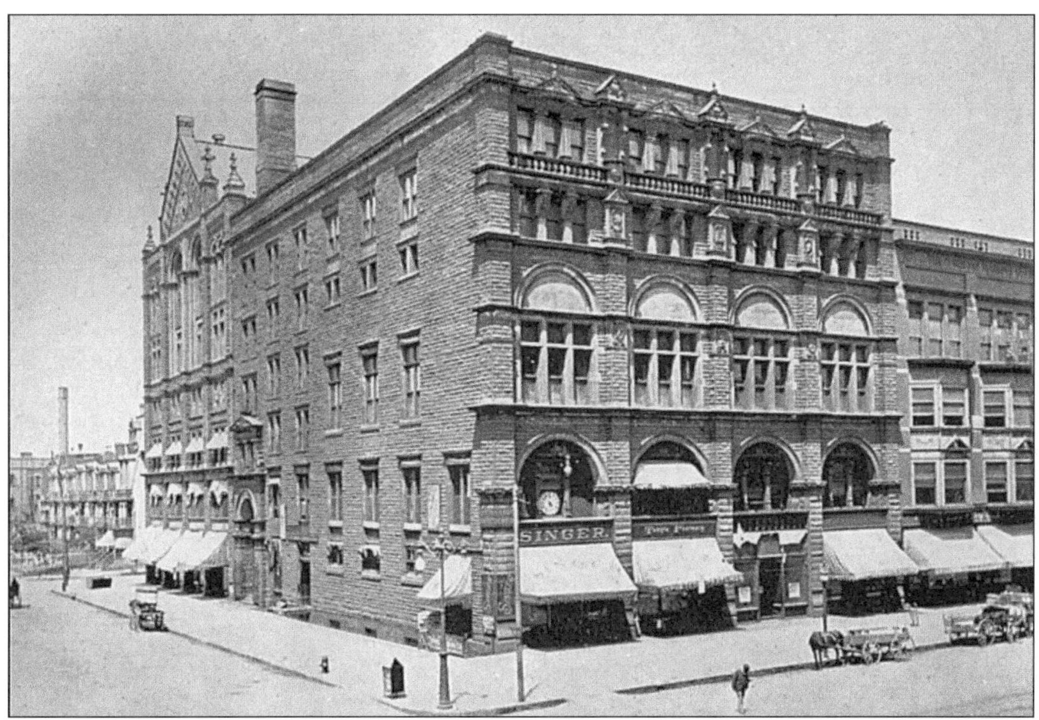

The Masonic Temple was built in 1886 at Superior and East Sixth, site of the current Federal Reserve Building. Note the Singer Sewing Machine shop on the corner.

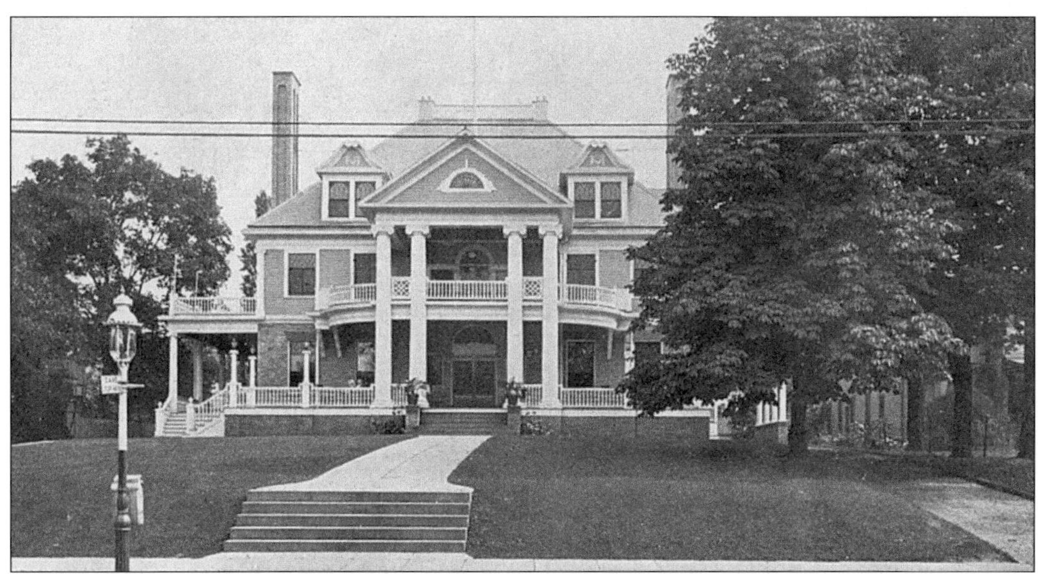

Social clubs were established as gathering places for Cleveland's prominent and well-to-do citizens. The Colonial Club, organized during the height of the Temperance movement, prohibited alcoholic beverages.

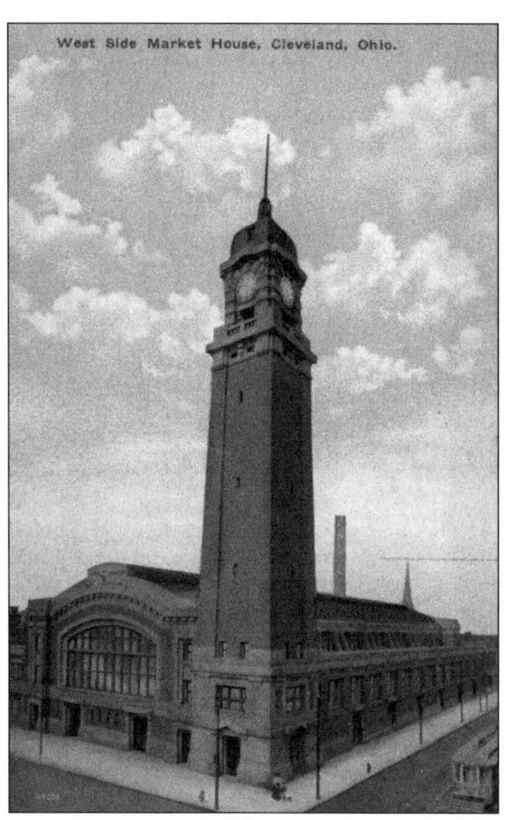

Dating to 1912, the West Side Market is Cleveland's oldest publicly owned market. It is one of Cleveland's most prominent landmarks and was touted as America's finest marketplace in the early 1900s. It still draws new generations of shoppers today.

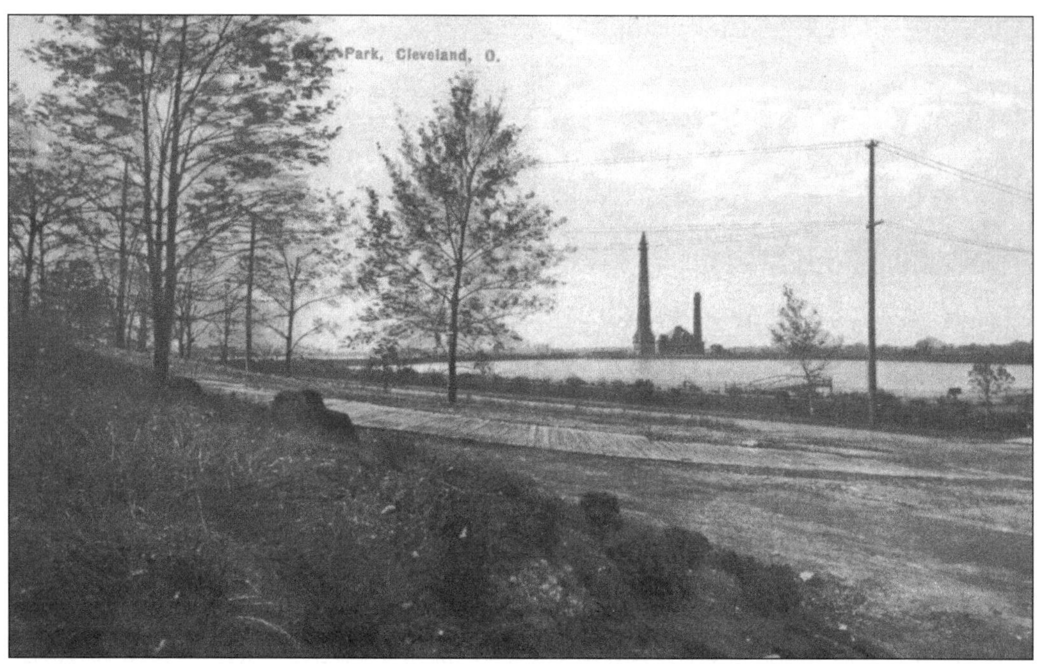

The Fairmont Reservoir and pumping station opened in 1855 to provide water for the city mains through a new, high-pressure supply system.

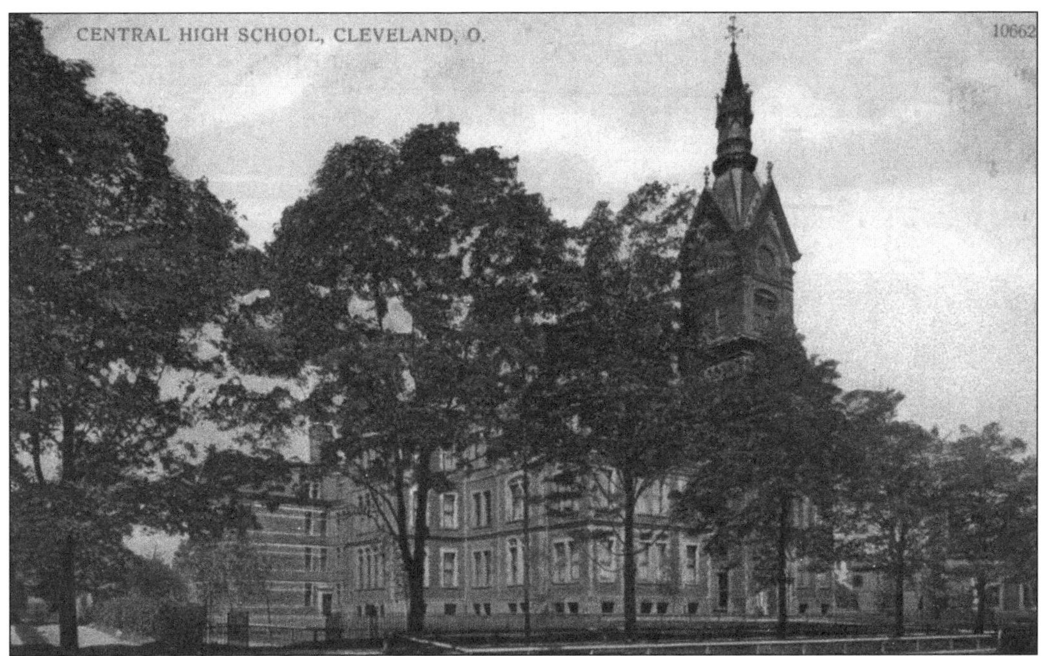

A clock tower without a clock crowned the new Central High School, opened in 1878 to replace the smaller school built in 1856. It was designed by noted architect Levi T. Scofield, who later built the Schofield Building which stood at Euclid and East Ninth.

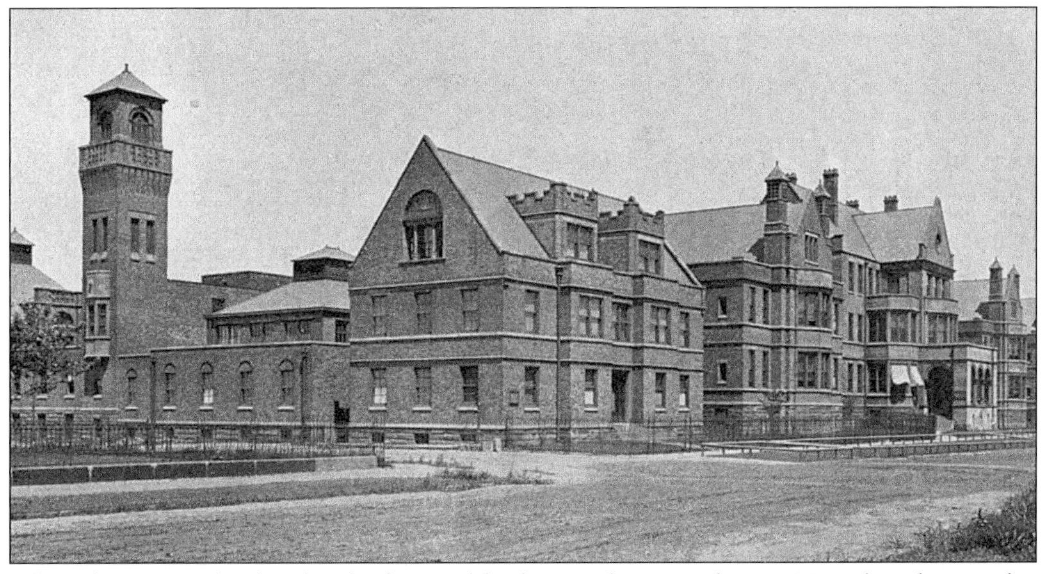

Lakeside Hospital, Cleveland's first public hospital, opened in 1898. Lakeside is today part of the highly rated University Hospitals of Cleveland.

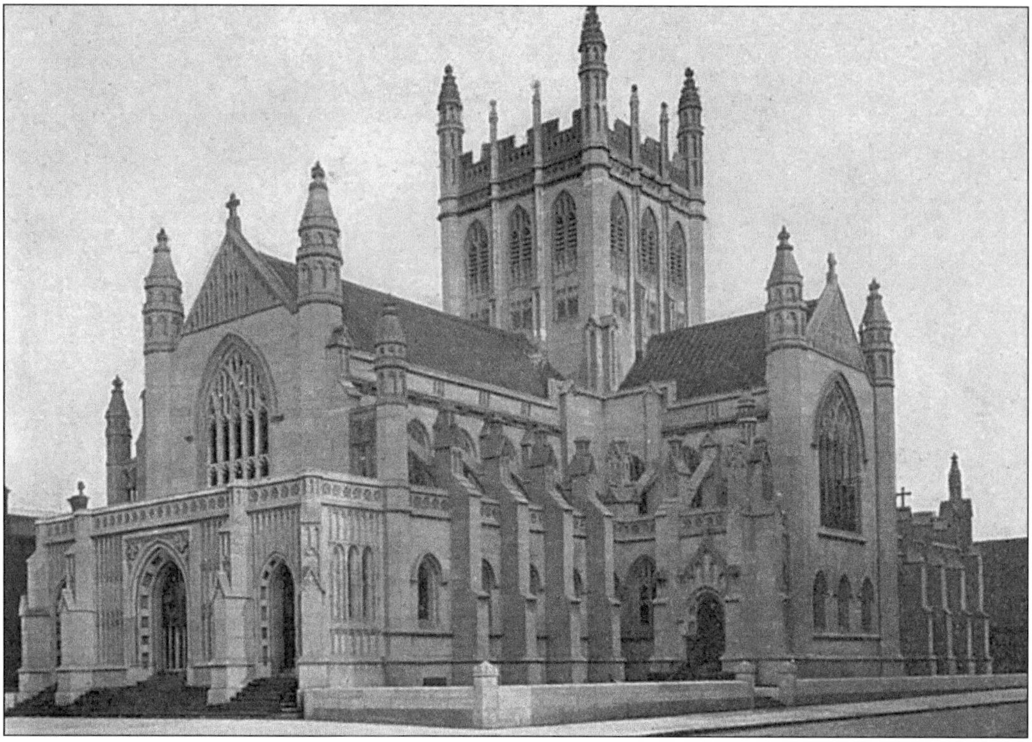

Trinity Cathedral, constructed in 1907, is today the seat of the Episcopal Diocese of Ohio. The church was one of Cleveland's original religious organizations, founded in 1816.

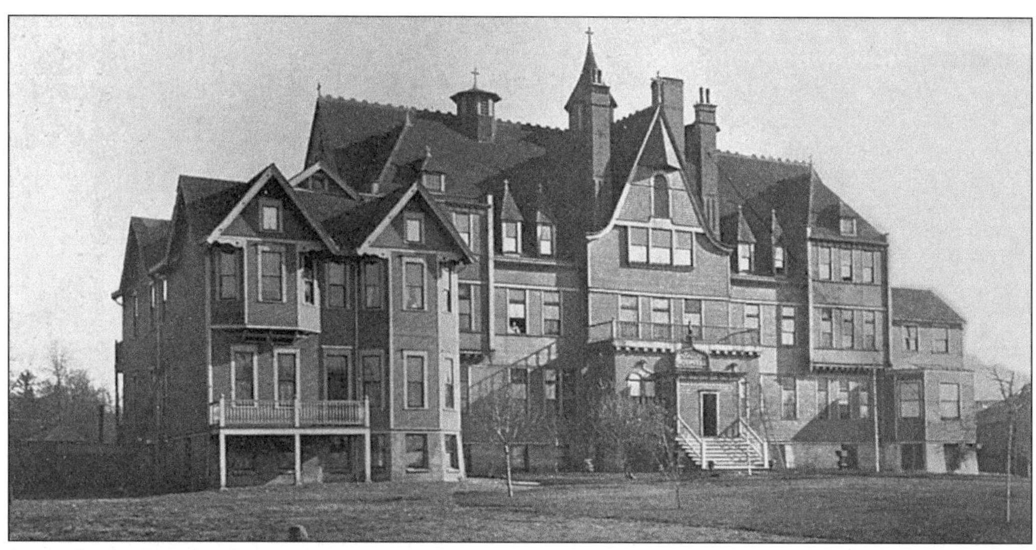

St. John's Hospital, on Detroit Avenue, was organized in 1892 to serve west side residents. In was run by the Franciscan Sisters.

Organized as the Sunday School of the First Baptist Church in 1846, the Erie Street Baptist Church became Euclid Avenue Baptist Church in 1871. John D. Rockefeller was Superintendent of Sunday Schools for a time and gave money for the church that succeeded this one.

Epworth Memorial church, located here at Fifty-fifth and Prospect, was descended from Cleveland's earliest Methodist congregation. The church merged with the Euclid Avenue Methodist Church in 1920 to form the Euclid–Epworth Methodist Church, a prominent University Circle landmark (the "oil can" church).

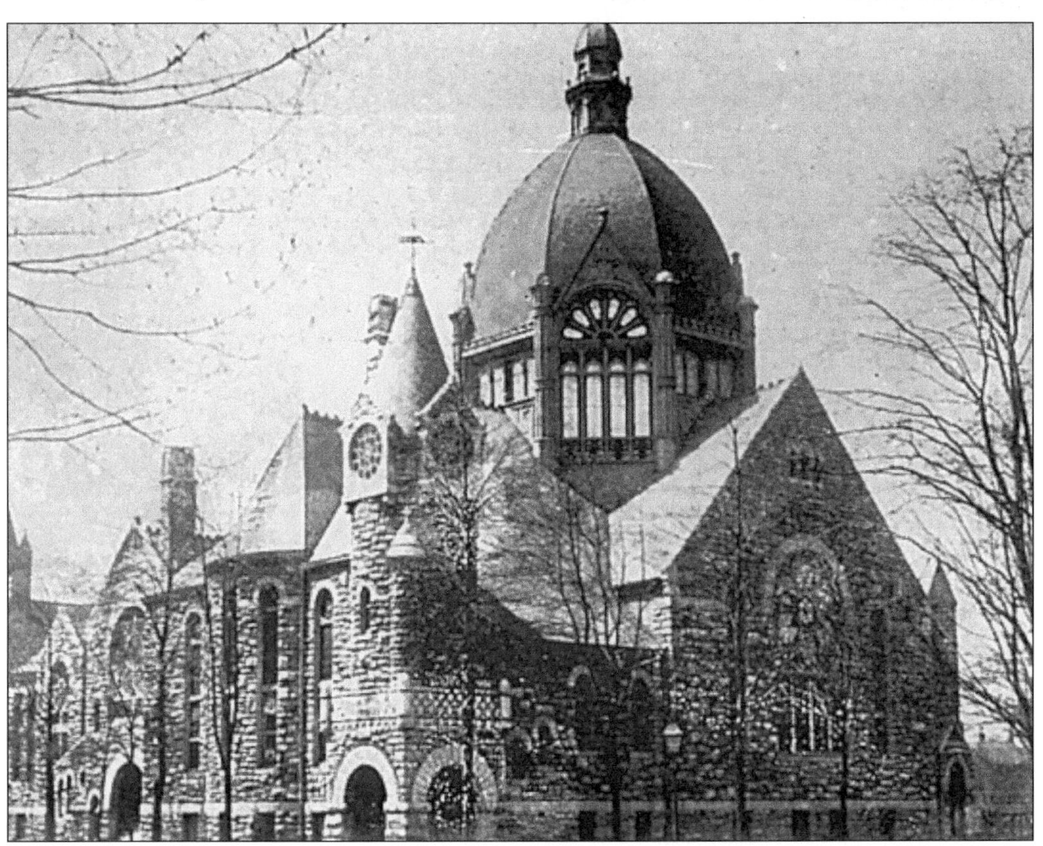

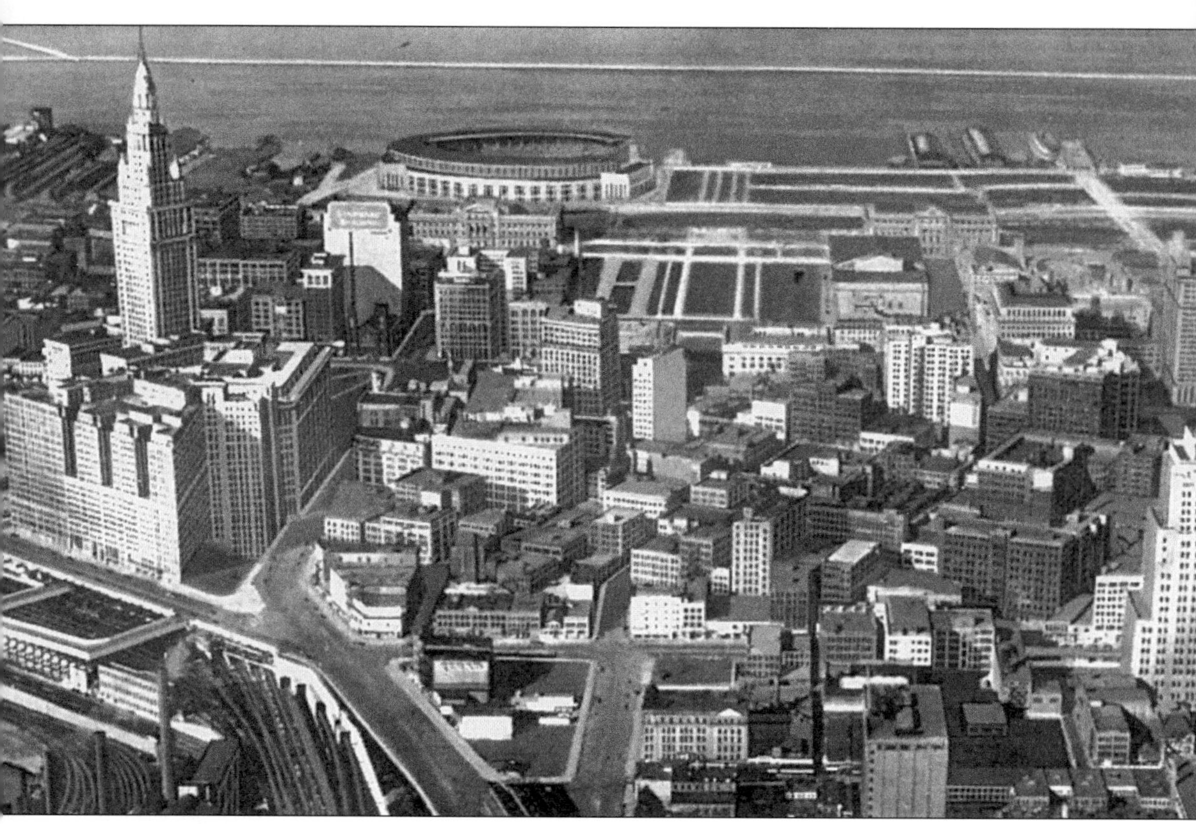

This 1940s aerial view of the city shows two landmarks, the Terminal Tower (at left) and Municipal Stadium on the lake, that were to define the city for decades. Terminal Tower became the unique identifying feature of the city, its image virtually synonymous with Cleveland. The Tower and adjacent buildings were constructed in the 1930s by the famed Van Sweringen brothers to anchor Public Square. The buildings housed Higbee's Department Store (now Dilliard's) and Hotel Cleveland (now Renaissance Plaza). The Tower building featured Cleveland's mammoth railroad station with offices on the upper floors. The rail terminal area is now Tower City, a very popular downtown shopping mall. The stadium featured Cleveland's professional NFL Browns and American League Indians, sources of pride that helped carry the city through the days of decay and default in the 1970s.

Six

UNIVERSITY CIRCLE

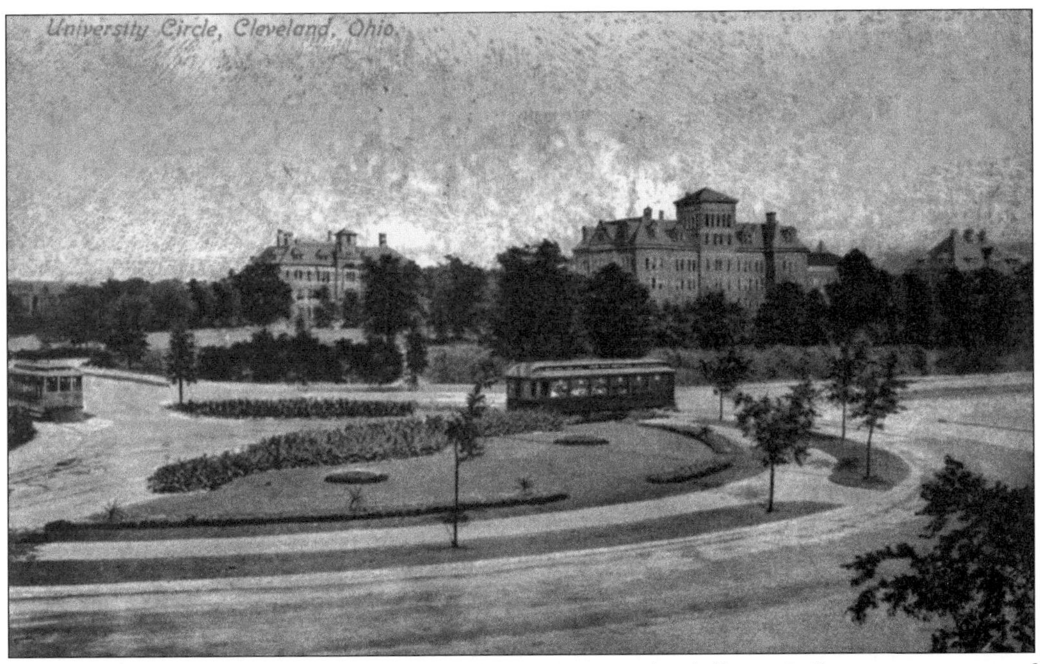

This University Circle bird's-eye view shows Case and Adelbert Colleges, now part of Case Western Reserve University. University Circle got its name from the trolley turnaround circle, shown here in 1910.

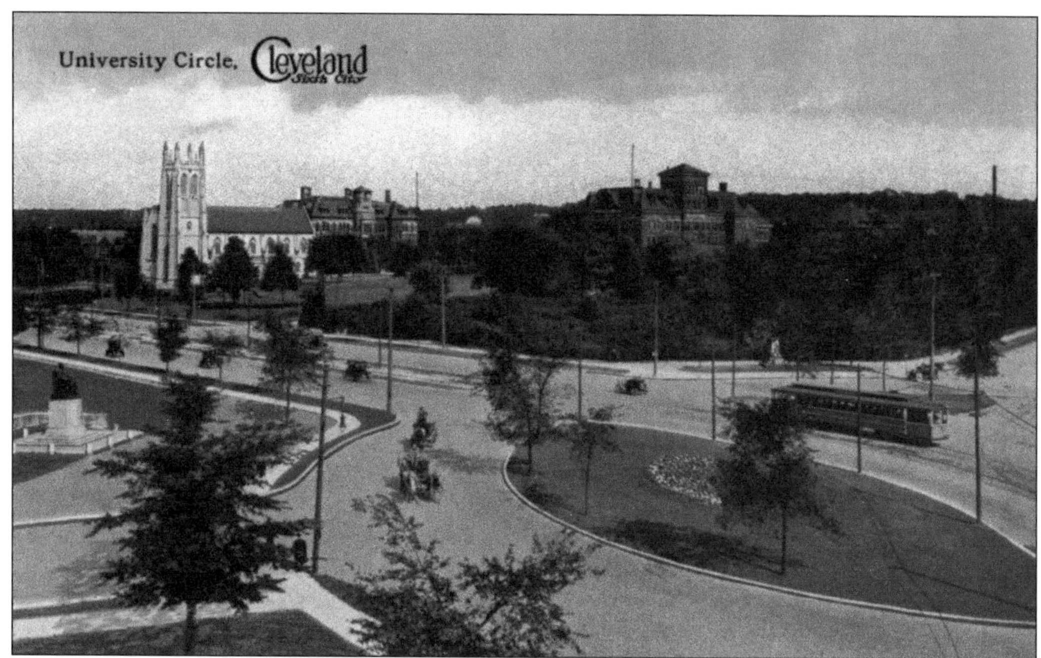

University Circle, known as the cultural heart of Cleveland, provides a park-like setting for Cleveland's prominent museums. It includes the campus of Case Western Reserve University, formed in 1967 as a merger of Case Institute of Technology and Western Reserve University.

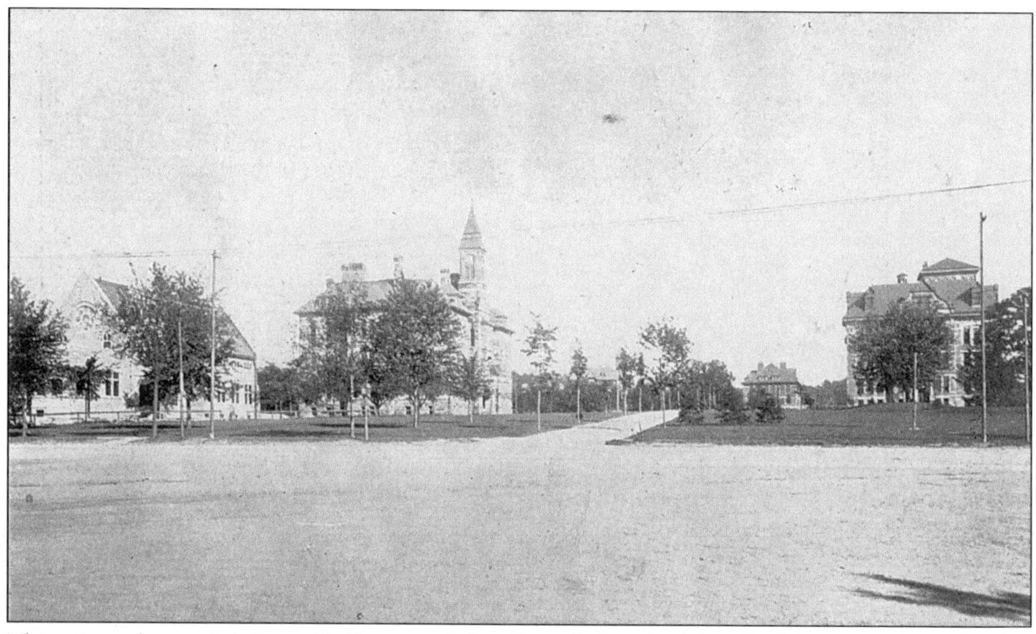

This view shows Adelbert College and the Case School of Applied Science from Euclid Avenue. Adelbert College was the men's undergraduate college of Western Reserve University. It was named after railroad magnate (and benefactor) Amasa Stone's son, who drowned while a student at Yale.

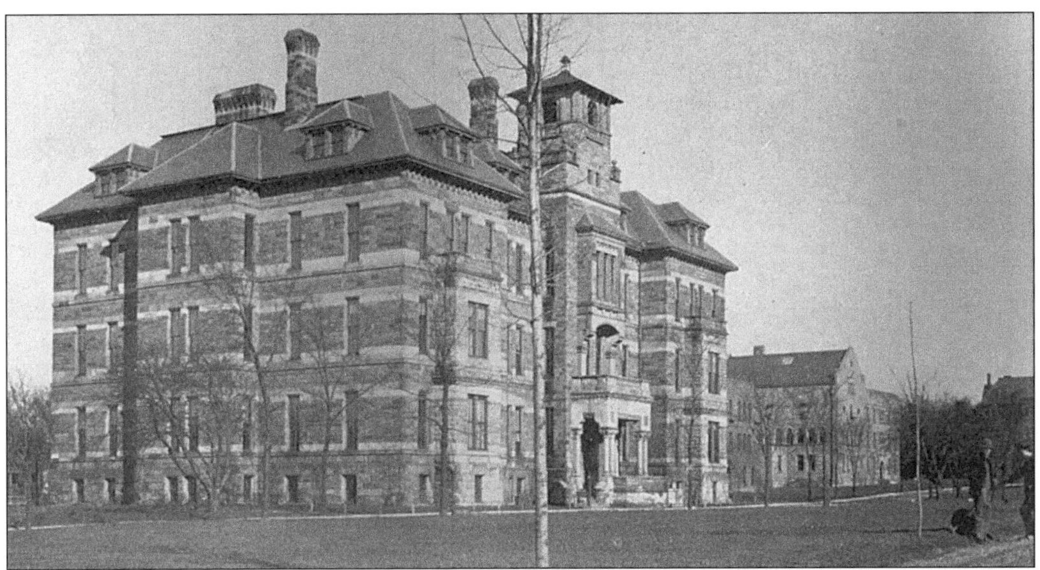

This view gives a close-up look at Adelbert College. Because higher education for women was not fully accepted in this era, it was decided to restrict Adelbert to men and establish a separate women's college.

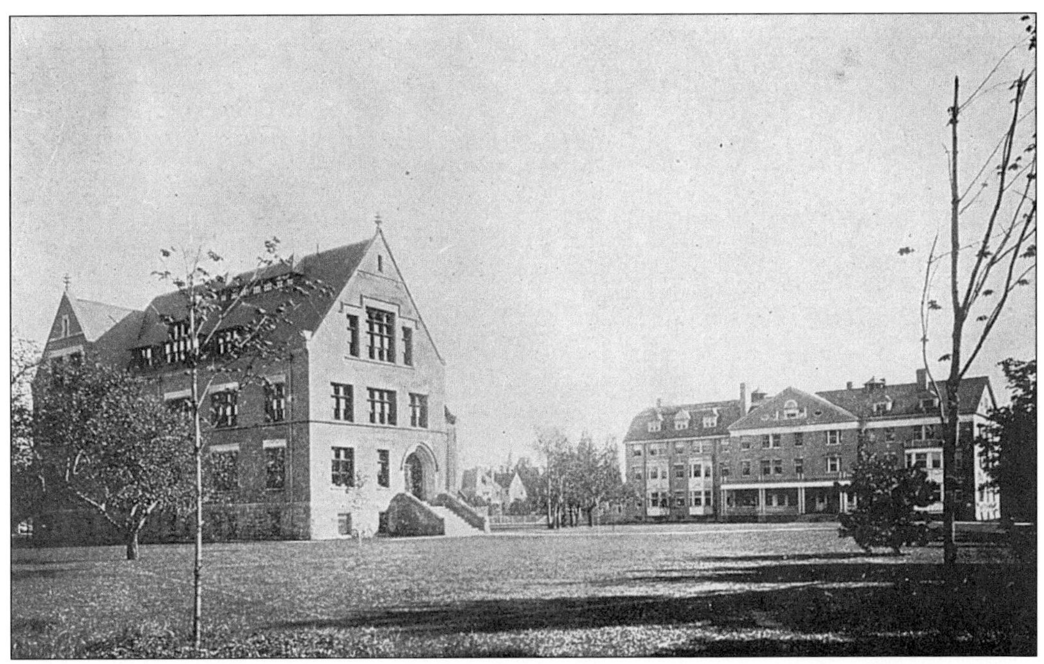

The women's college of Western Reserve University is shown here. The college opened in 1888 in the Ford Homestead with 40 students, and was considered to be a pioneering educational institution for women.

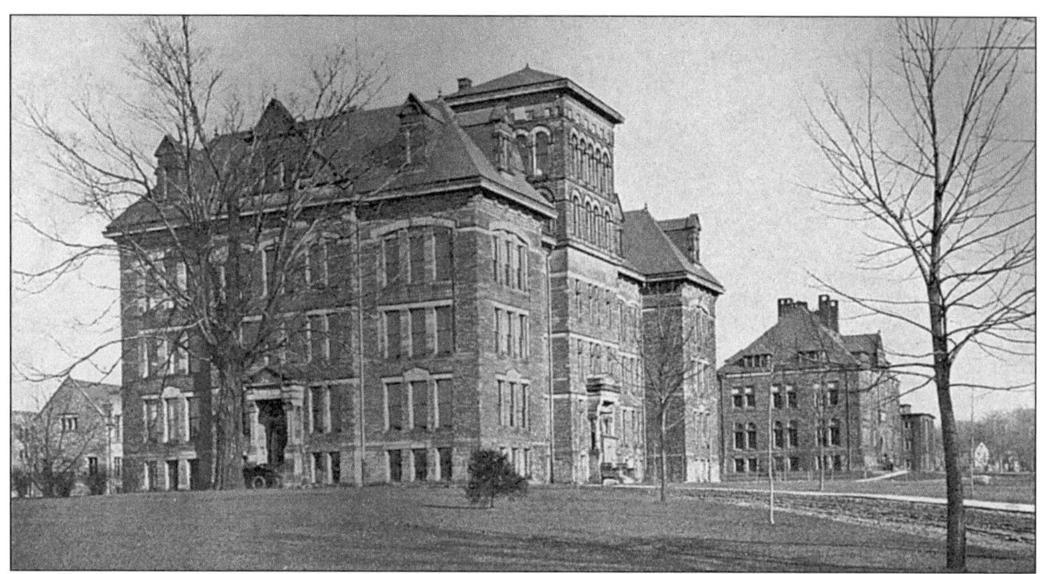

Case School, which later became Case Institute of Technology, was founded in 1880 by Leonard Case Jr. to provide advanced technical education. The school grew to become a leading technical university and greatly expanded its University Circle campus through the years. It is now part of Case Western Reserve University.

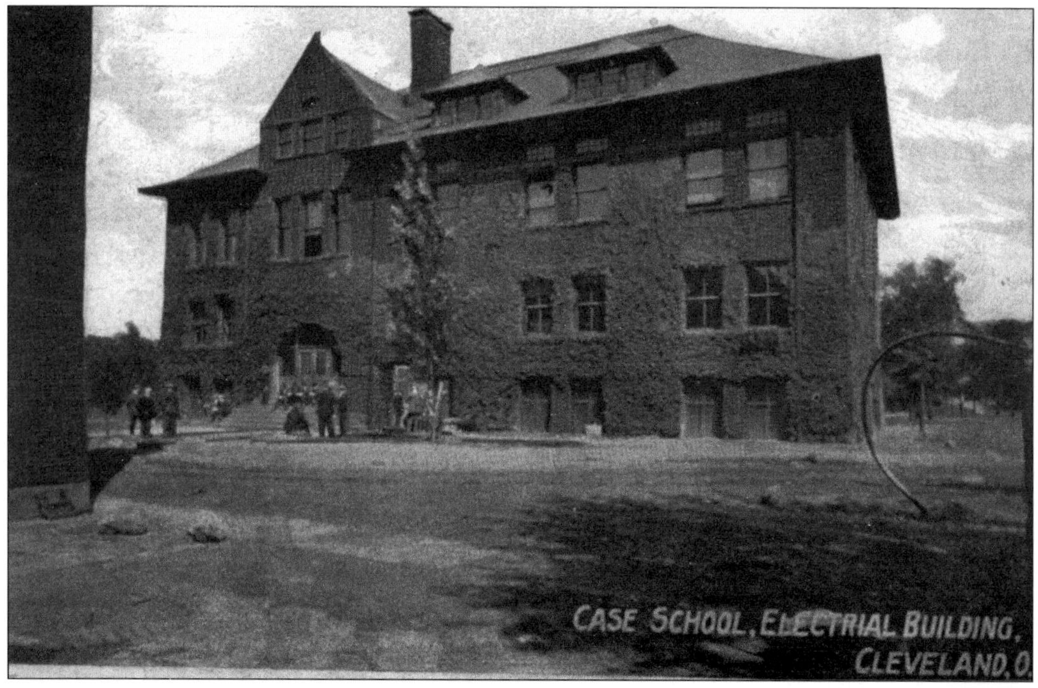

The Electrical Building at Case School was one of the early sites for training engineers.

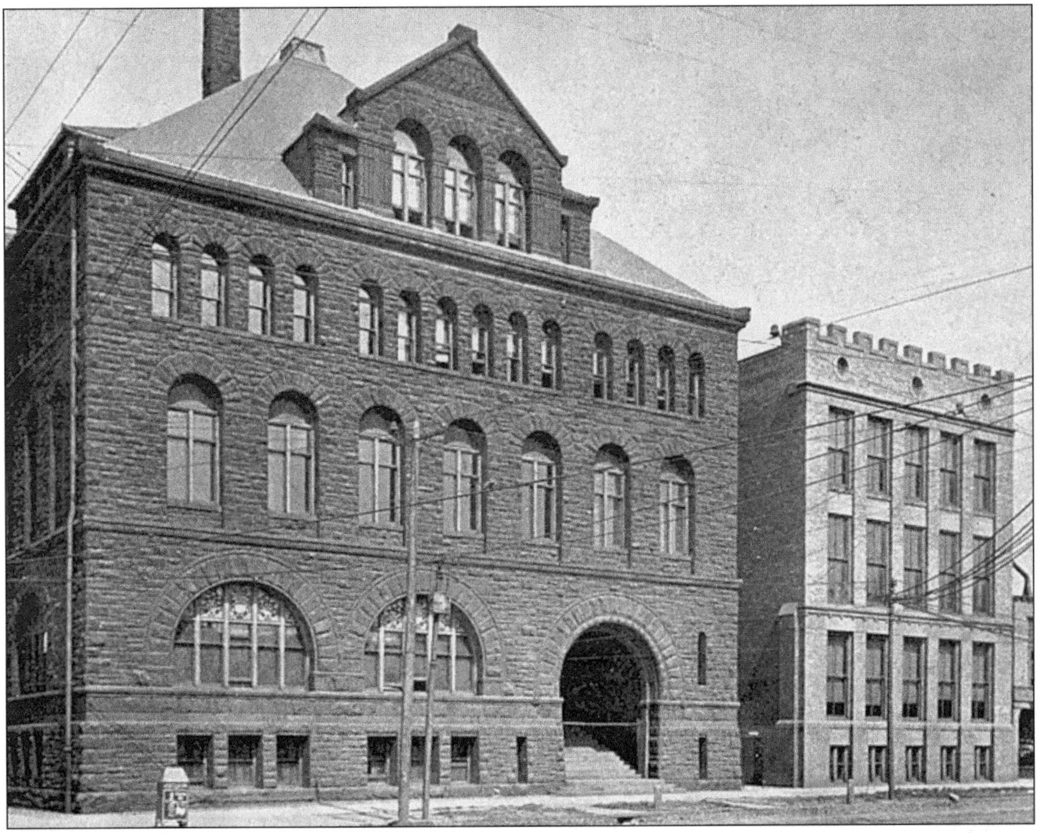

Western Reserve College was founded in 1821 in Hudson, Ohio, and was moved to Cleveland in 1880 after outgrowing its Hudson campus.

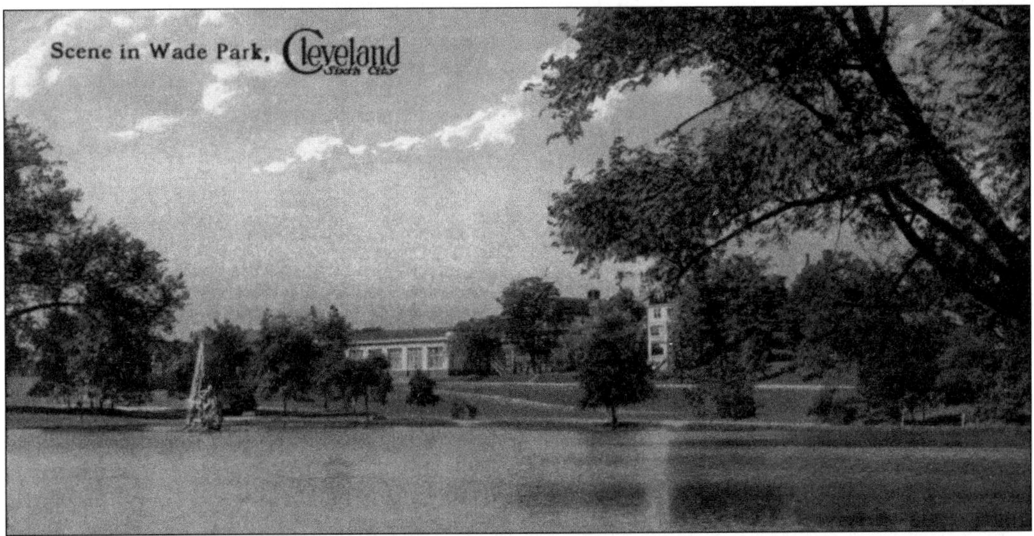

Wade Park, in University Circle, was developed from the estate of Jeptha H. Wade in the 1880s. It is bordered today by the Cleveland Museum of Art and remains a delightful summer promenade.

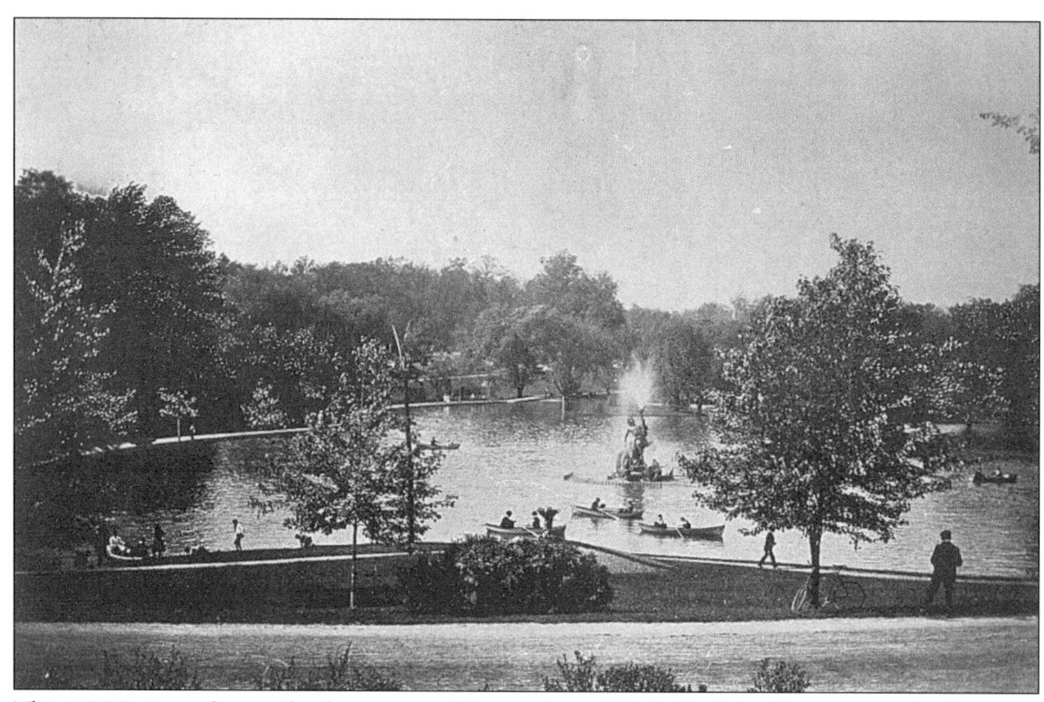

This 1908 view shows the lagoon and fountain at Wade Park in University Circle.

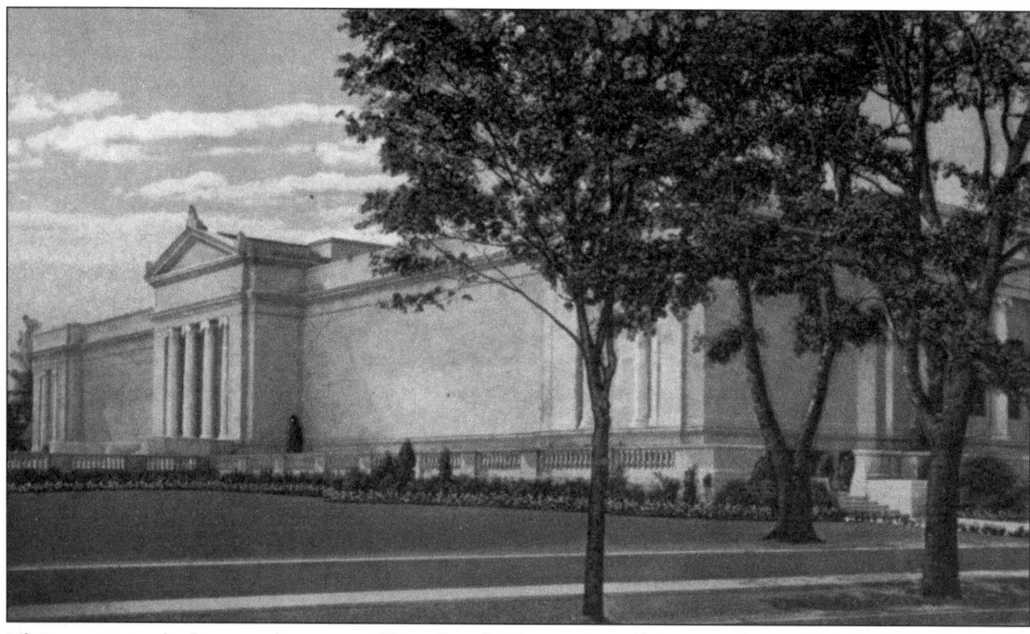

This postcard shows the new Cleveland Museum of Art in the 1920s. The museum opened in this neoclassical marble building, built at a cost of $1.25 million in 1916. The building, now larger due to several additions through the years, still houses the museum's splendid collections.

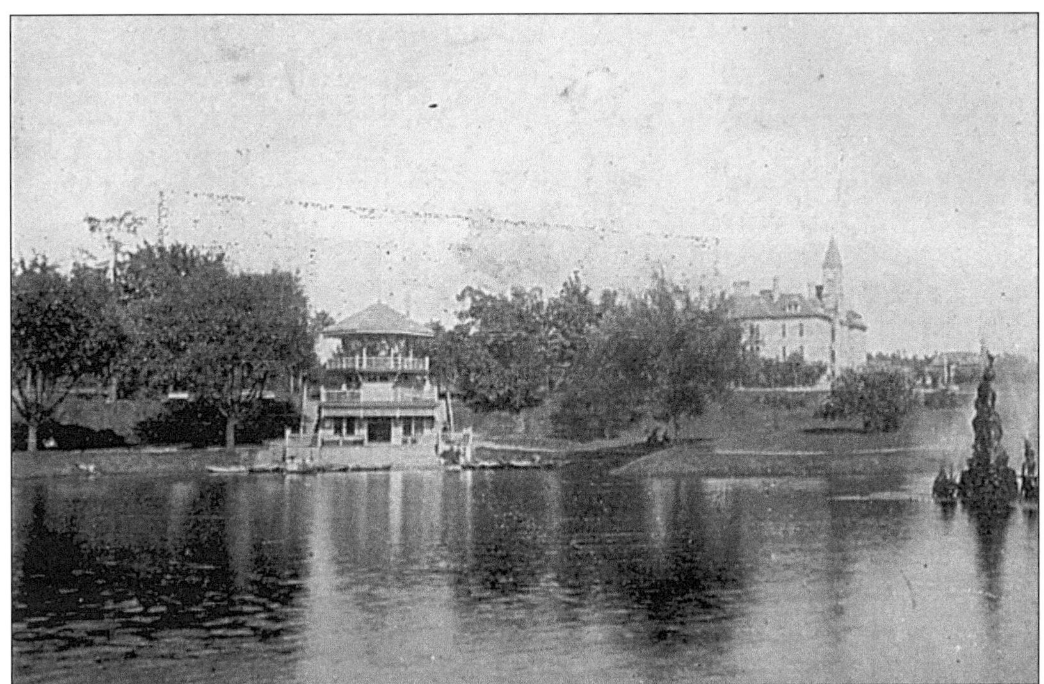

This University Circle view shows the fountain in Wade Park lagoon and a now long-gone boathouse. In the background is Adelbert College.

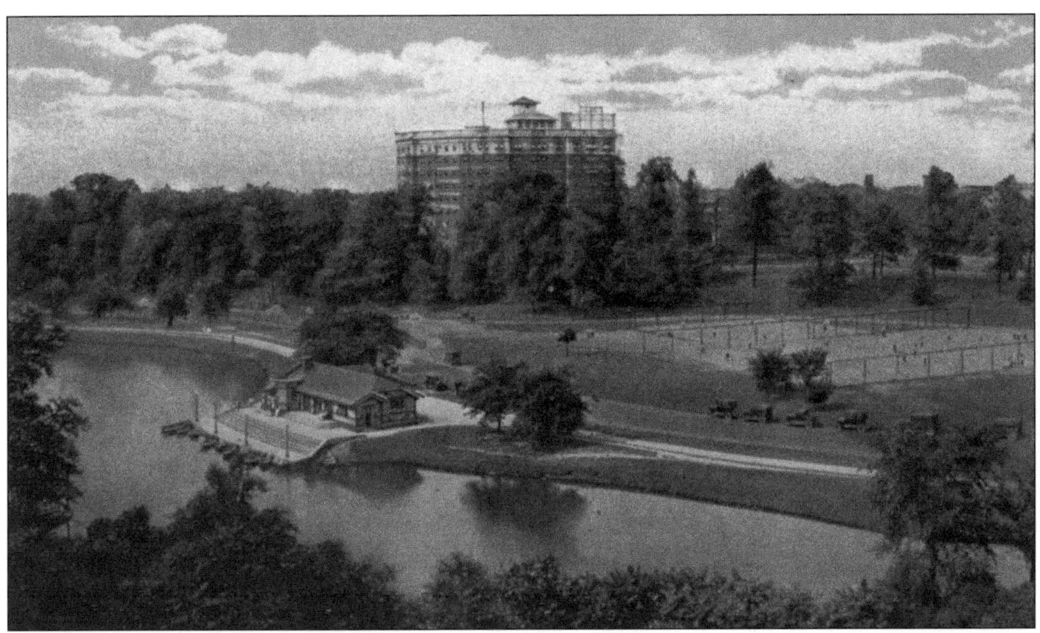

Wade Park connects to Rockefeller Park at East 105th Street in University Circle. The park is named for John D. Rockefeller, who donated the land to the city in 1897. This bird's-eye view shows the Rockefeller Park lagoon with the Sovereign Hotel in the background. Note the boats for rent at the foot of the pavilion.

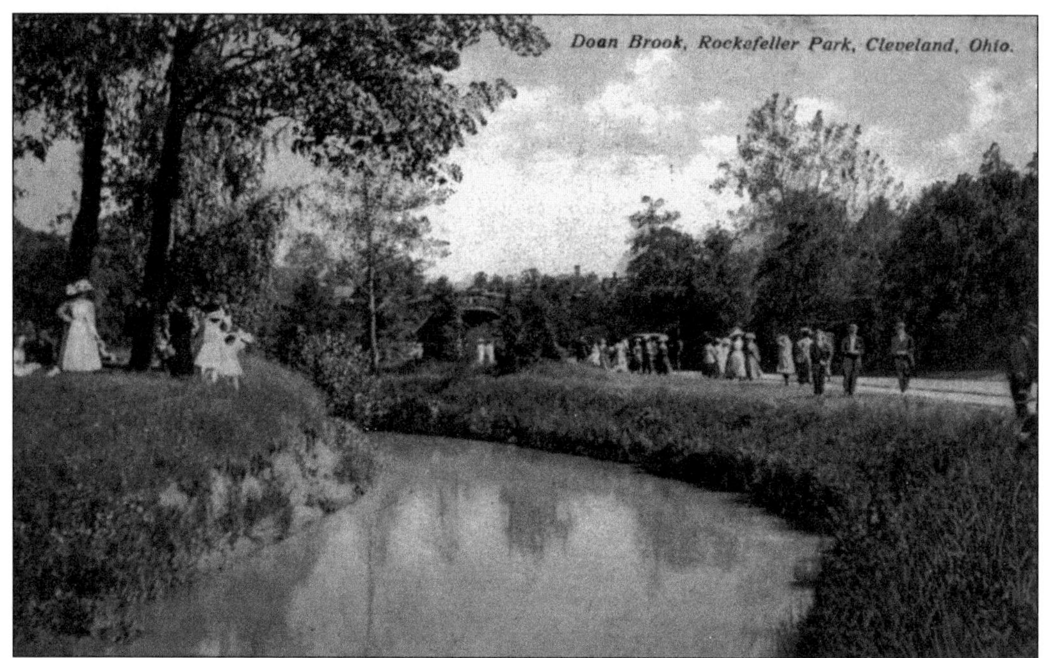

Strollers in their Sunday best picnic and promenade along Doan Brook at Rockefeller Park.

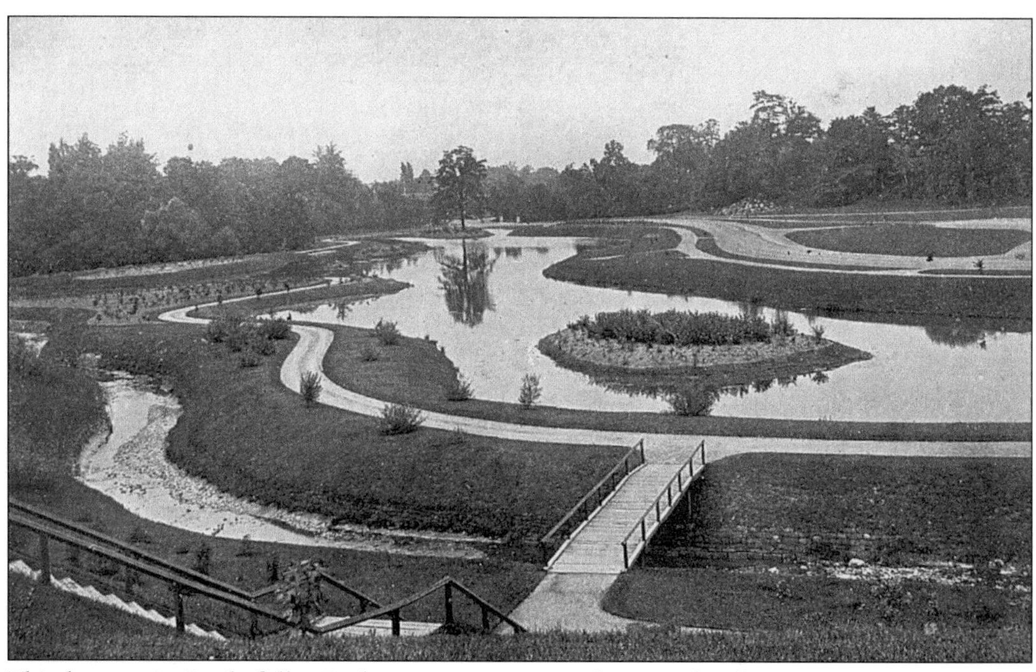

This lagoon in Rockefeller Park was a quiet oasis for city dwellers.

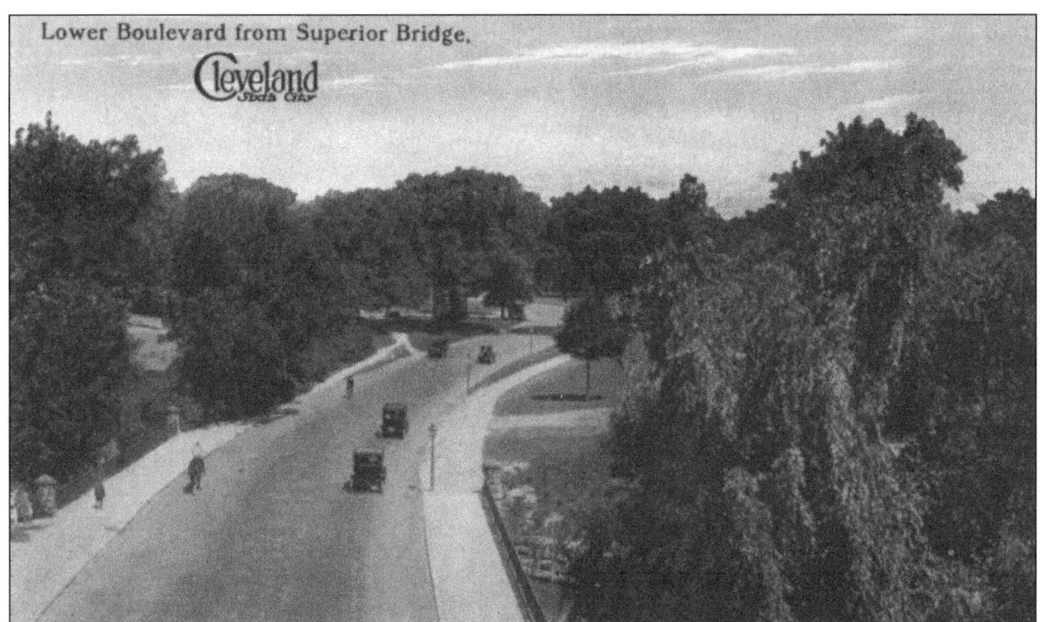

The boulevard through Rockefeller Park is the link between Gordon Park on Lake Erie and Wade Park in University Circle. It is now home to Cleveland's famed Cultural Gardens (developed in the 1930s), representing each of Cleveland's major ethnic groups.

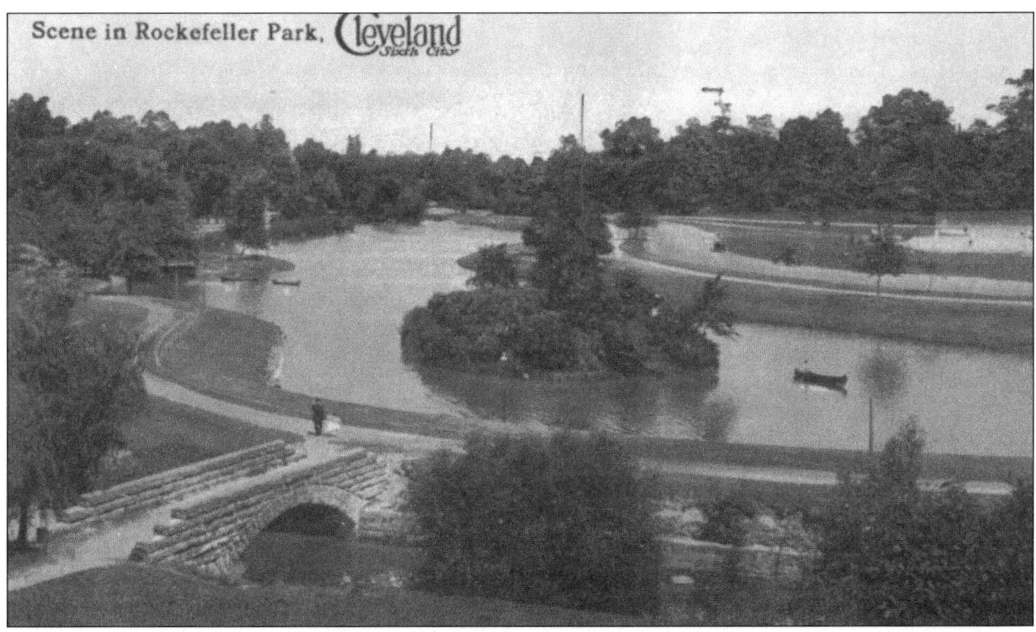

Canoes ply the lagoon at Rockefeller Park in this 1918 postcard. Contrast this scene with the earlier view, opposite.

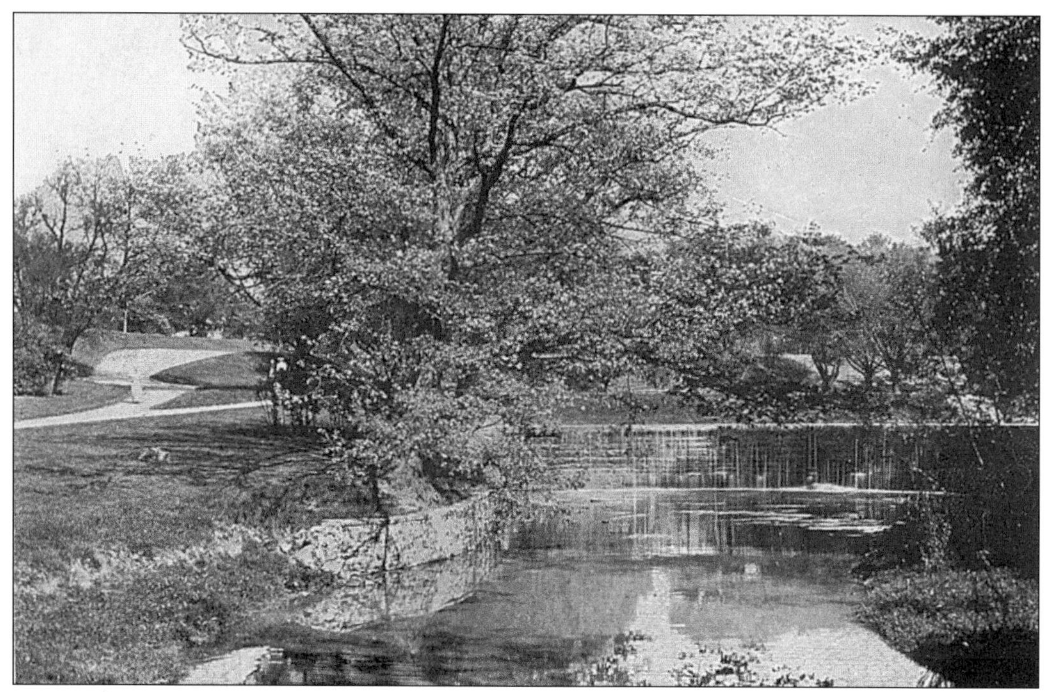

This view of Doan Brook was taken at Wade Park. The brook flows through Rockefeller Park and enters into Lake Erie at Gordon Park.

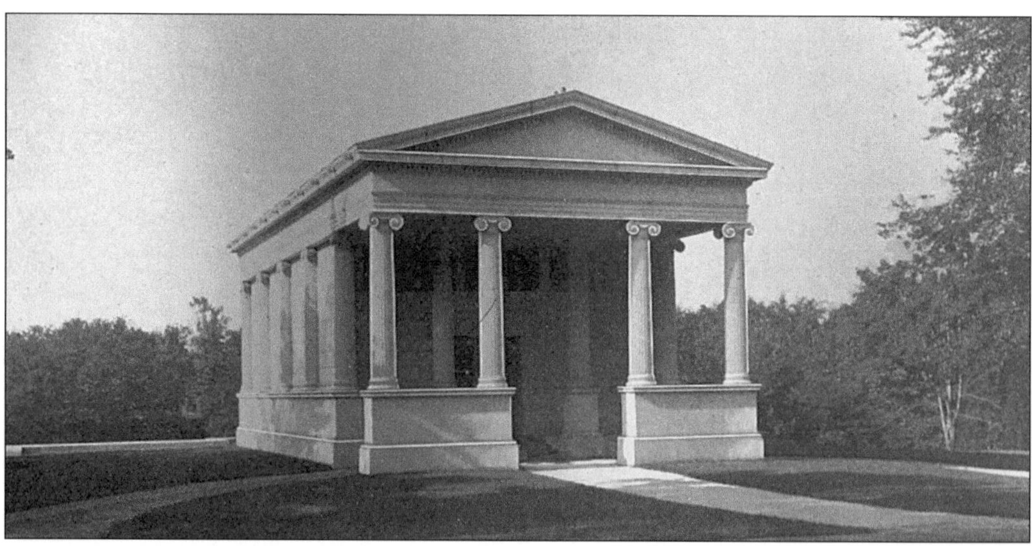

Wade Memorial Chapel at Lakeview Cemetery honors railroad builder and financier Jeptha H. Wade (namesake of Wade Park).

The Garfield Monument in Lakeview Cemetery on the edge of University Circle, completed in 1890, was said to be the first mausoleum dedicated to an American statesman. The crypt at the base of the monument contains the remains of slain President James A. Garfield, his wife, and his mother. Stained glass windows in the memorial chapel depict the thirteen original states and Ohio.

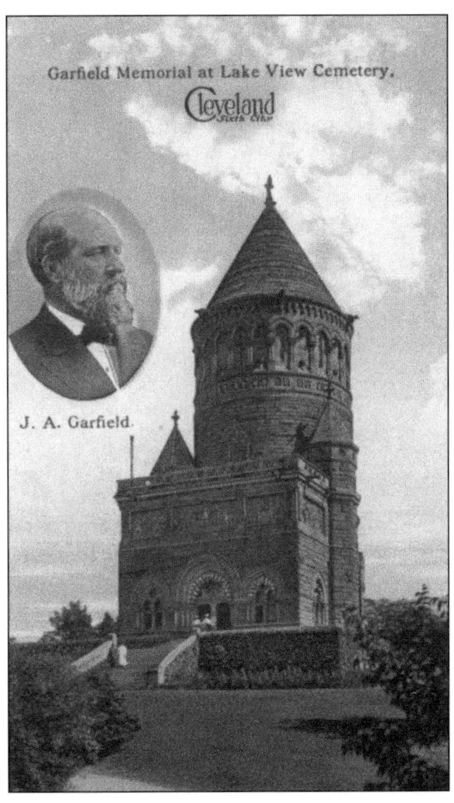

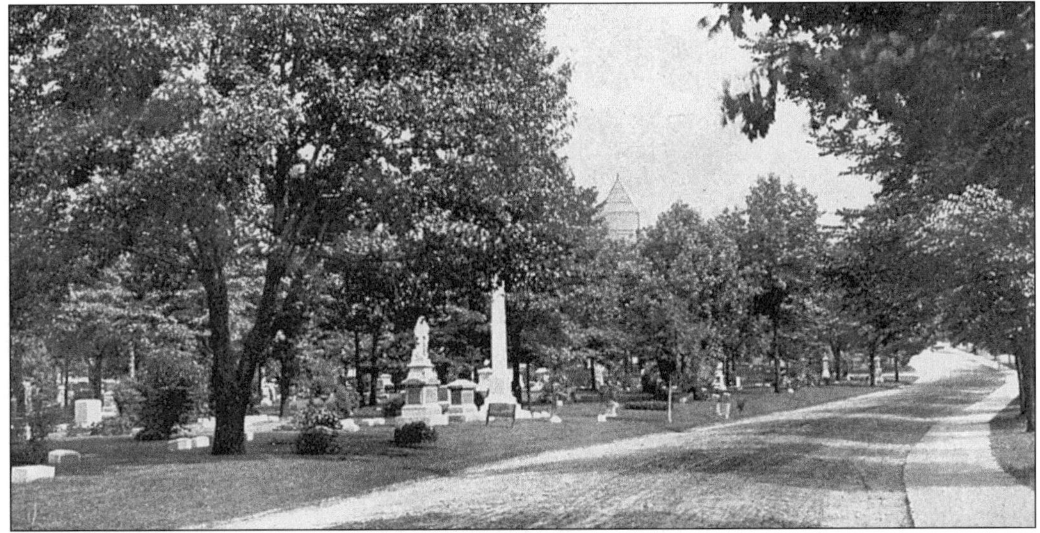

Lakeview Cemetery, founded in 1870, is the resting place of many prominent Clevelanders. Numerous monuments dot its shady, picturesque grounds, the Garfield and Rockefeller memorials being among the most conspicuous.

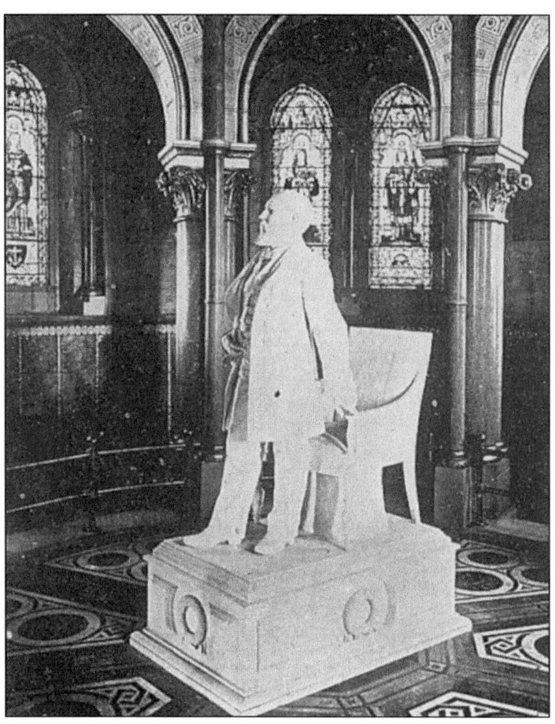

The Garfield Statue, in the center of the Memorial Chapel, was created by renowned sculptor Alexander Doyle of New York.

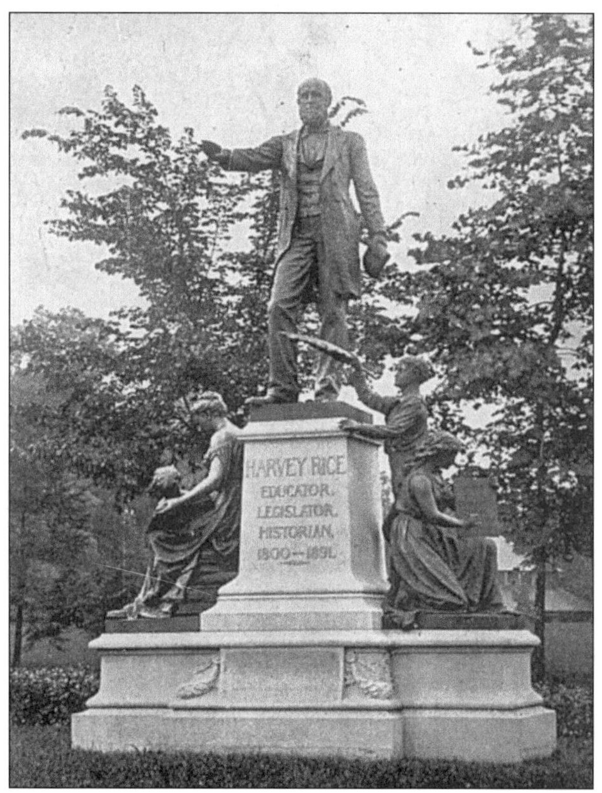

This monument honors Harvey Rice, who, through his pioneering educational plans, became known as the father of Ohio's public schools.

Seven

Residential Cleveland

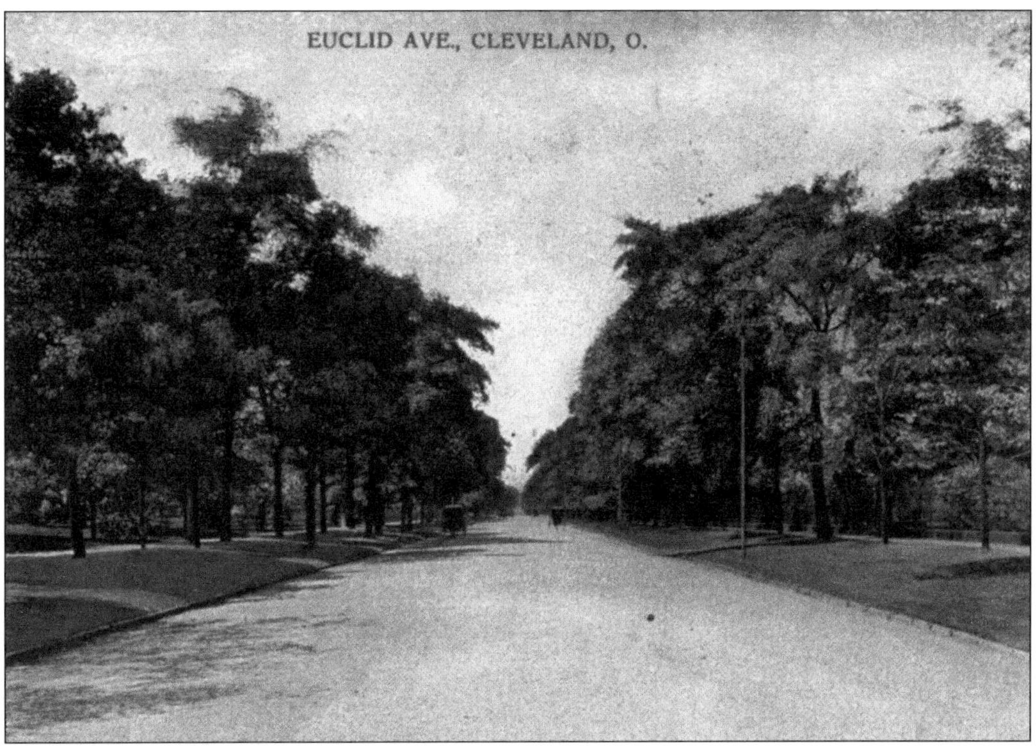

Euclid Avenue beyond the downtown commercial district looks like a park in this pastoral scene. But behind the greenery stand mansions of the rich and famous.

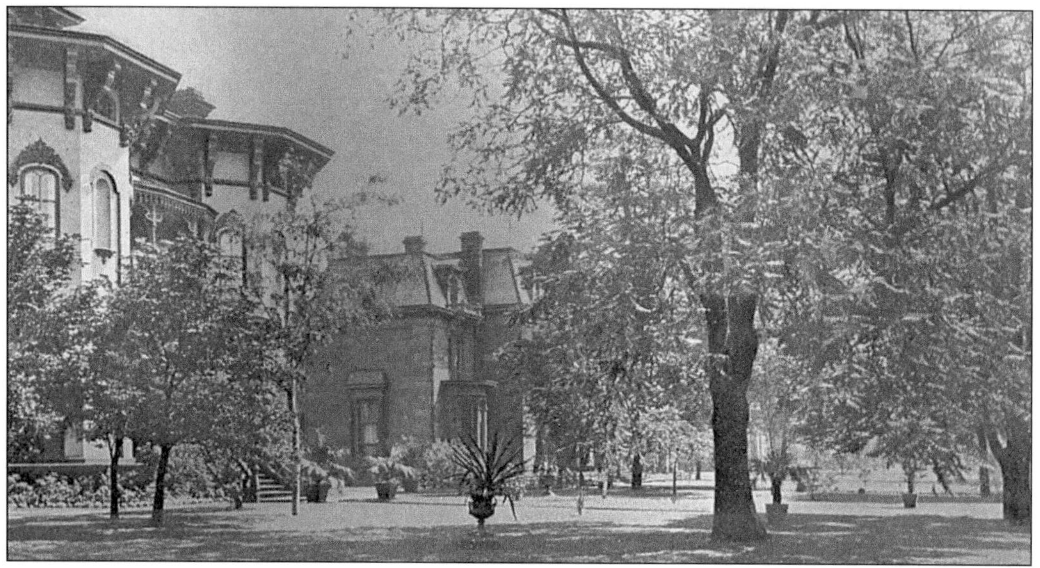

Hailed as "the most beautiful avenue in the world," Euclid Avenue was home to the industrial giants who made their money in the Flats. John D. Rockefeller bought a home here in 1868, and by the late 1800s the street was known as Millionaire's Row.

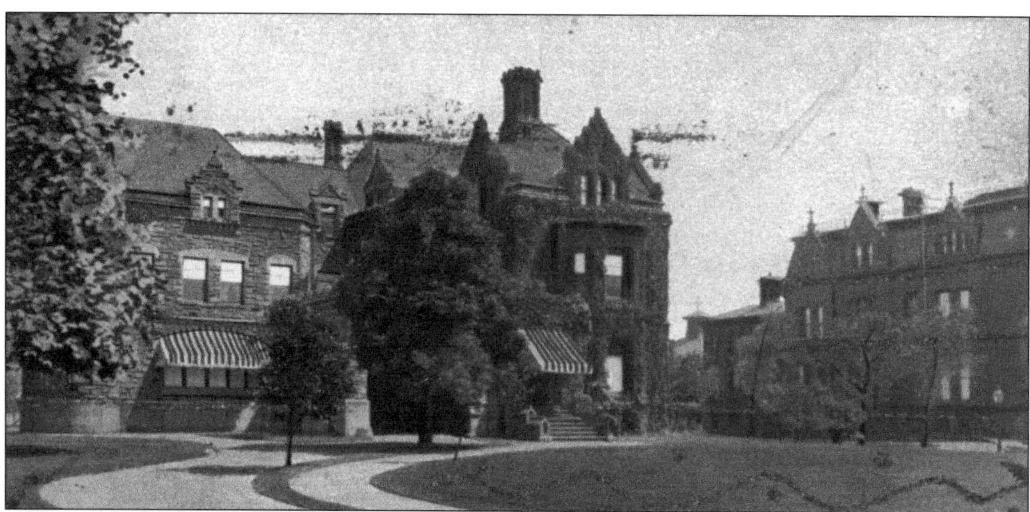

Tom L. Johnson, mayoral giant, owned this home, one of the showplaces of Euclid Avenue. The colorful mayor dramatically influenced Cleveland's development during his four terms in office (1901–1909).

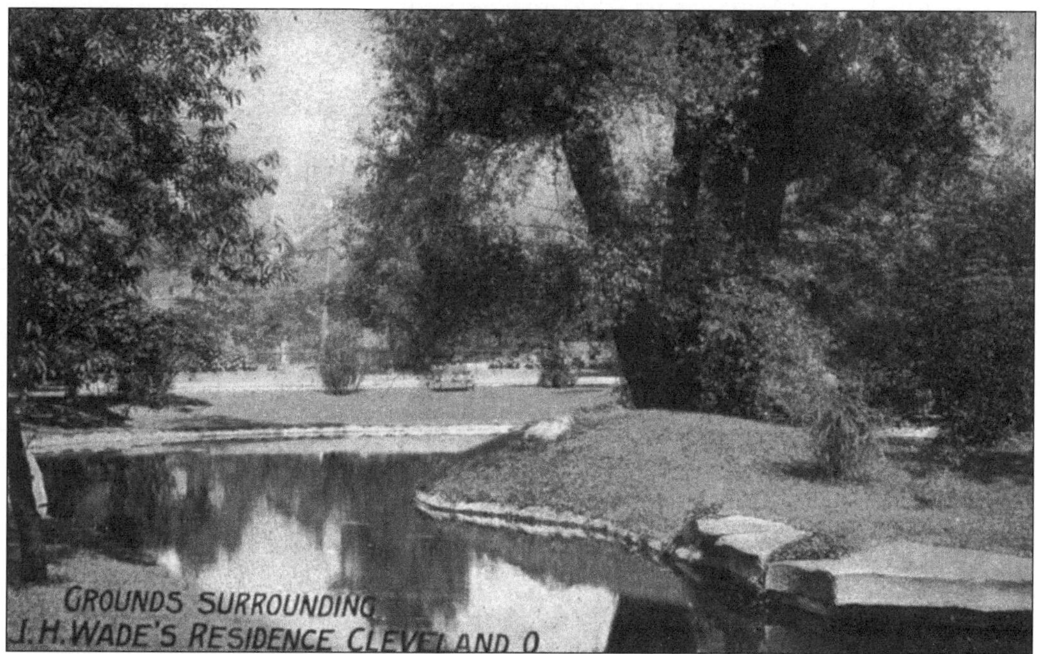

Spacious grounds surrounded most of the homes. Cleveland banker Jeptha H. Wade's estate included a small lake. Wade's mansion was located at Euclid and Case Avenues.

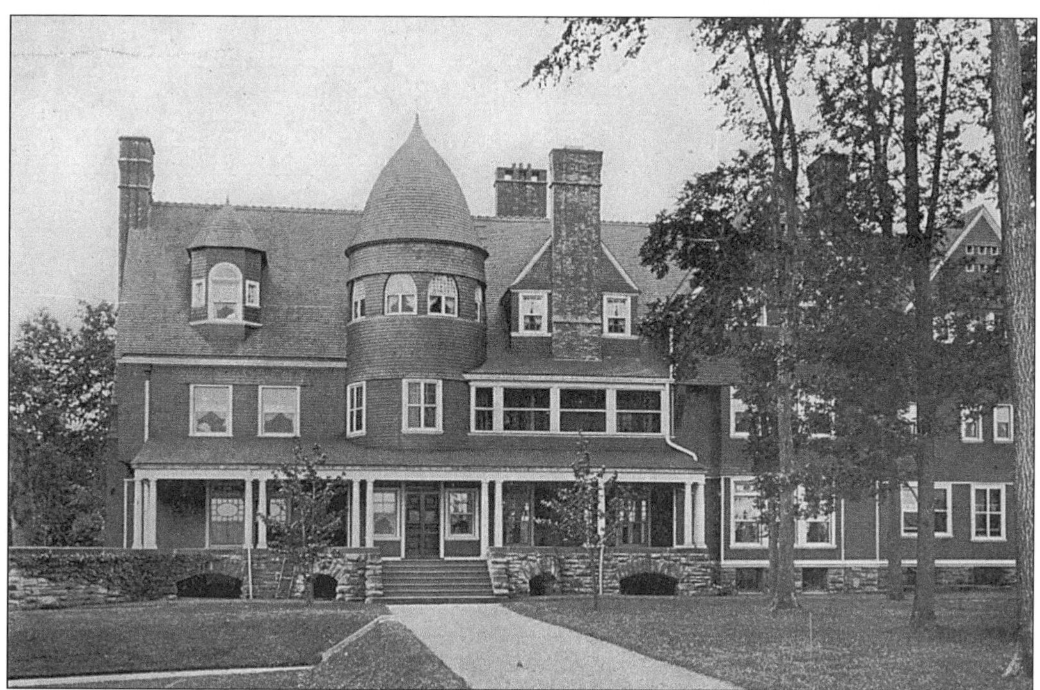

Not all millionaires lived on Euclid Avenue. On Cleveland's West Side, Lake Avenue on Lake Erie was lined with mansions that included the homes of Henry Winton, founder of the Winton automobile, and Mark A. Hanna, Cleveland industrialist and U.S. Senator (1897-1904), whose home is shown here.

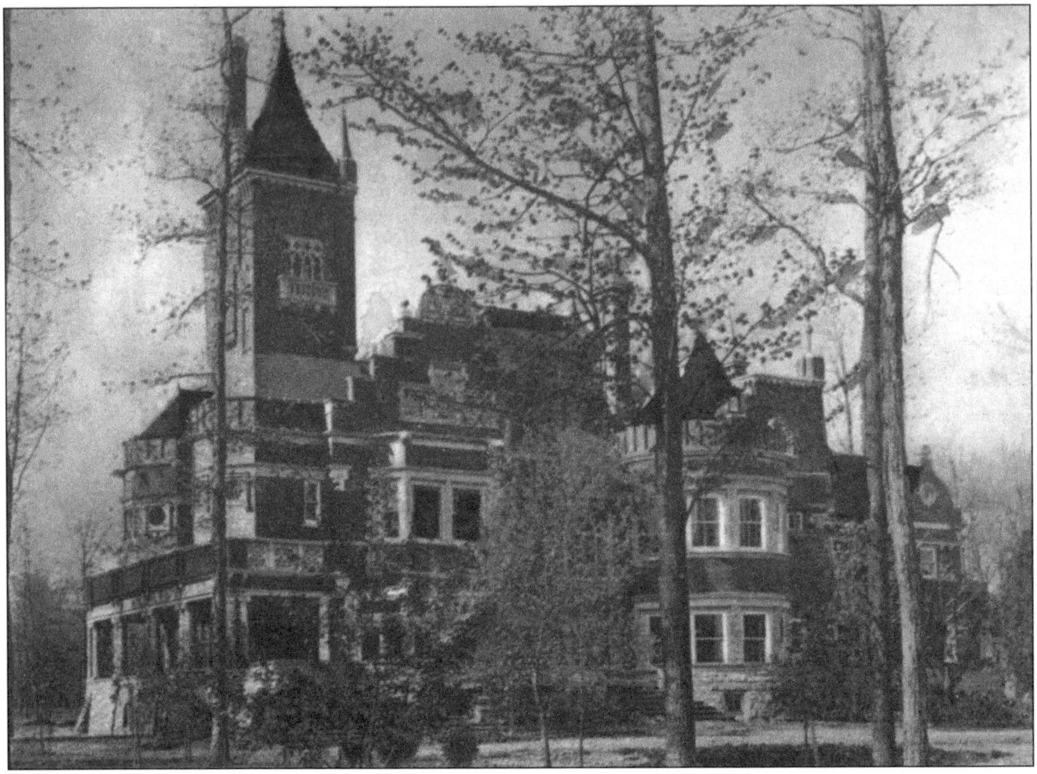

Theodor Kundtz came to Cleveland from Hungary in 1873. He established the Theodor Kundtz Co., which made cabinets for White Sewing Machines. He built this Lake Avenue residence as a millionaire.

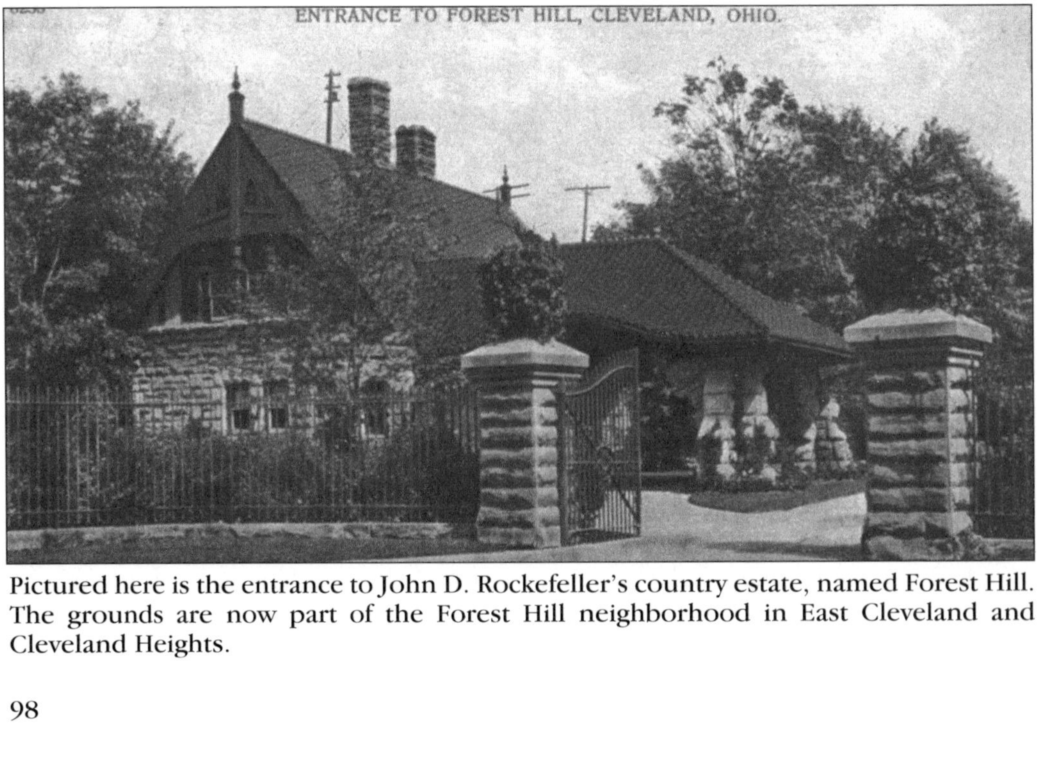

Pictured here is the entrance to John D. Rockefeller's country estate, named Forest Hill. The grounds are now part of the Forest Hill neighborhood in East Cleveland and Cleveland Heights.

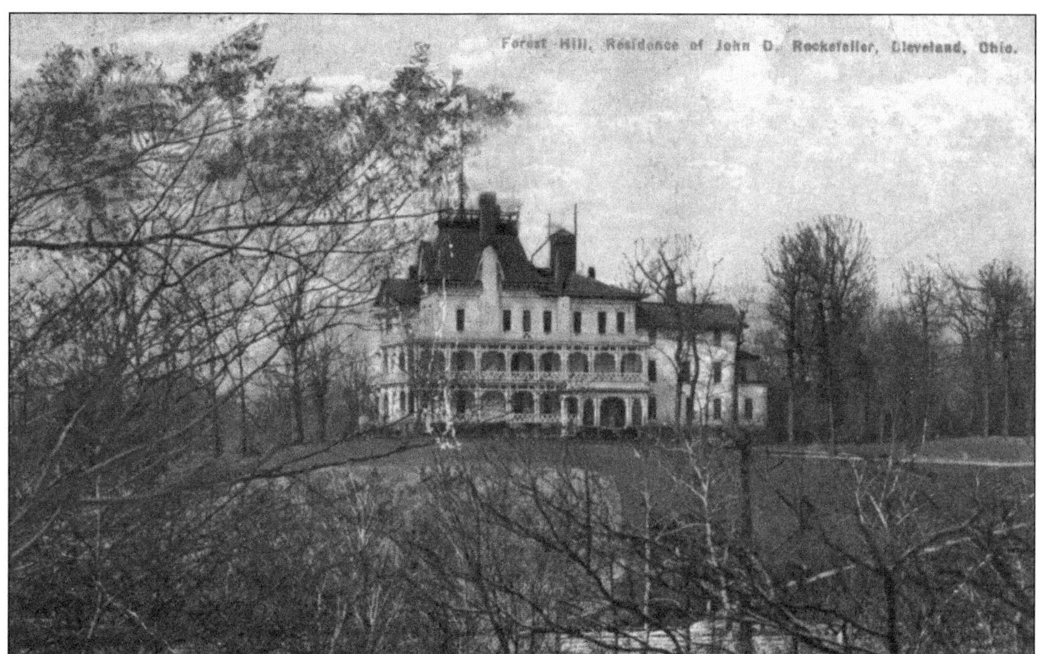

Rockefeller purchased this estate, which was originally intended to be a health resort, in 1879, and maintained it as a summer residence for many years.

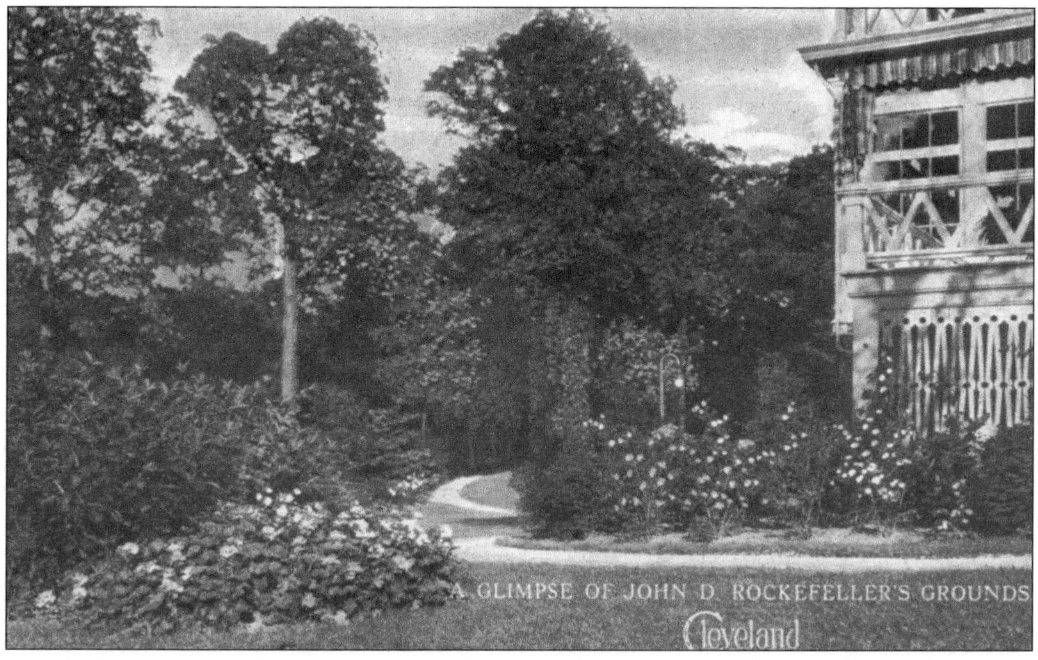

Lushly landscaped grounds bordered the Rockefeller country house. The estate included several lakes and even a nine-hole golf course.

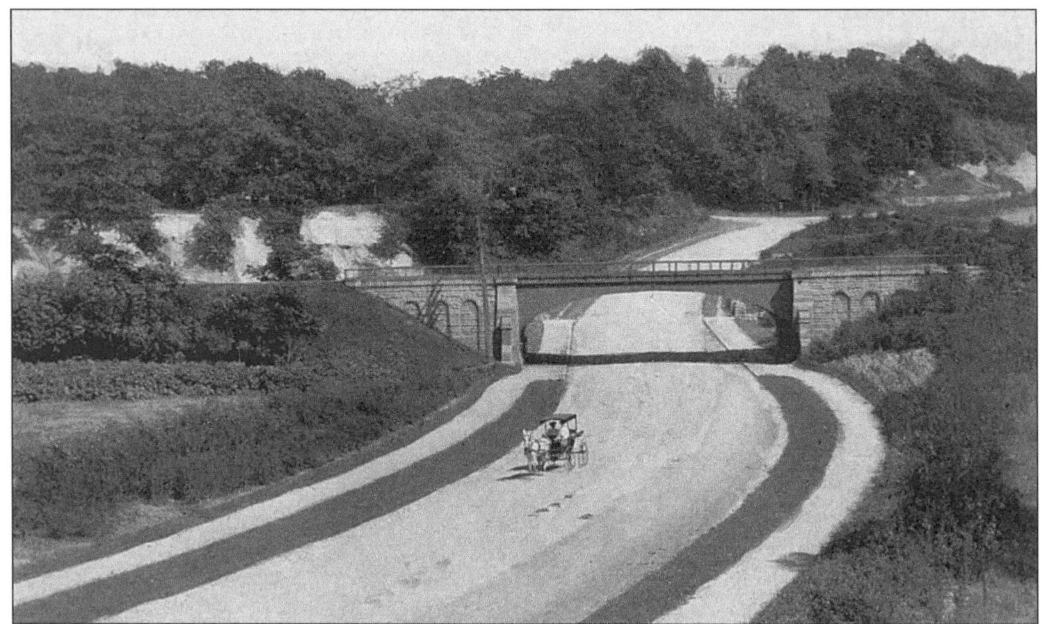

This "Boulevard to Shaker Heights" was one of several scenic drives through the Heights neighborhoods.

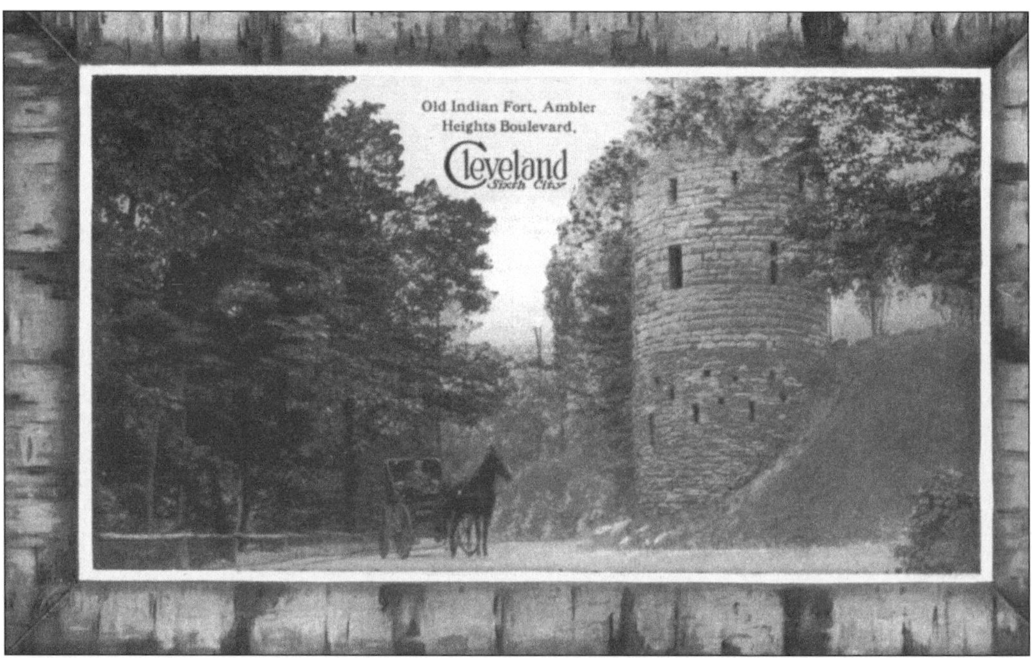

Ambler Heights, in the southwestern part of Cleveland Heights, was named after Dr. Nathan Ambler, a Cleveland dentist who owned land in the area. The suburb was developed by Ambler's nephew, William Eglin Ambler, and Daniel Caswell, his adopted son.

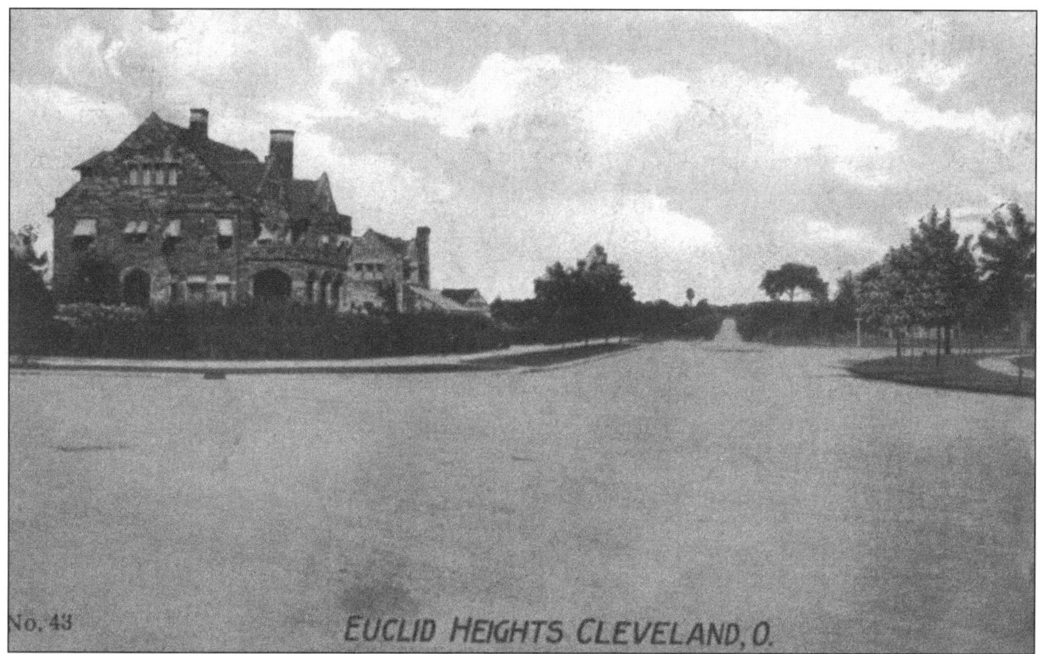

Euclid Heights was developed by real estate magnate Patrick Calhoun as one of Cleveland's first suburbs. The area is now part of the Coventry Road neighborhood.

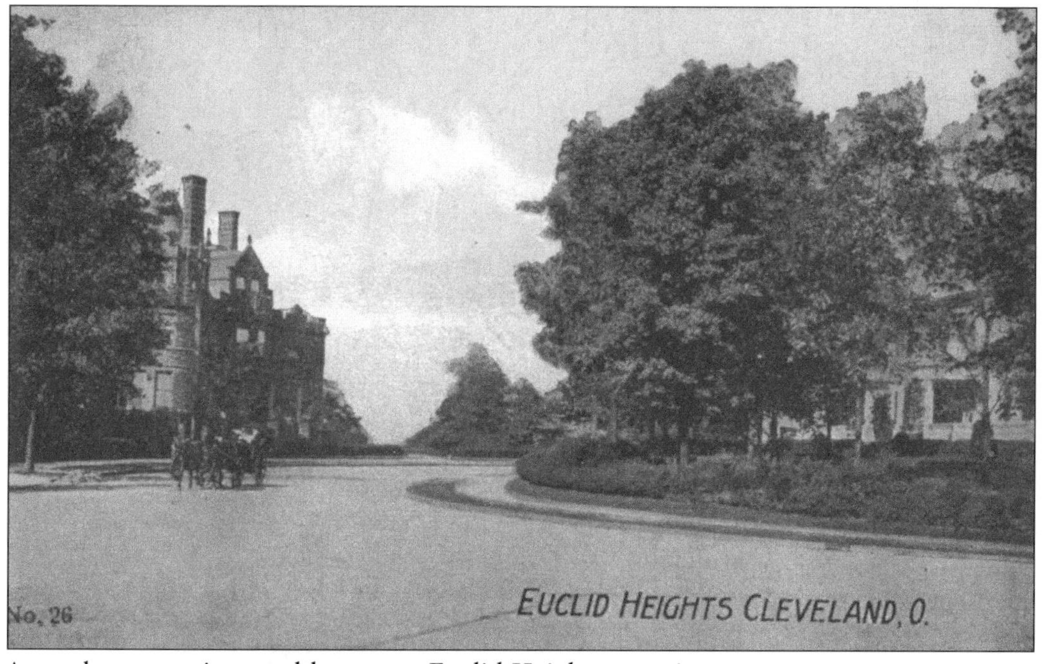

A two-horse carriage ambles past a Euclid Heights mansion.

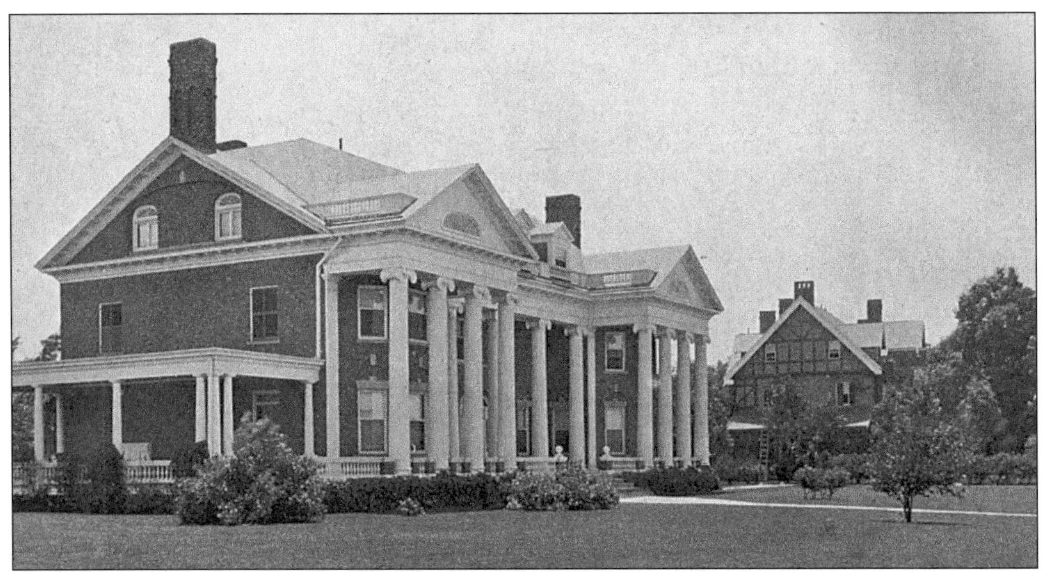

Stately homes with spacious grounds made Euclid Heights one of Cleveland's most desired addresses in the early 1900s.

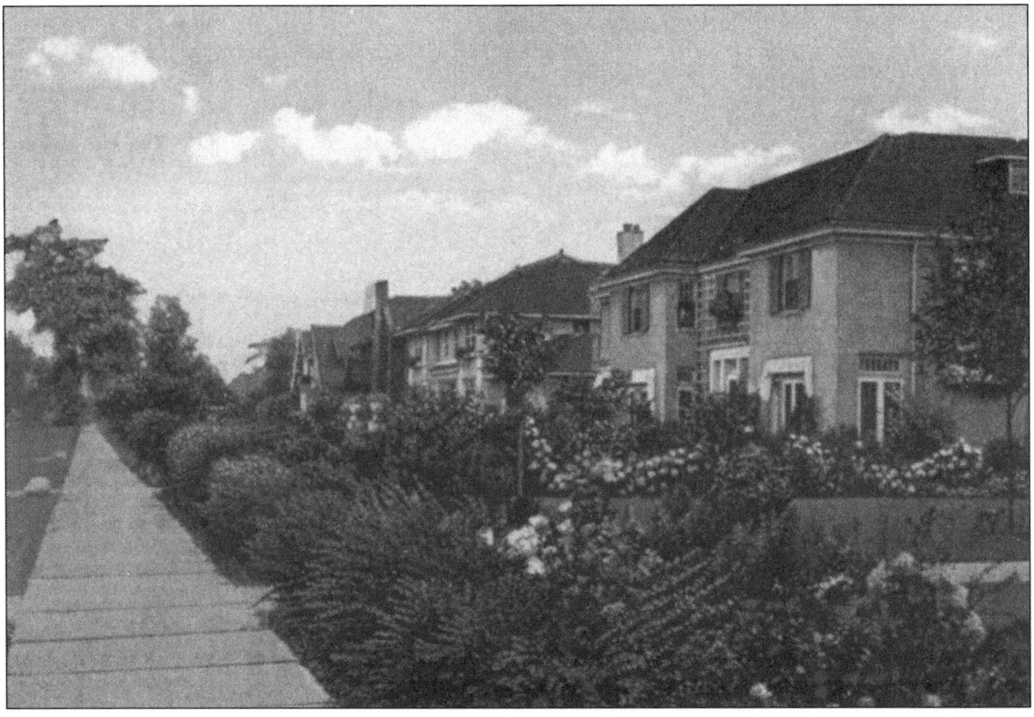

These homes are on Coventry Road in Cleveland Heights.

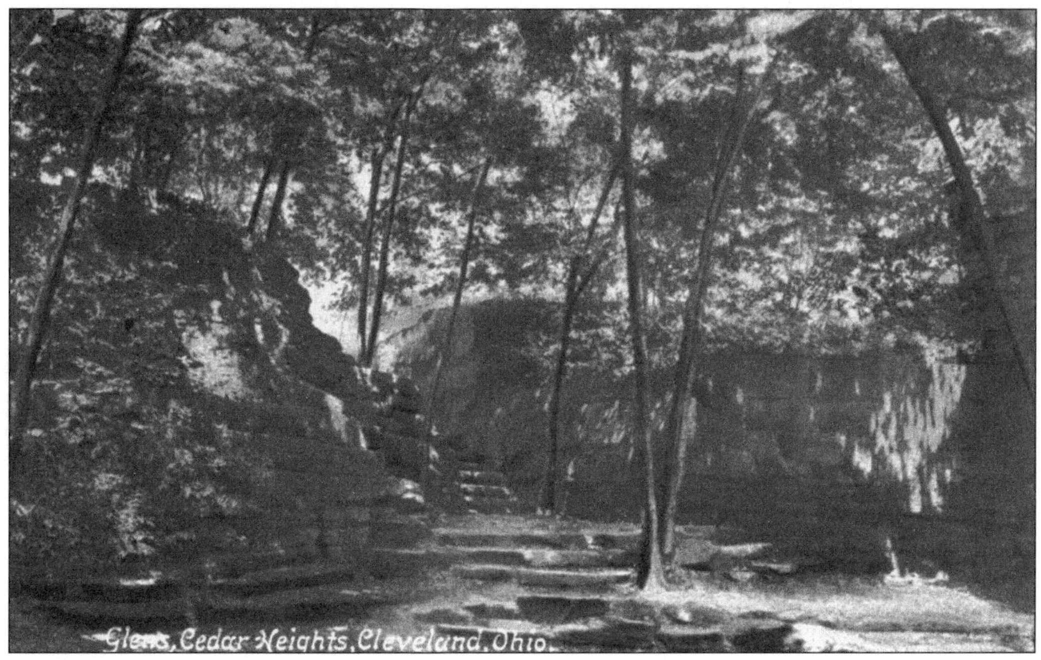

Cedar Glen, south of University Circle in Cedar Heights, featured a natural spring producing "healthful" sulfur water.

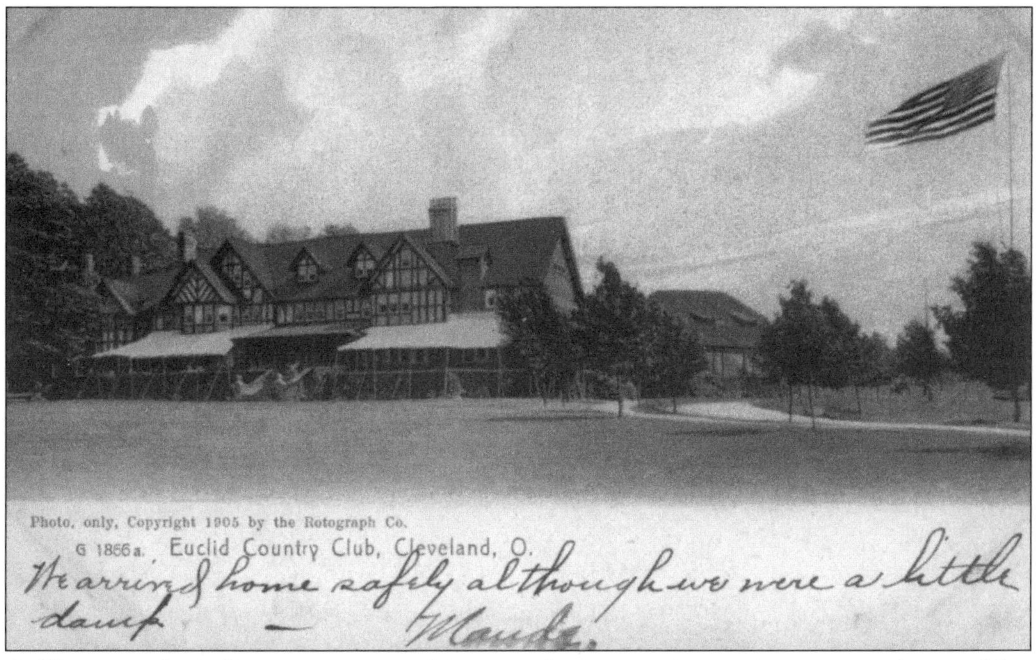

Golf was a relatively new sport, and its popularity was increasing among the wealthy. The Euclid Country Club in Euclid Heights was the second club in Cleveland devoted exclusively to golf. The club, opened on July 4, 1900, boasted one of the finest clubhouses in the country.

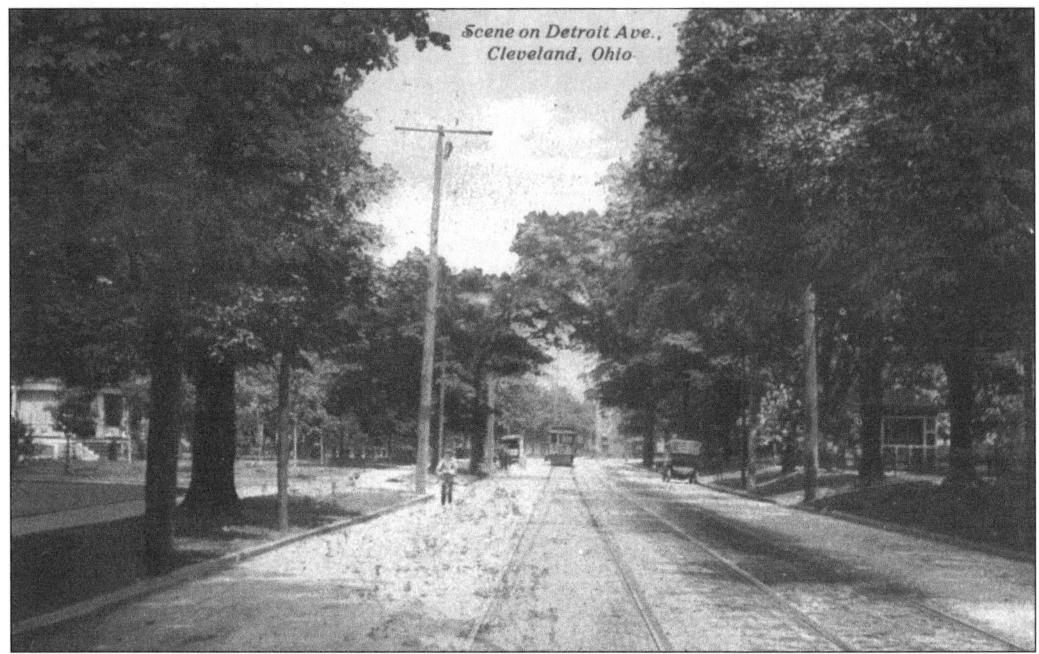

Detroit Avenue was one of Cleveland's early west side thoroughfares. Trolley tracks crisscrossed the city, carrying residents to and from jobs, shopping, and entertainment.

This Space For Writing Messages

Dearest, - I'll see you Fri. night if nothing prevents. Don't bother to meet the train. I know the way up and will find you sure.
Lovingly,
Nellie

Sept 13, 1910.

CLEVELAND SEP 13 1910 OHIO
POST CARD
CLEVELAND CIRCUIT R.P.O.
U.S. POSTAGE ONE CENT

Mrs. Wm. C. Bartlett,
109 Euclid St.,
Salem,
Ohio.

This side for the Address only

The "R.P.O." postmark on this card indicates it was mailed on board an interurban streetcar.

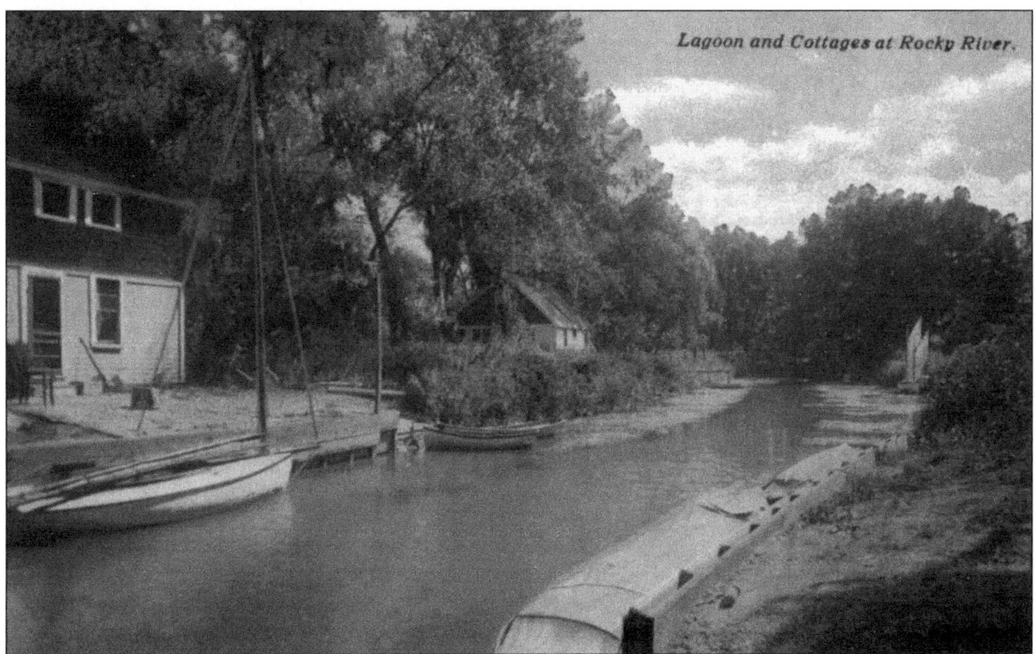

These cottages on the Rocky River lagoons were the forerunners of the tony Clifton Lagoon beach houses of today.

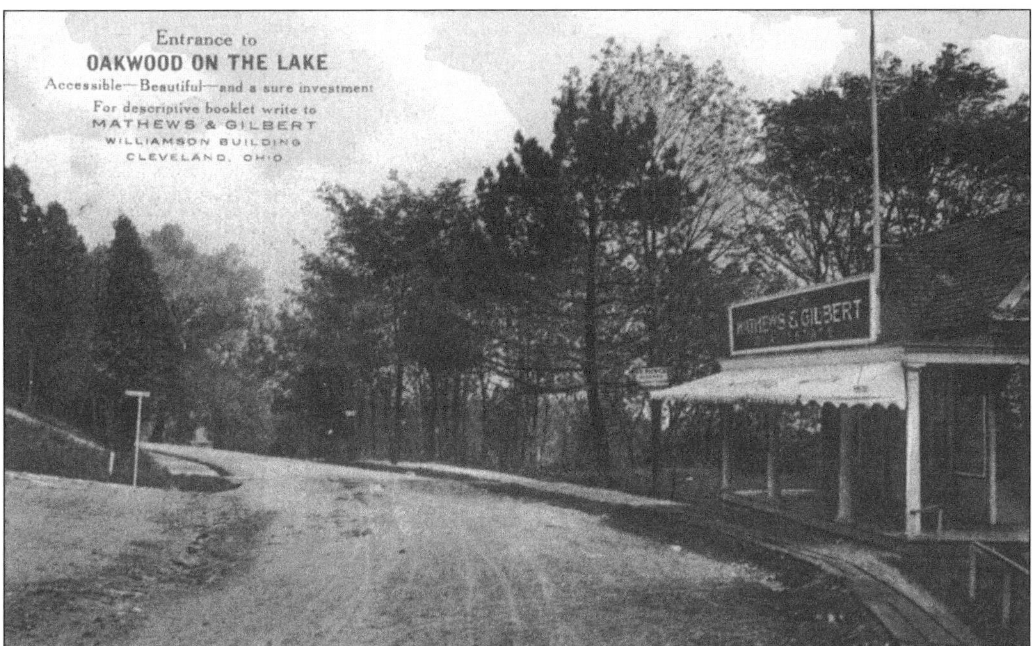

Suburban residential developments proliferated during the real estate boom of the 1920s. This postcard promotes Oakwood on the Lake, described as a "sure investment." It shows the on-site real estate office and directs prospects to write to the firm's headquarters in the Williamson Building on Public Square for the "descriptive booklet."

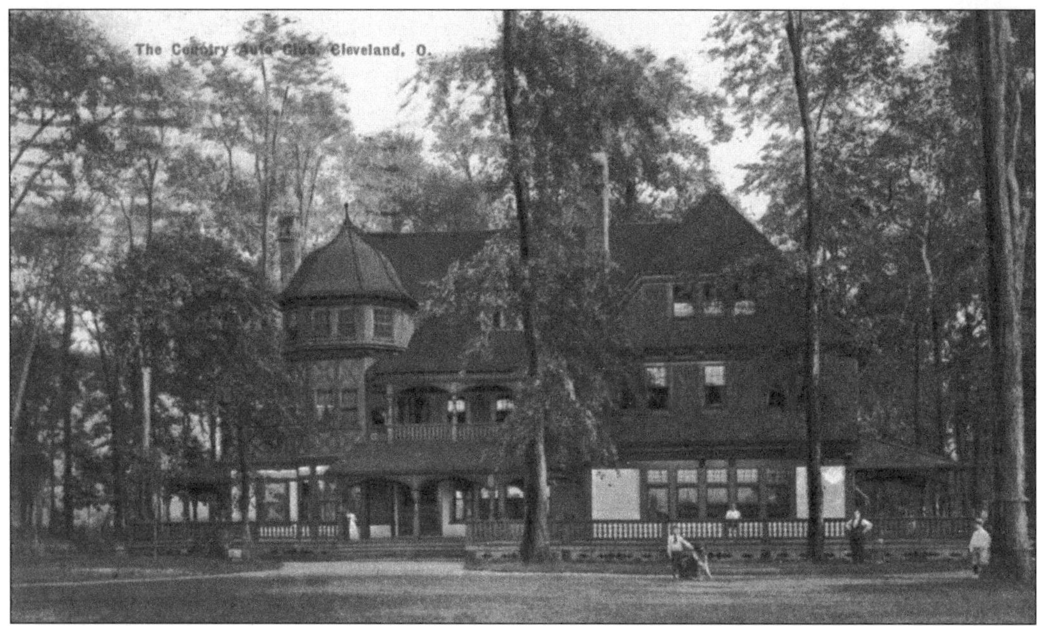

As the birthplace of the automobile, Cleveland had its share of auto enthusiasts. Pictured here is the Country Auto Club.

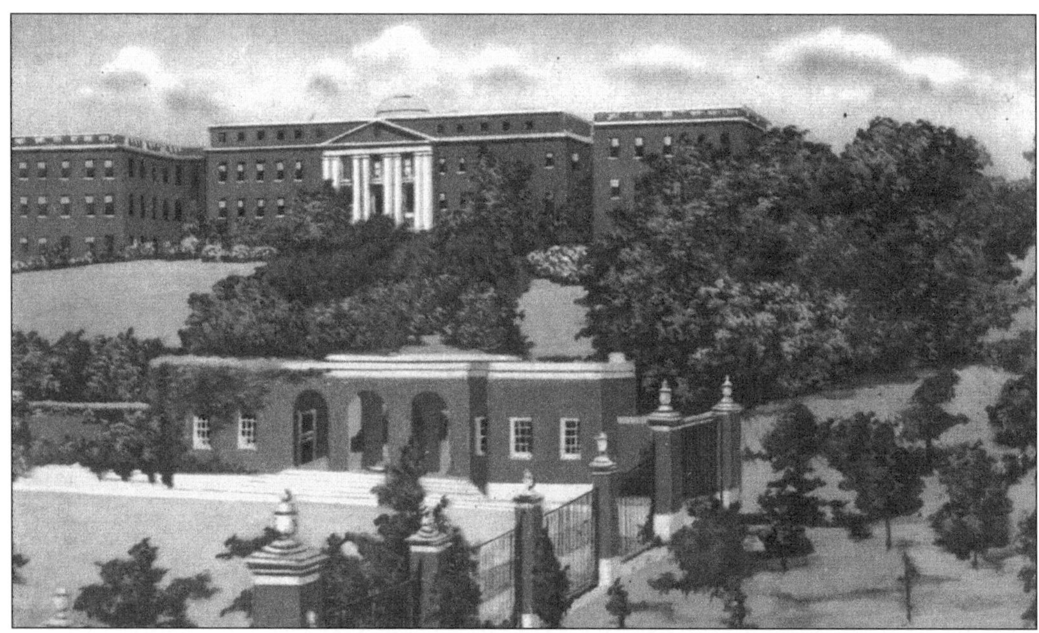

Nela Park in East Cleveland was the nation's first industrial park. Nela (National Electric Lamp Association) was a consortium of independent lamp companies that banded together in the early 1900s to coordinate and promote the sale of light bulbs. Nela Park was designed and built as a park-like "campus" in 1912–1913. The company became part of General Electric and Nela Park is today a National Historic Landmark and the world headquarters of GE Lighting.

Eight

WESTERN RESERVE

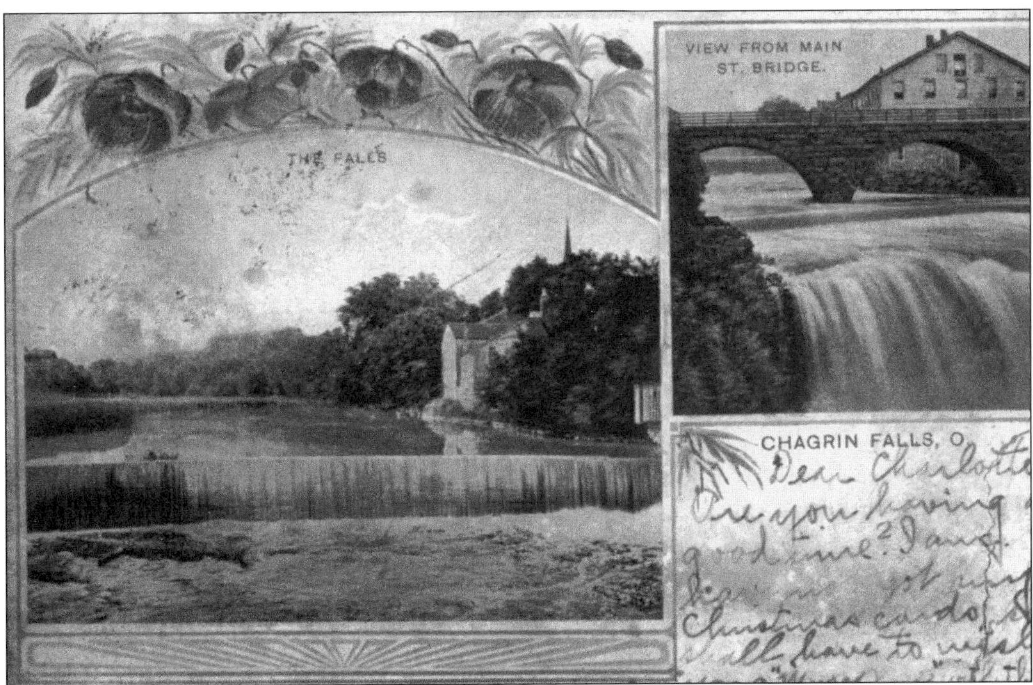

The Falls of Chagrin Falls afforded mill sites that were the early economic foundation of this picturesque village southeast of Cleveland in the Chagrin River Valley. Western Reserve architecture is predominant in the area, especially along River Road in the adjoining villages of Hunting Valley and Gates Mills. This view, from 1907, shows the two falls in the town.

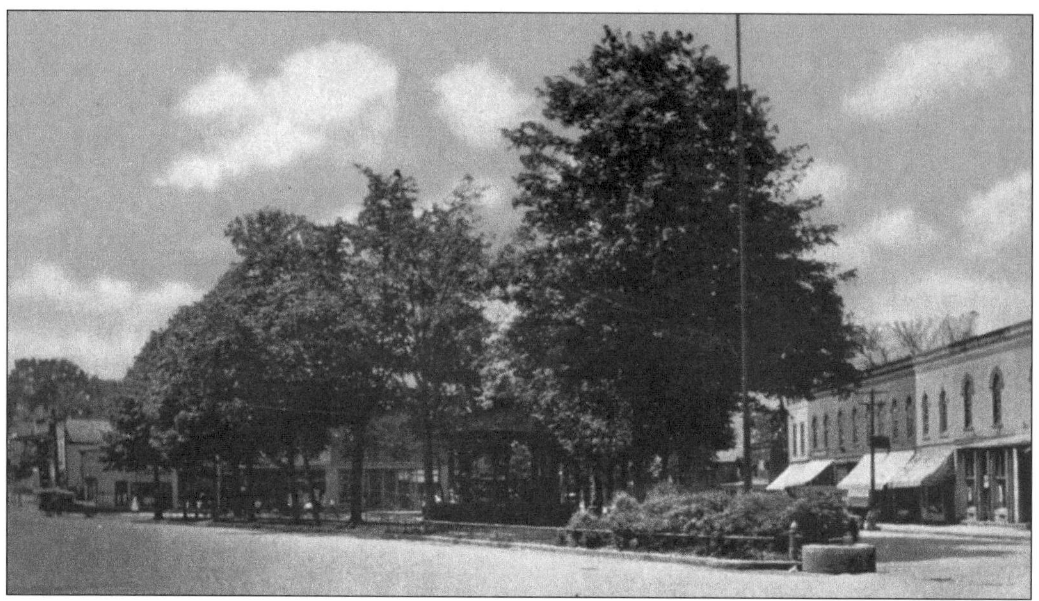

The triangle with the gazebo at the center of Chagrin Falls looks much the same today. The green area is a popular spot for band concerts, art shows, and holiday events.

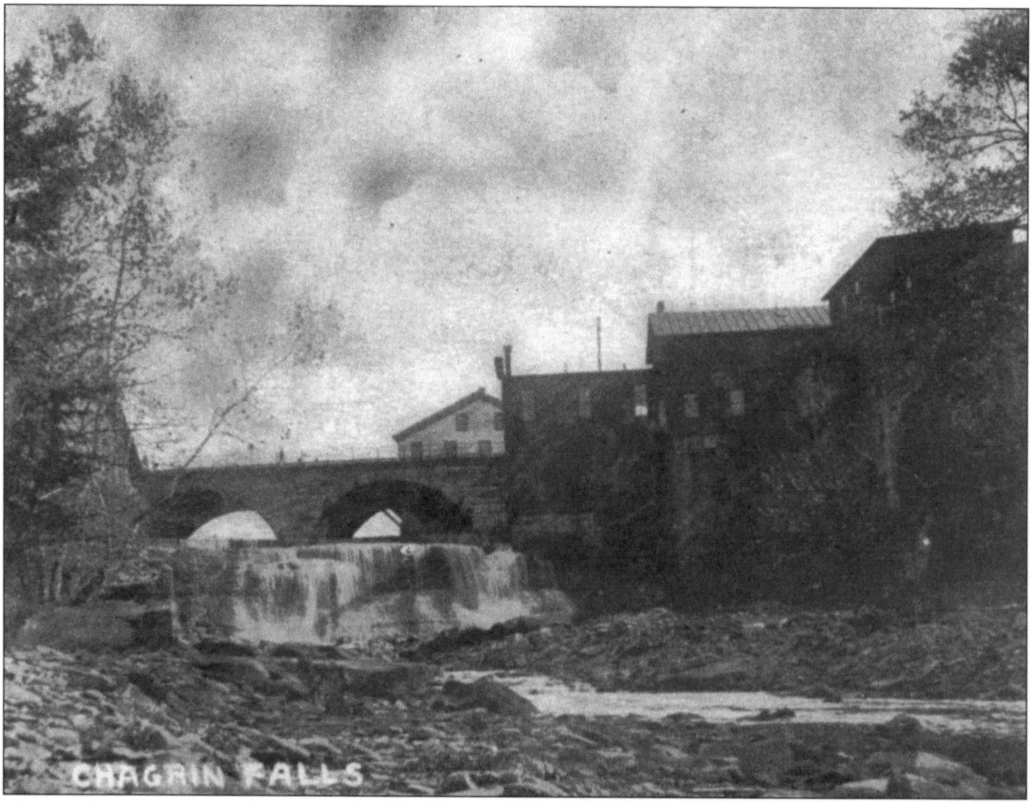

The Falls are seen during a dry period when the river is barely a stream.

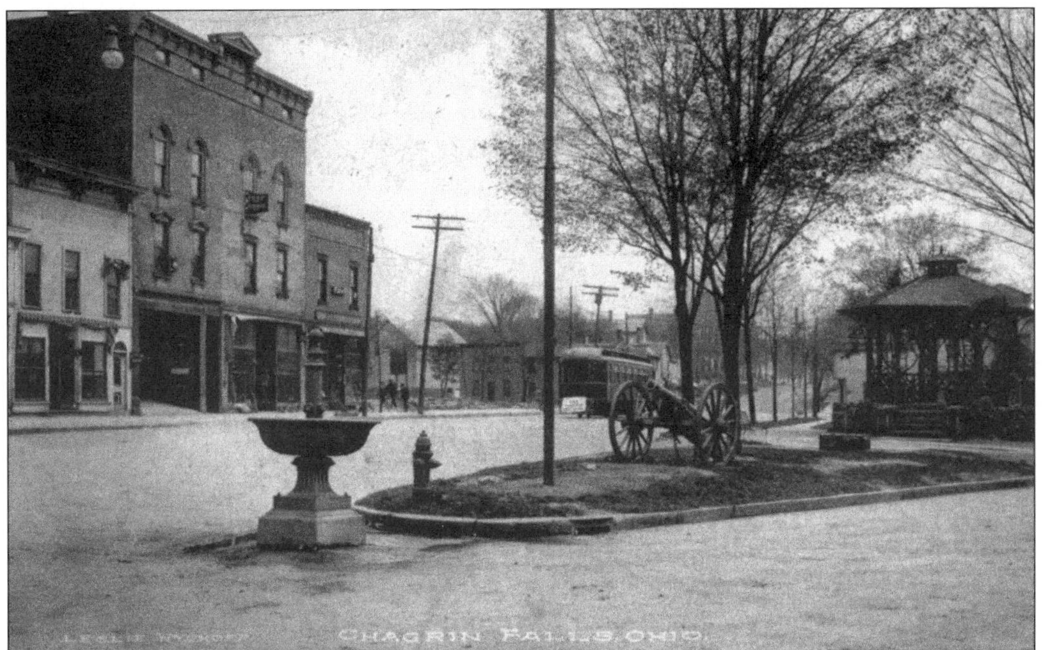

This image of Chagrin Falls around 1910 shows a horse-watering trough and an early streetcar. Streetcars were a primary means of transportation at that time and residents were able to travel significant distances, to Cleveland for example, on the numerous car lines.

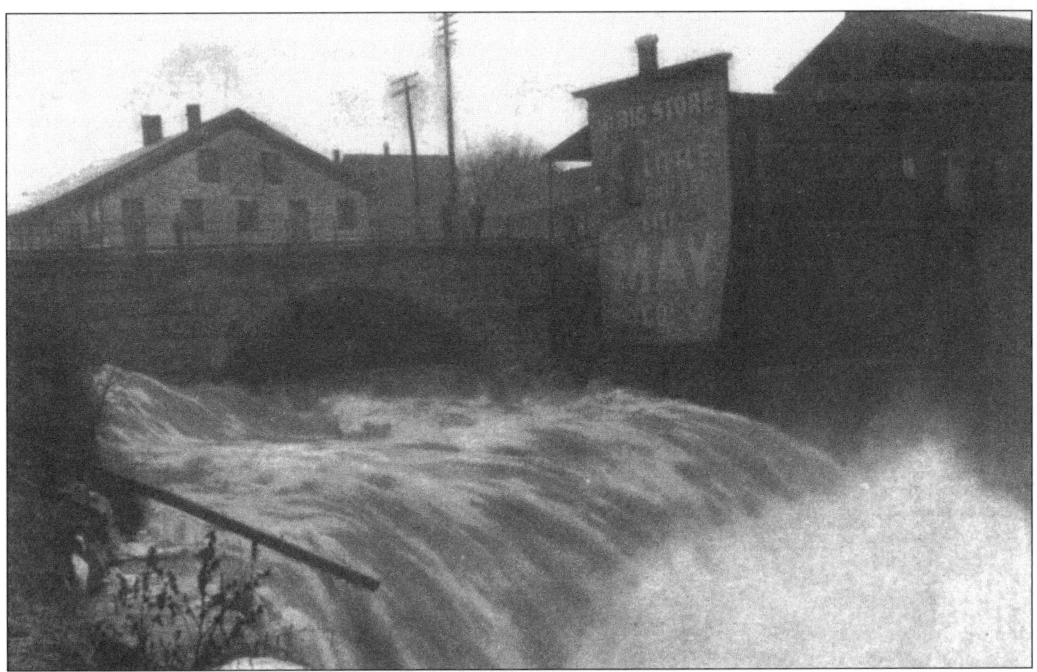

These rushing torrents show quite a different river from the previous view on the opposite page. The building to the right is serving as a billboard for the May Co. store on Public Square in downtown Cleveland.

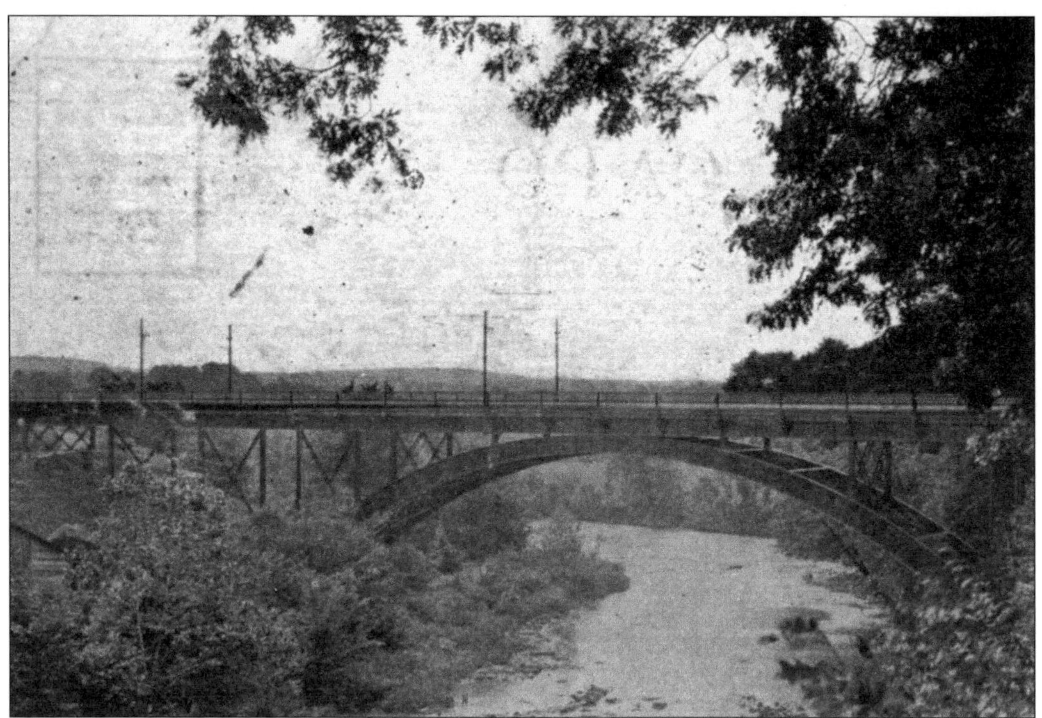

Chagrin Falls' High Level Bridge carried traffic over the Chagrin River.

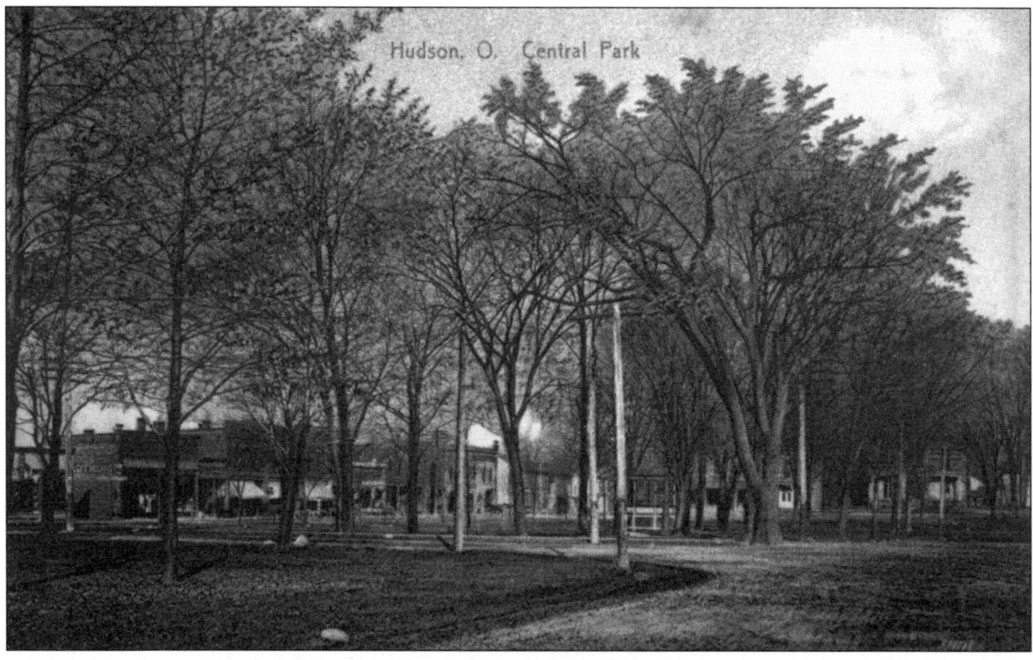

True to their New England heritage, Western Reserve towns were typically laid out on a village green that featured retail stores on one side only. Hudson, founded in the 1790s, has been beautifully preserved through civic planning. The village today features hundreds of Western Reserve homes dating to the early 1800s.

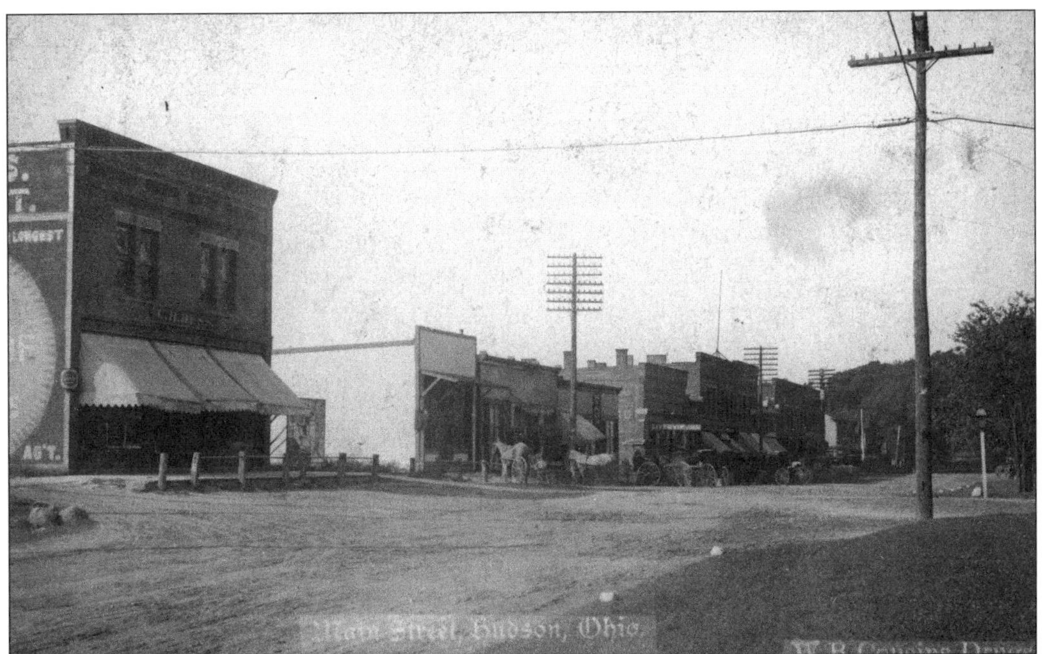

A rare, early view of Main Street in Hudson, before the fire of 1892, shows horse-drawn carriages and an unpaved roadway along with buildings later destroyed in the fire. The north end of the downtown area today contains structures dating to the 1830s that survived the blaze.

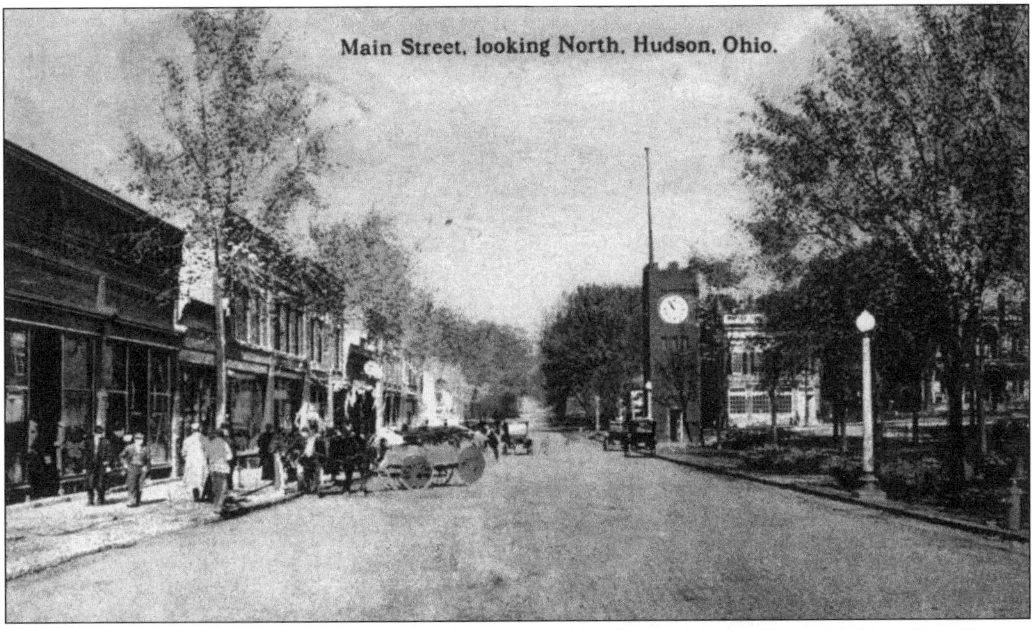

A later view of downtown, *c.* 1920, shows the clock tower, built in 1912. Main Street has been bricked at this time and a few Model Ts are in evidence among the horse carts.

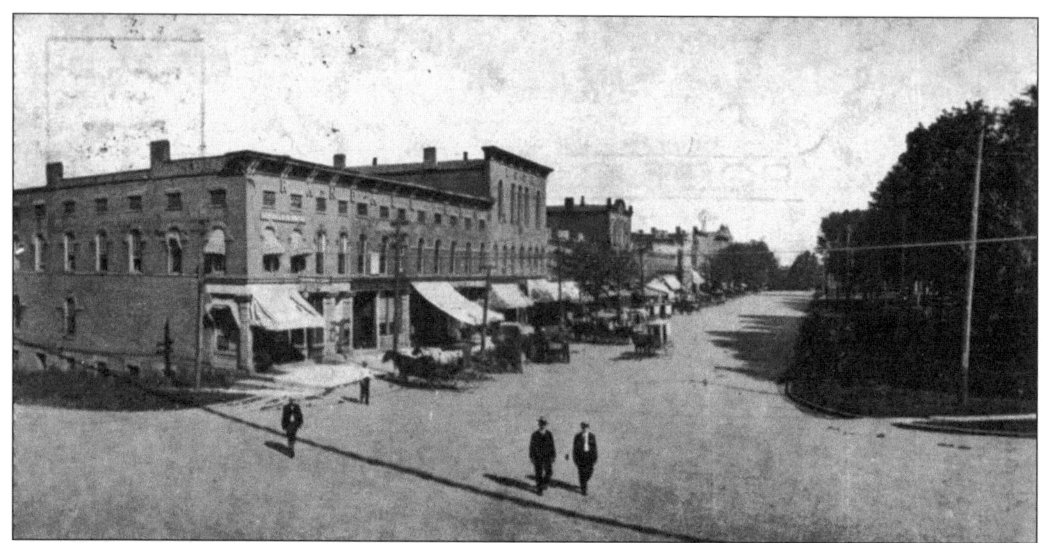

Disastrous fires were common in the mostly wooden downtown areas of cities and towns across America during the 1800s, leaving volunteer fire departments largely helpless to control their spread. Downtown Chardon, in the heart of the Western Reserve east of Cleveland, was totally destroyed by fire in the 1860s. A largely planned Victorian downtown, seen here in 1909, arose and remains very much intact today.

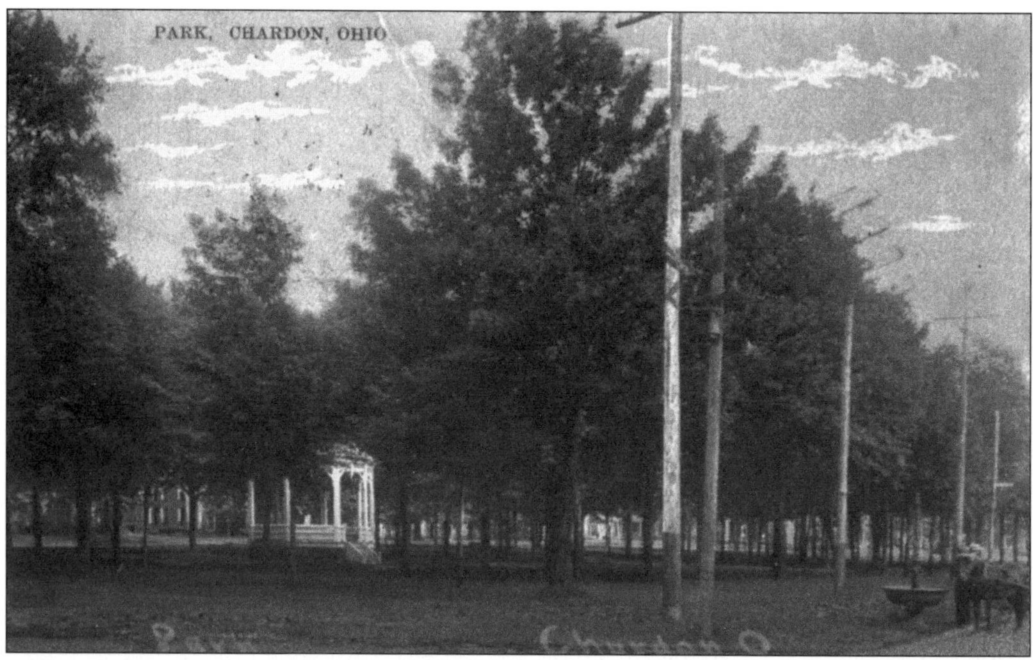

Chardon, like many other Western Reserve towns, was laid out on a village green with its requisite gazebo. The green is the site of the yearly Maple Festival, a longtime spring event celebrating the production of maple syrup, a key industry in the area. Note the horse-watering trough at right.

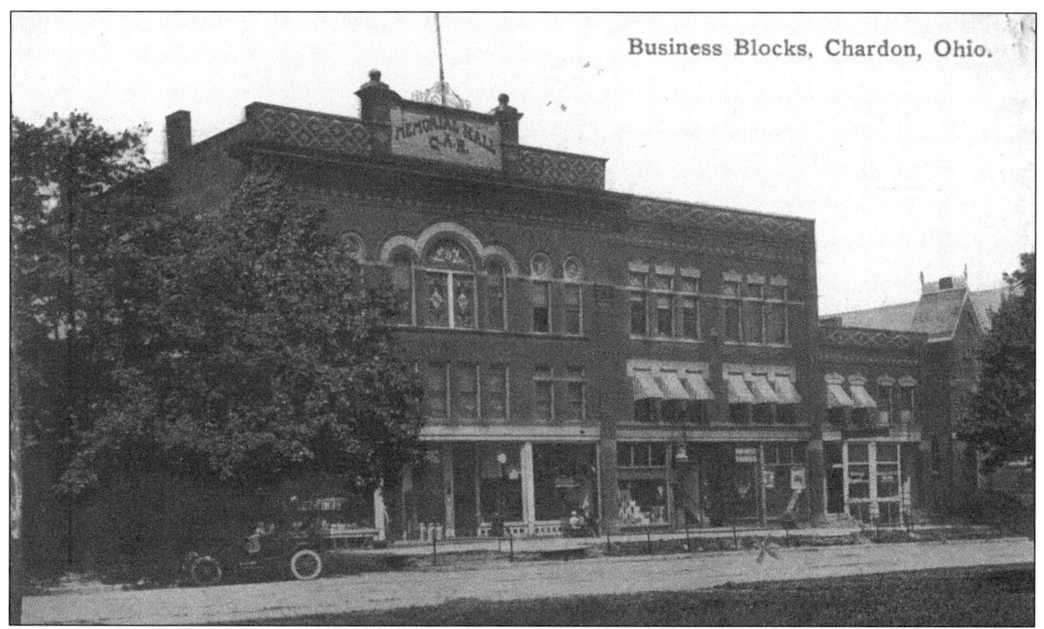

This closer view of downtown Chardon highlights the intricacies of Victorian design. The building shown now houses a popular antique mall.

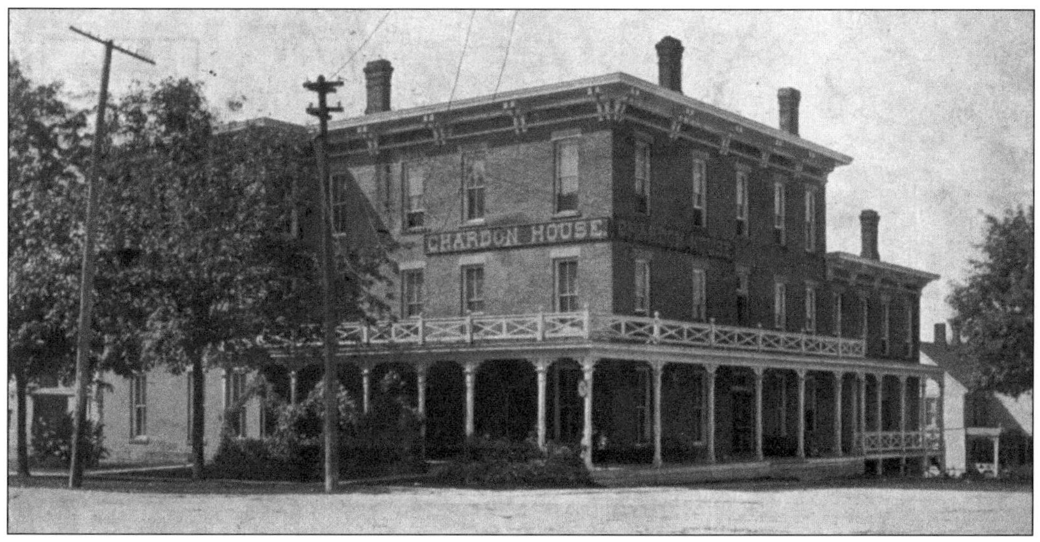

The Chardon House welcomed guests early in the century.

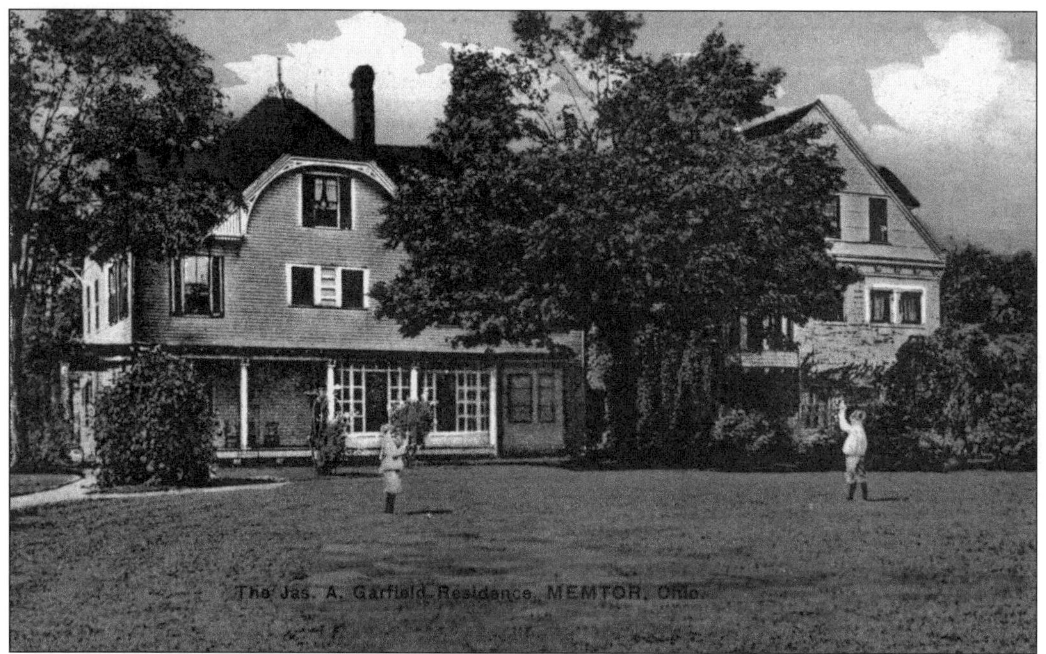

James A. Garfield, 20th president of the United States, purchased Lawnfield, his residence in Mentor, while a member of Congress. Originally a small farmhouse, it was enlarged by the Garfields to its present size. The porch across the front, used by Garfield for campaigning, was where the term "front porch campaign" originated. The home is now operated by the National Park Service as a National Historic Site.

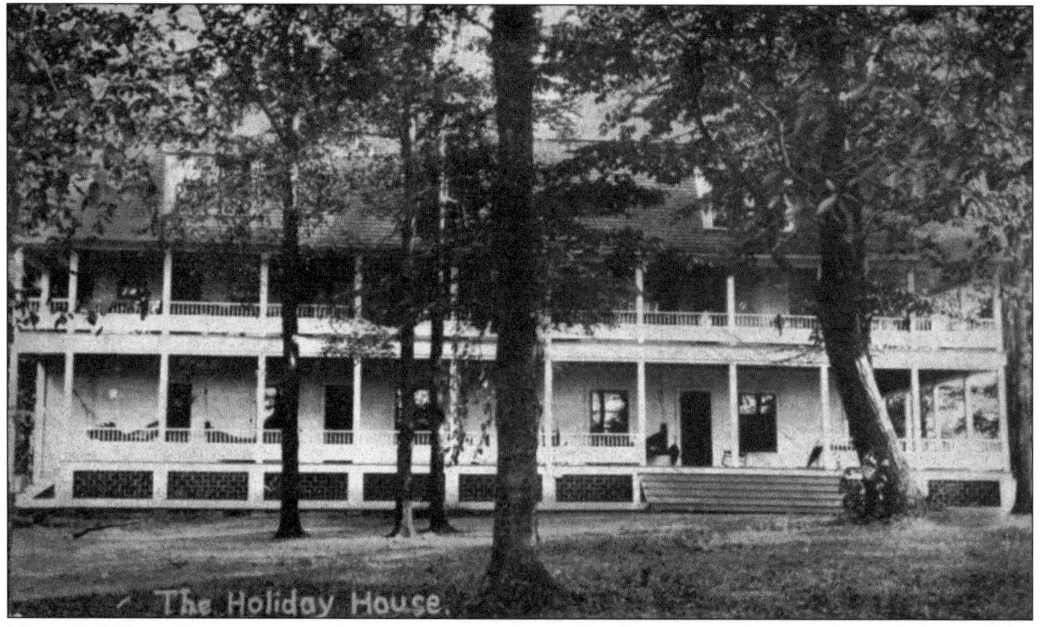

The Holiday House near Mentor was a typical, country-style hotel, complete with verandahs lined with rocking chairs and a hammock. The verandah provided a cool spot for relaxing and socializing in the days before air conditioning.

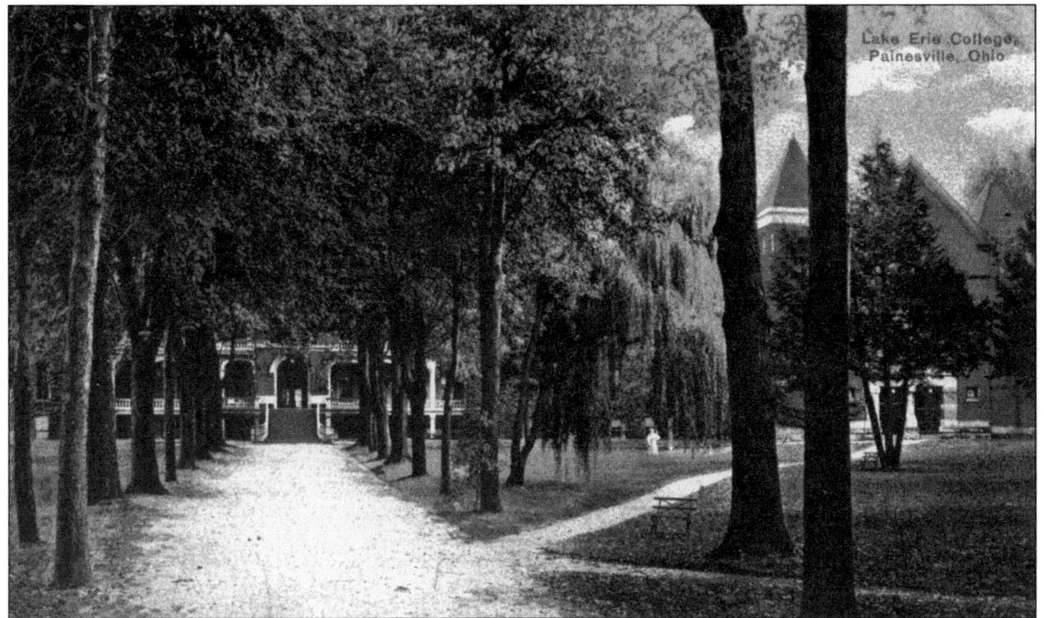

The Connecticut settlers of the Western Reserve brought with them their commitment to higher education, as exhibited by the many small liberal arts colleges found throughout the area. Lake Erie College in Painesville, the county seat of Lake County, was an early women's institution. The well-respected school is now co-educational. Its campus is little changed from this view.

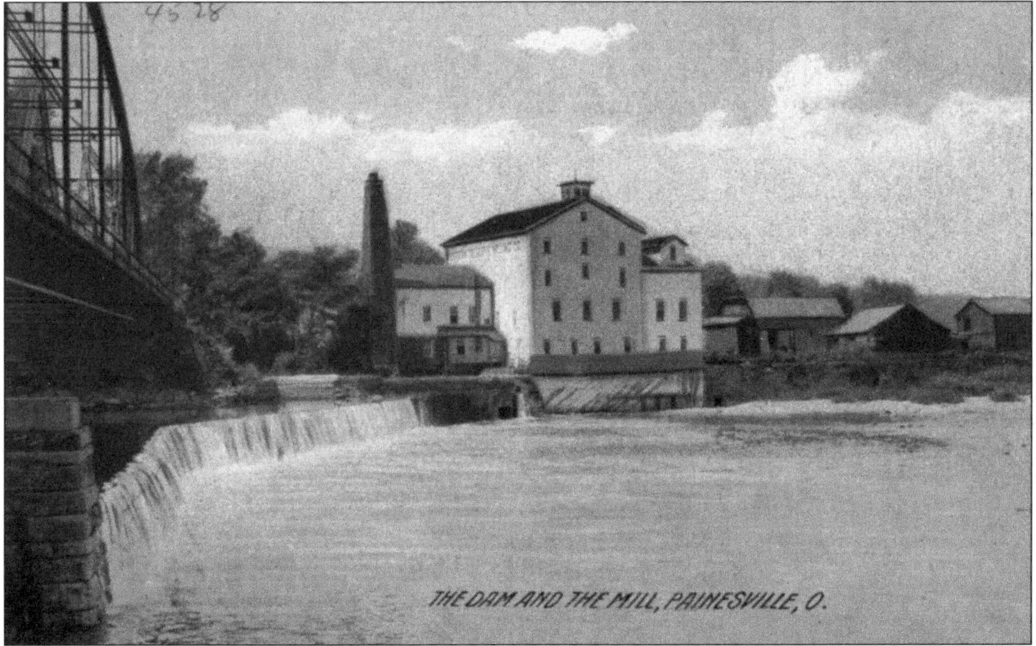

Rivers flowing through the Western Reserve provided mill sites that were the basis for early industry in many towns. This view shows the Western Reserve Mill on the Grand River near Painesville.

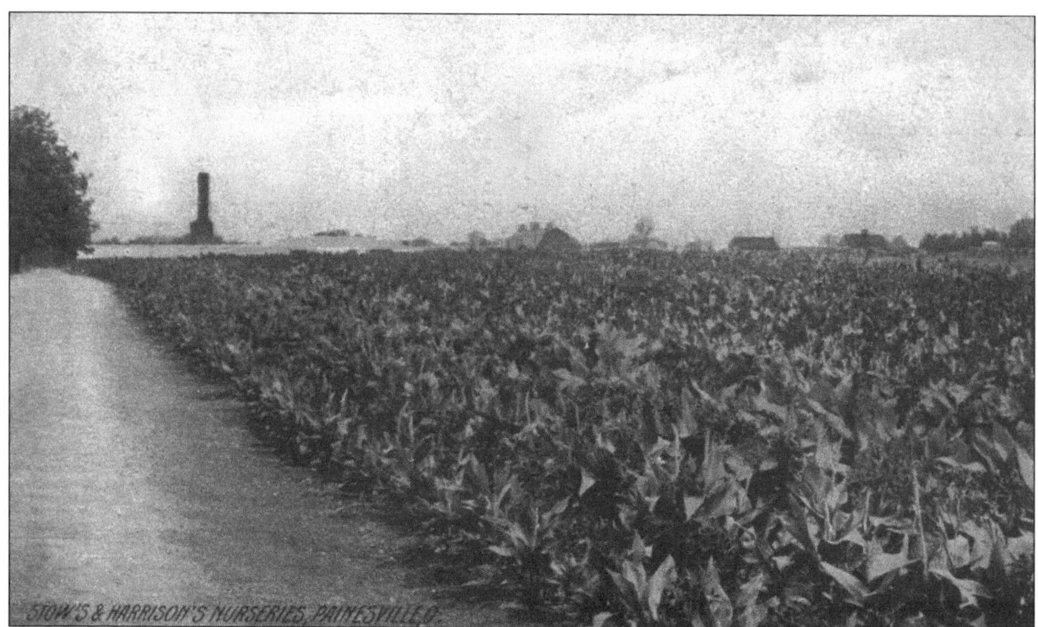

The moderating influence of Lake Erie made eastern Lake County a prime location for nurseries. This 1908 card shows Storrs' and Harrison's Nurseries near Painesville, founded by Jesse Storrs of Cortland, New York in the 1850s. Many local nurserymen served their apprenticeship at Storrs, Harrison, and Co., and by 1927 the partners had developed the largest departmental nursery in the world. The nursery thrived until the 1940s.

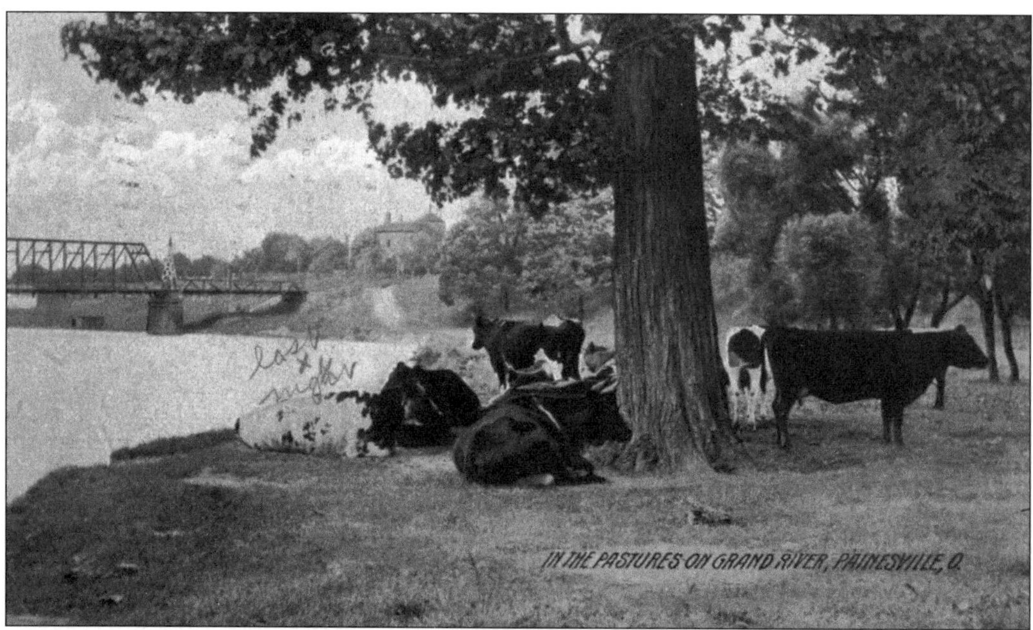

Cattle find a spot in the shade on the banks of the Grand River at Painesville. An iron bridge spanning the river can be seen on the left in this 1908 scene.

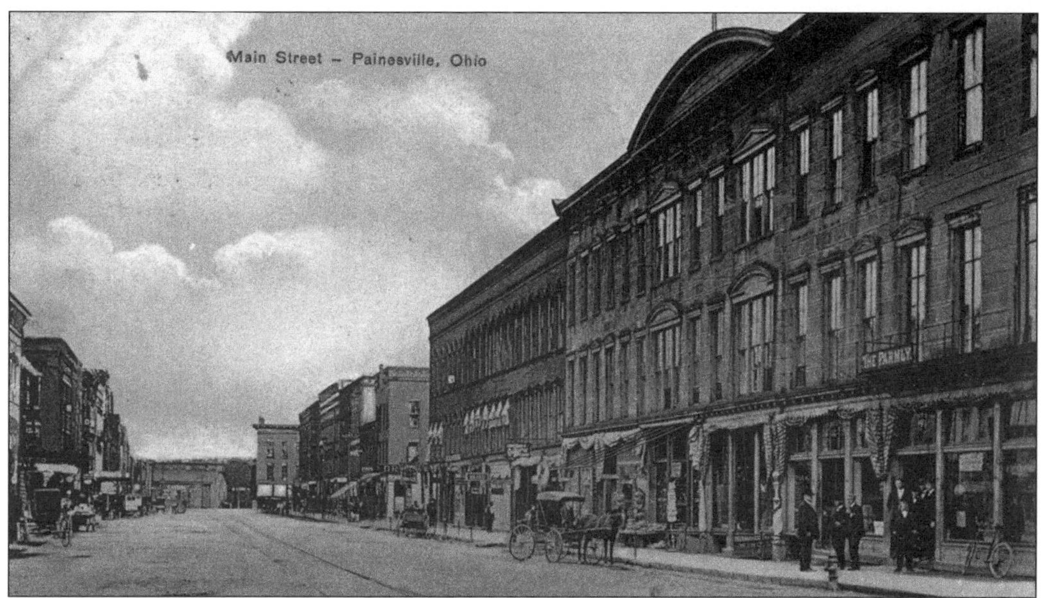

The Parmly Hotel, a drugstore, and the Bijou Theater are visible in this 1911 view of Main Street in Painesville. The Parmly, at right, was built by Eleazer Parmly in 1861. The Parmly family came to Lake County in 1817 and became known for their contributions to the undeveloped field of dentistry.

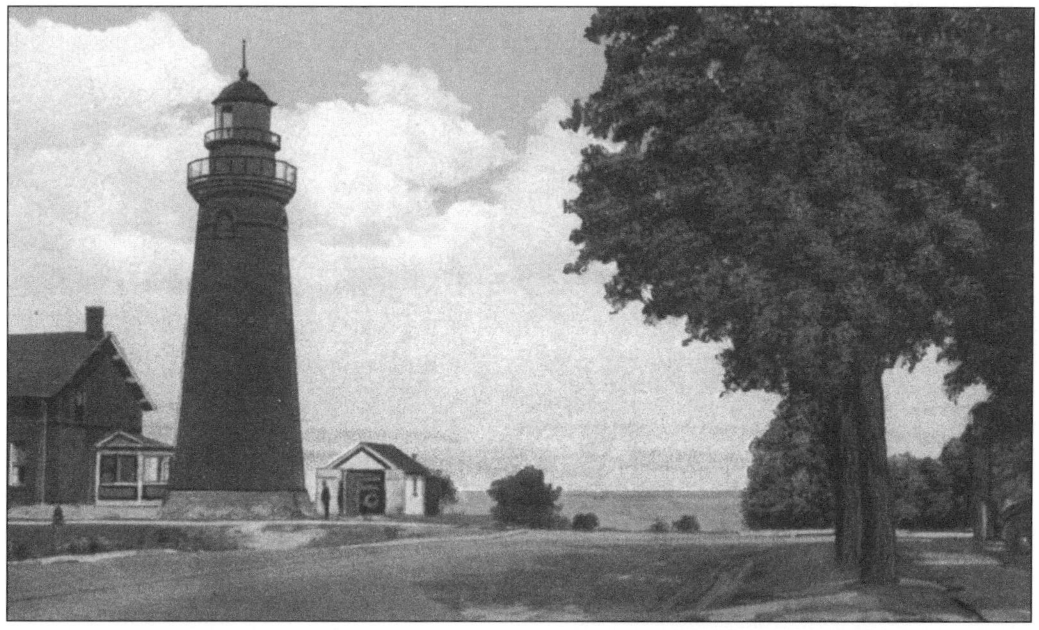

Fairport Harbor lighthouse, erected in 1925, was the fourth light in that location. Today the complex is home to the Fairport Harbor Historical Society.

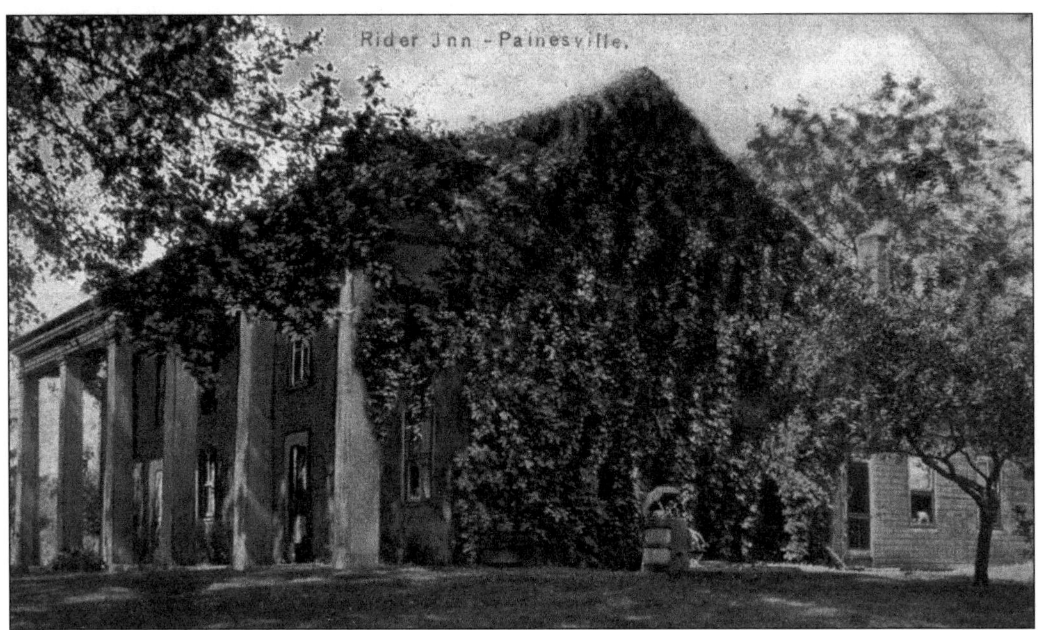

Taverns were common on the Western Reserve stagecoach routes from Cleveland to Pittsburgh and Buffalo. One of the more well known was Rider's, built by noted architect Jonathan Goldsmith around 1820. Located in Painesville on the Buffalo Road, it was patterned after George Washington's home in Mount Vernon. The inn still operates as a restaurant and B & B, and its latest restoration has captured its original beauty. It is shown here in 1907.

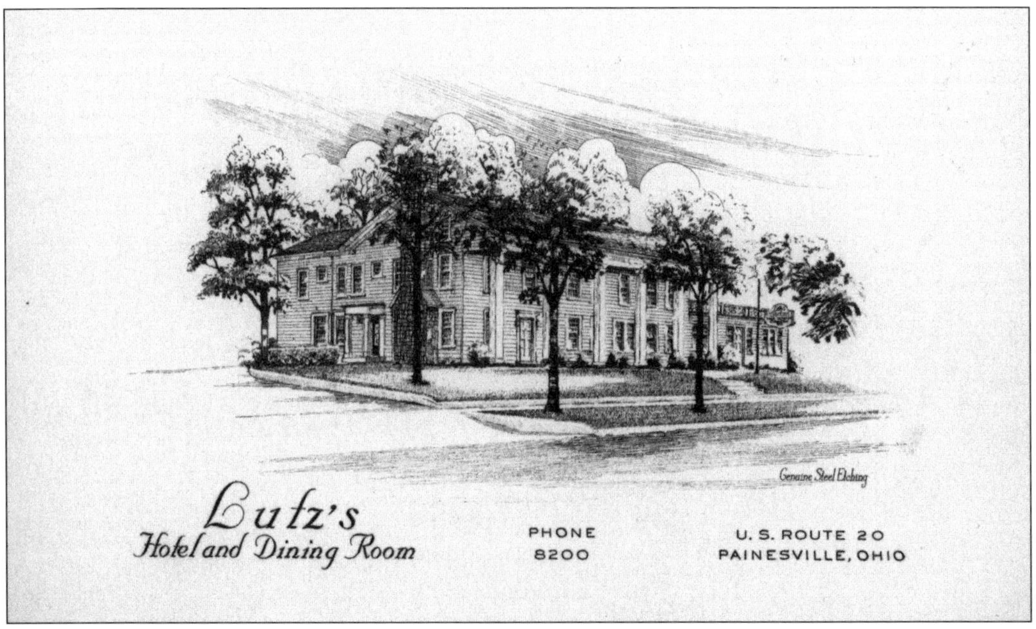

Rider's was bought by the Lutz family and operated from the early 1940s until the 1970s as Lutz Inn.

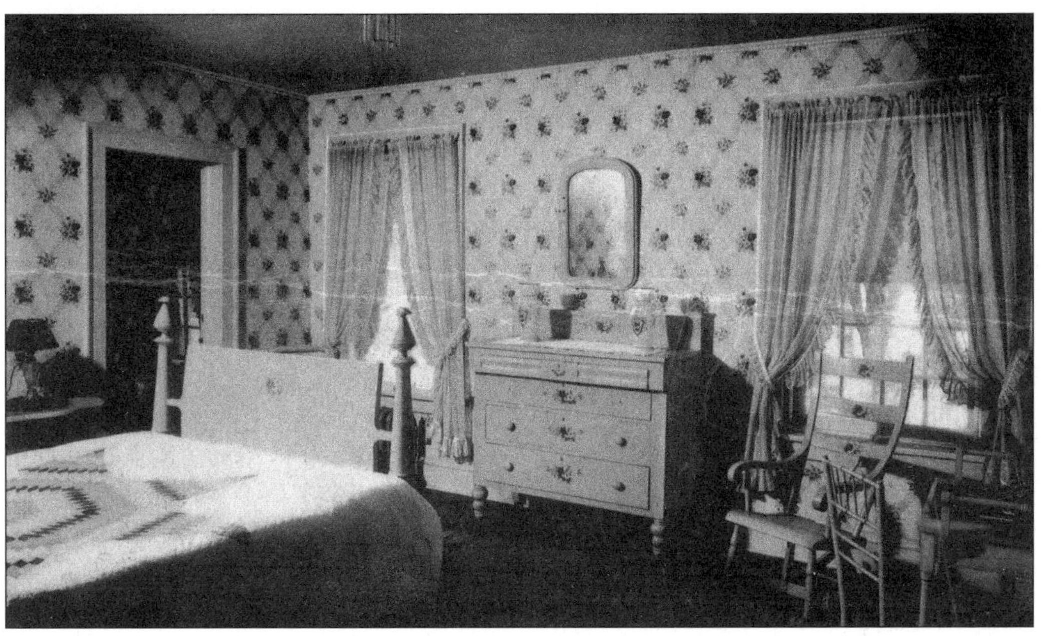

Most taverns were not as sumptuous on the inside as these scenes from the Randell Tavern in Painesville. Multiple beds usually occupied the rooms and guests often shared beds with strangers. The Randell Tavern was a stop on the Cleveland–Buffalo stage route.

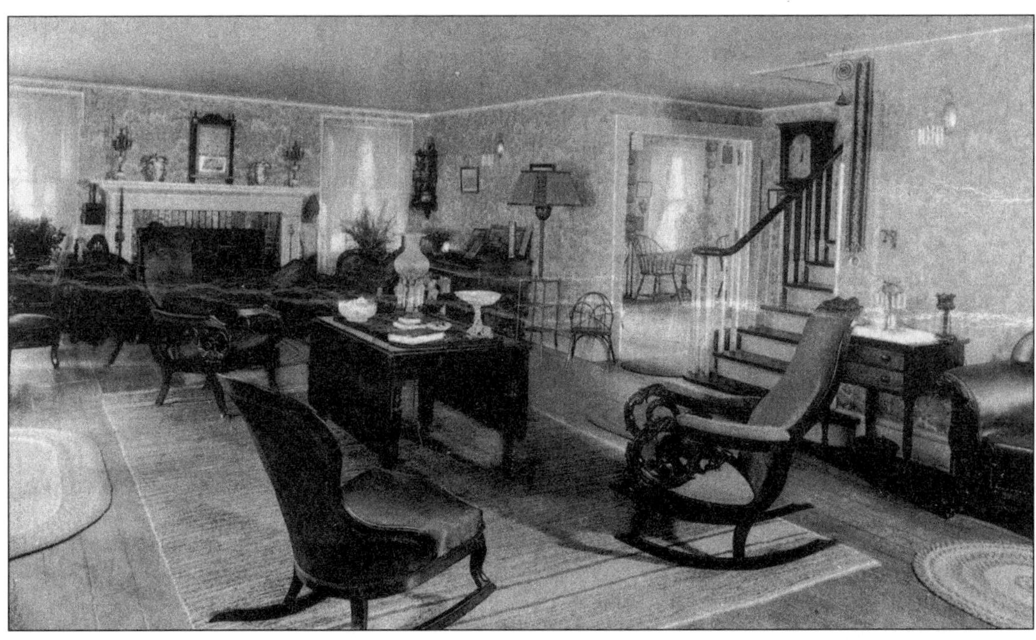

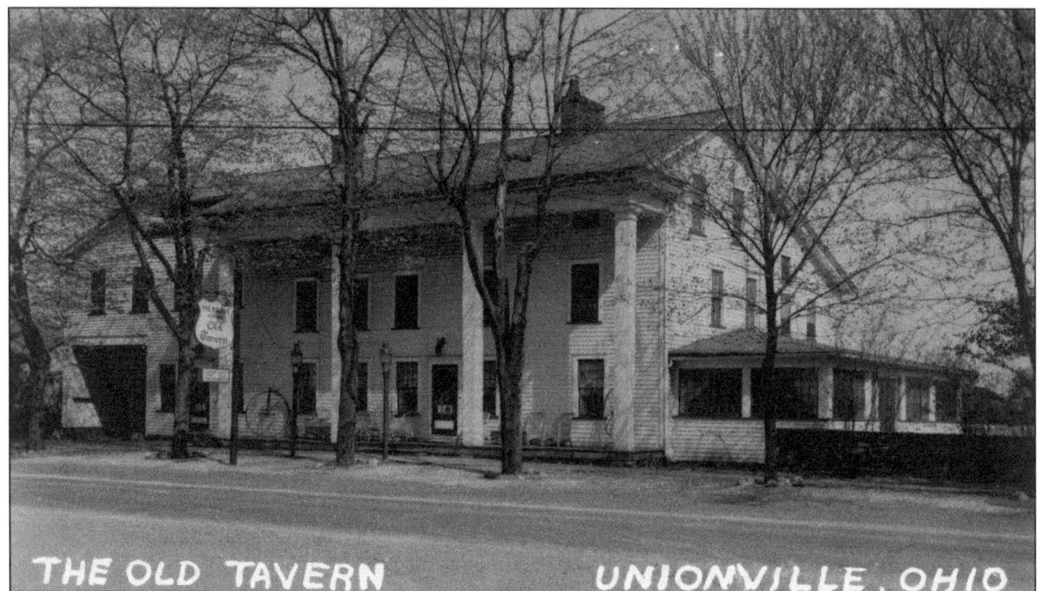

Another famous old inn was the Old Tavern at Unionville on the Cleveland–Buffalo route. Built in 1797, the inn was a station on the Underground Railroad in pre-Civil War days. It, too, was modeled after Mount Vernon. The structure has remained virtually unchanged throughout the years and is today a well-known country inn serving home-style meals.

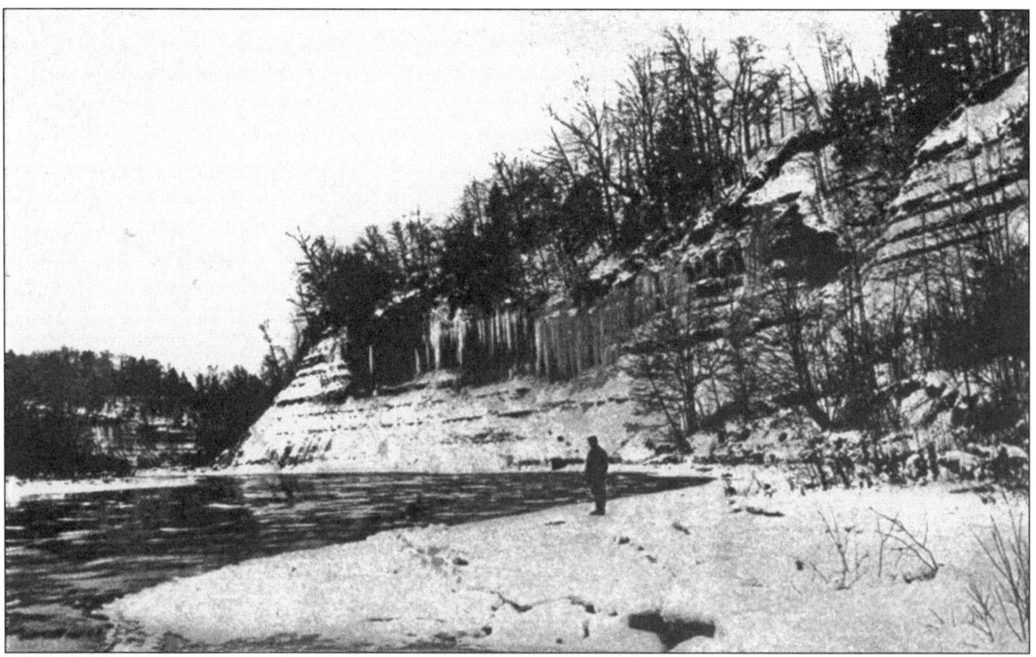

The Grand River was a stream of some importance in the early Reserve, providing a number of choice mill sites. Among the towns that developed along its banks were Painesville and Unionville. Here, a lone onlooker surveys its frozen shores near Unionville.

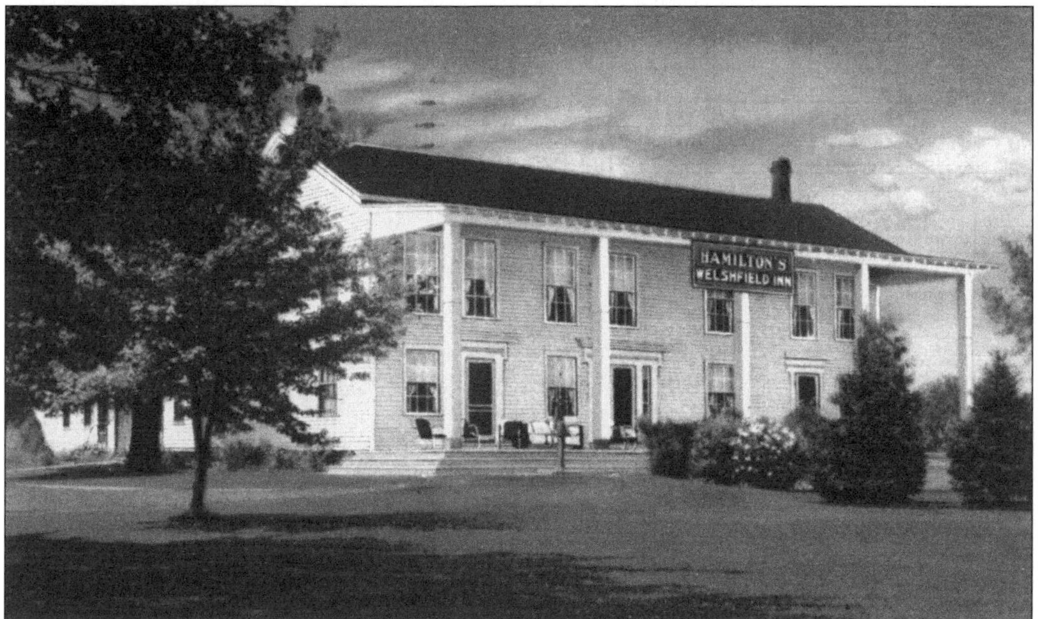

The Welshfield Inn was the center of activity for the town of Welshfield, on the Cleveland–Pittsburgh stagecoach route. Built around 1812, the Inn today is a famous eatery in the heart of the Western Reserve.

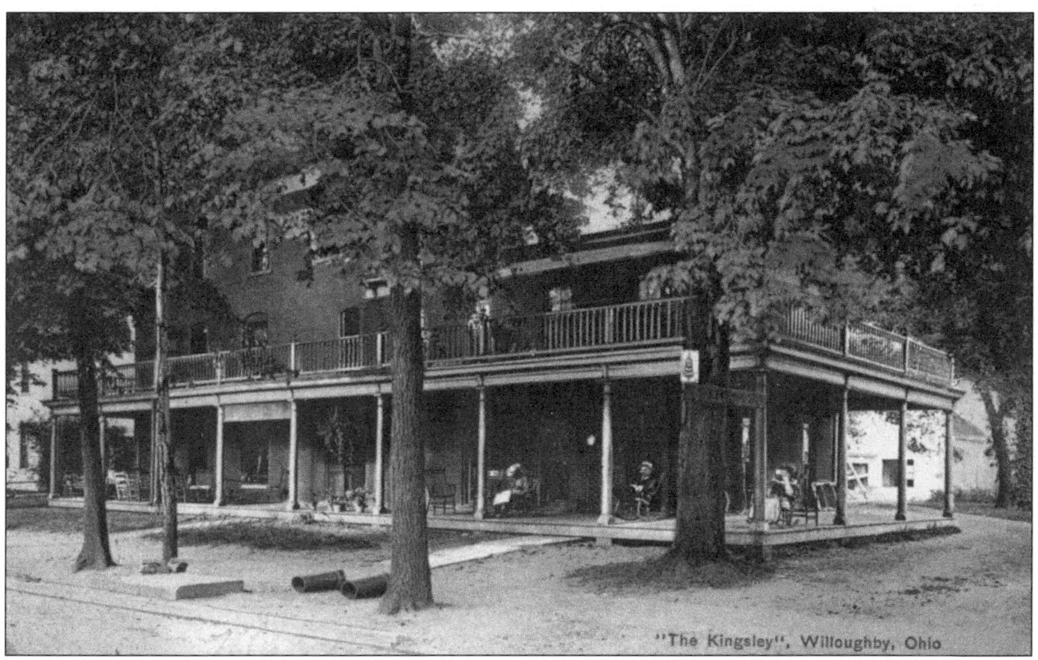

Rockers and Windsor-style chairs line the verandah of the Kingsley in Willoughby, east of Cleveland. The town developed as the medical center for the Reserve and today still retains fine examples of Western Reserve architecture. The first gristmill in the Reserve was established here in 1798.

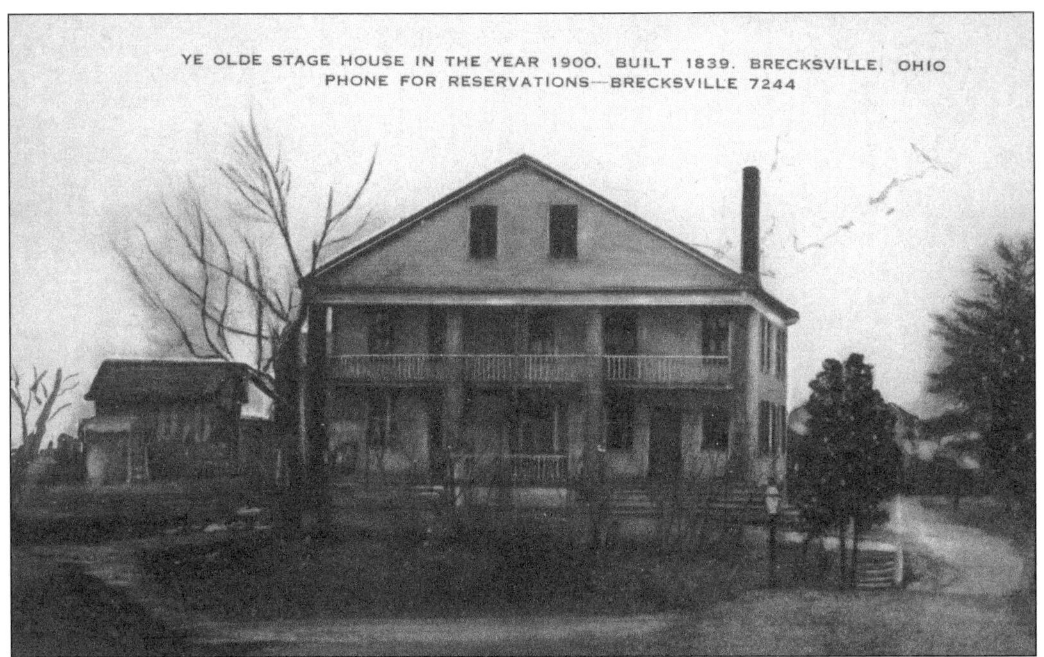

The Brecksville Inn, here called Ye Old Stage House, was built in 1839 by Theodore Breck, pioneer member of the Ohio State Senate. The Inn served Brecksville, a Western Reserve village on the southern border of Cuyahoga County.

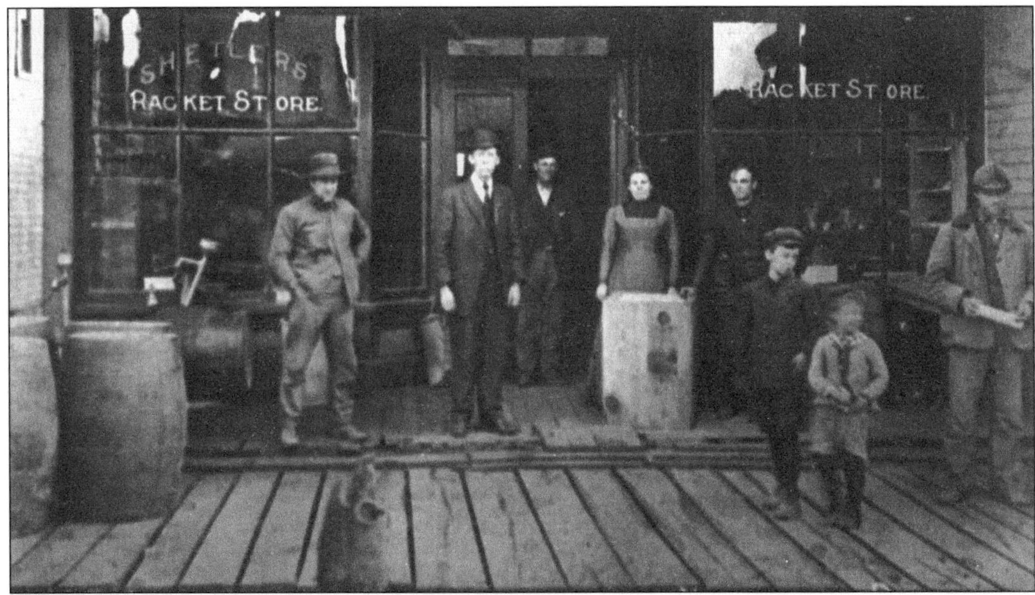

This photo from Middlefield, in the heart of Geauga County's Amish country, shows a typical local store with a few characters in front. Stores such as this served the needs of the largely agricultural community at that time.

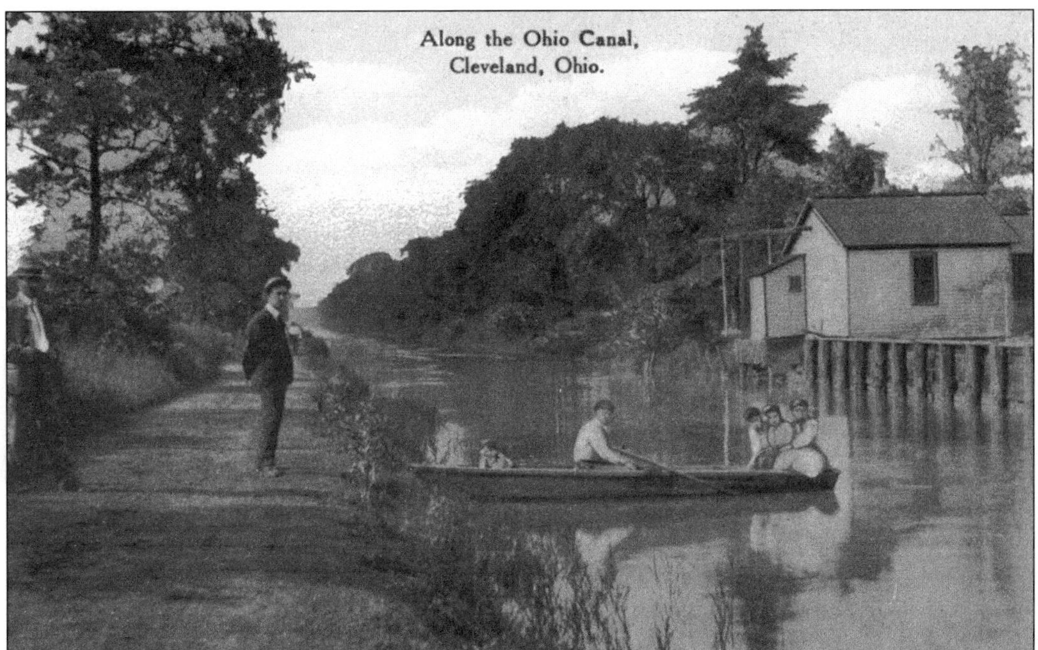

The Ohio Canal was constructed during the years 1825 through 1832. It ran from Lake Erie to the Ohio River and was a vital link in a shipping network that connected the East Coast via the Erie Canal with the Ohio and Mississippi Rivers, terminating at New Orleans.

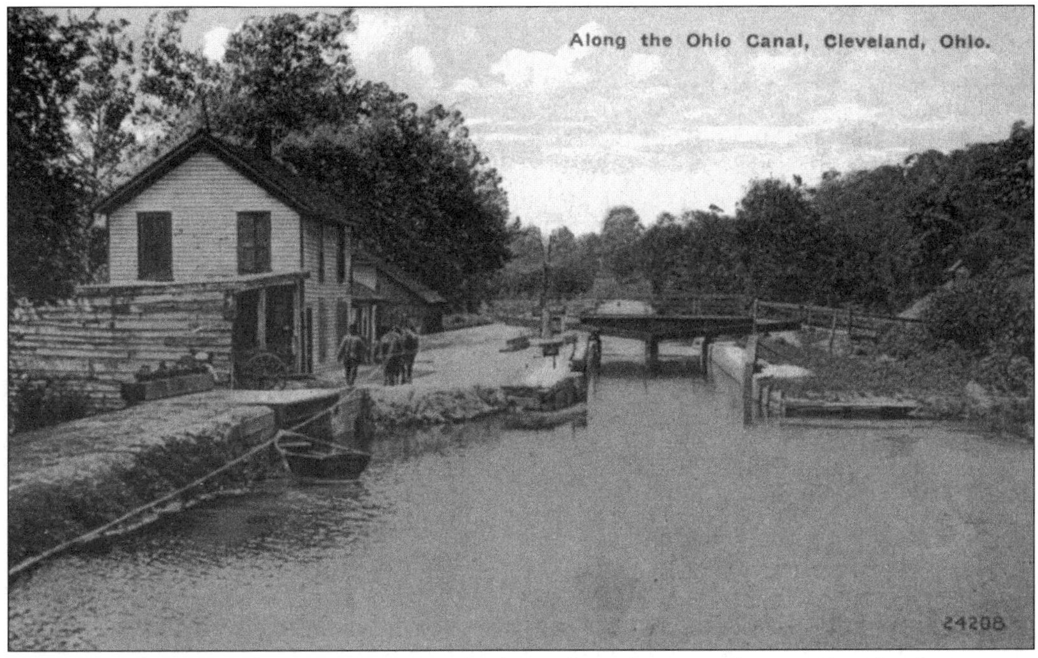

A mule team pulls a boat toward a lock along the Ohio Canal near Cleveland.

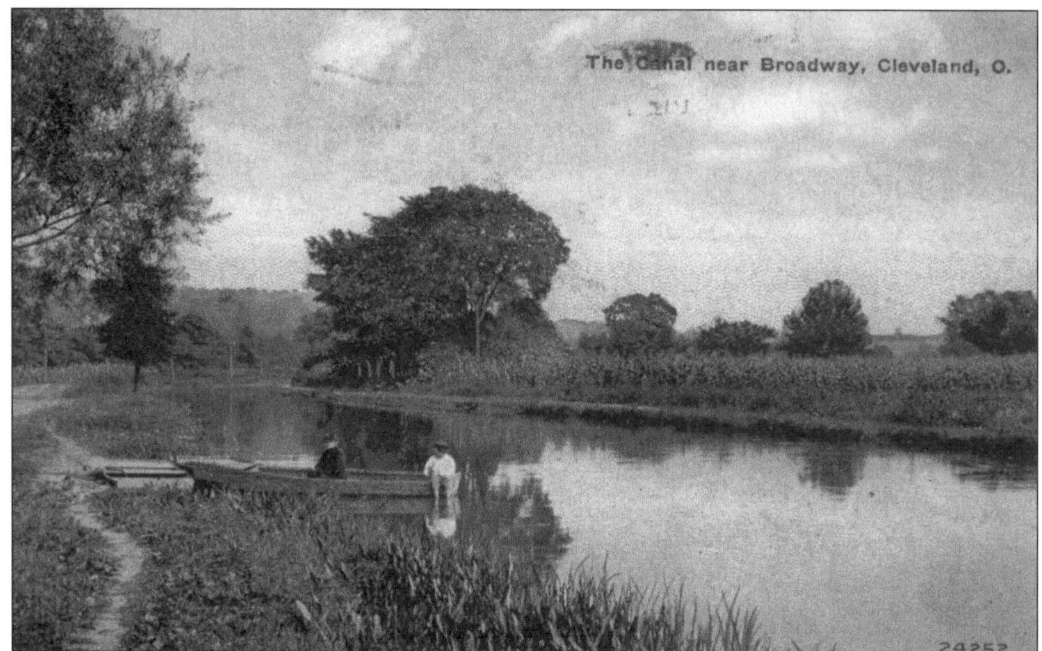

This pastoral scene along the Canal is near the current site of the Canal National Historic Corridor Visitors Center, today a bit of forest in the heart of Cleveland's industrial Flats.

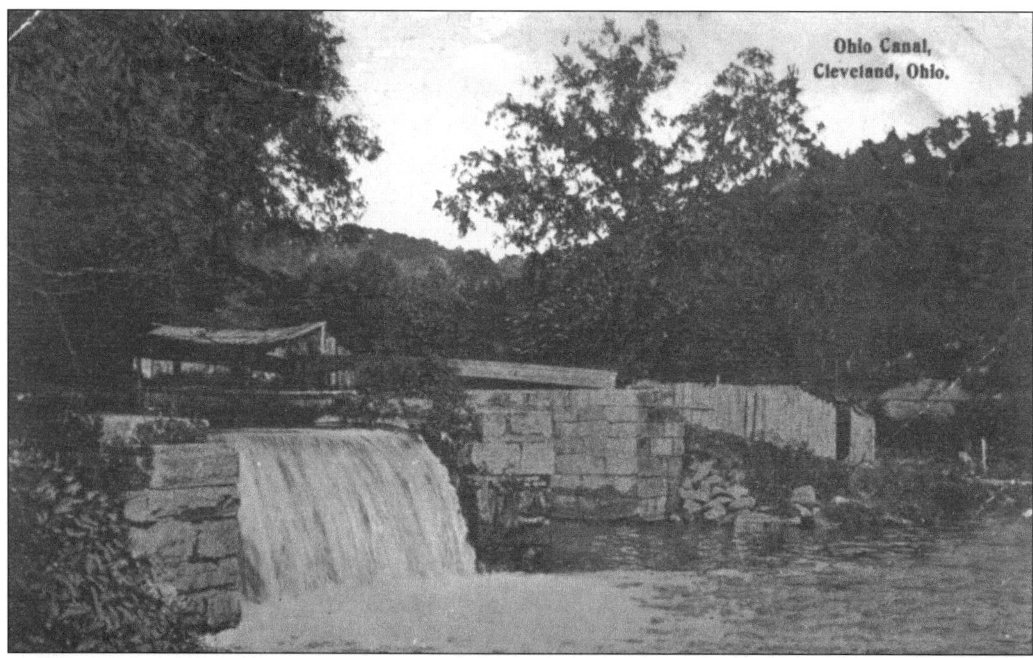

This lock near Cleveland is one of many along the Canal which reflect the changes in elevation as the Canal moved from the flatlands along Lake Erie to the higher elevations south.

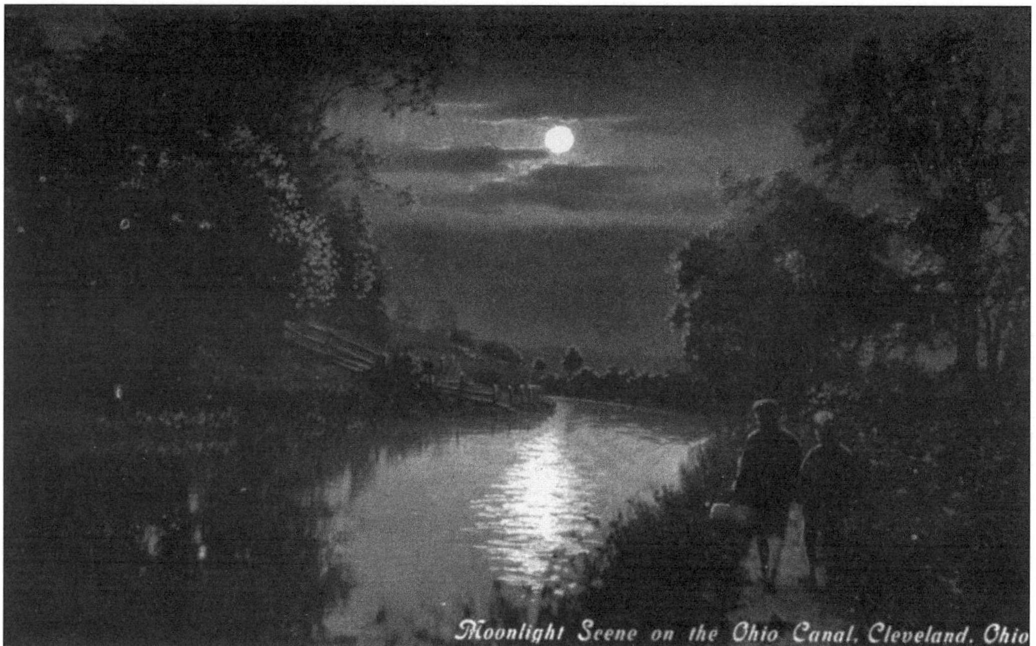

Two boys walk the horse path along the canal in this moonlit setting.

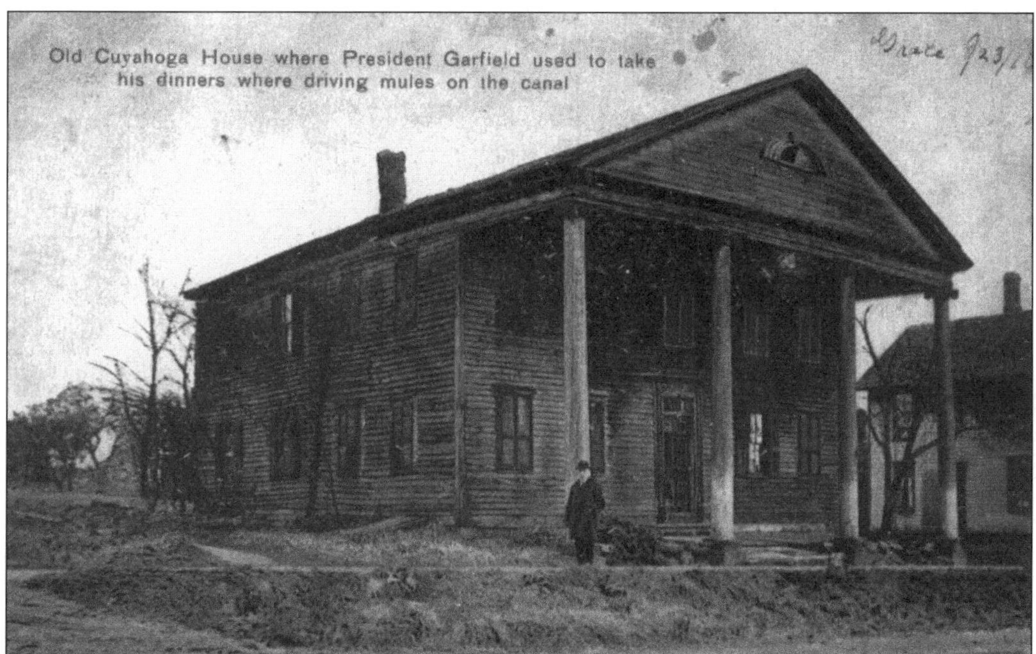

The Old Cuyahoga House, an early canal tavern, appears dilapidated in this 1910 view. According to the card, it was where "President Garfield used to take his dinners where [*sic*] driving mules on the canal."

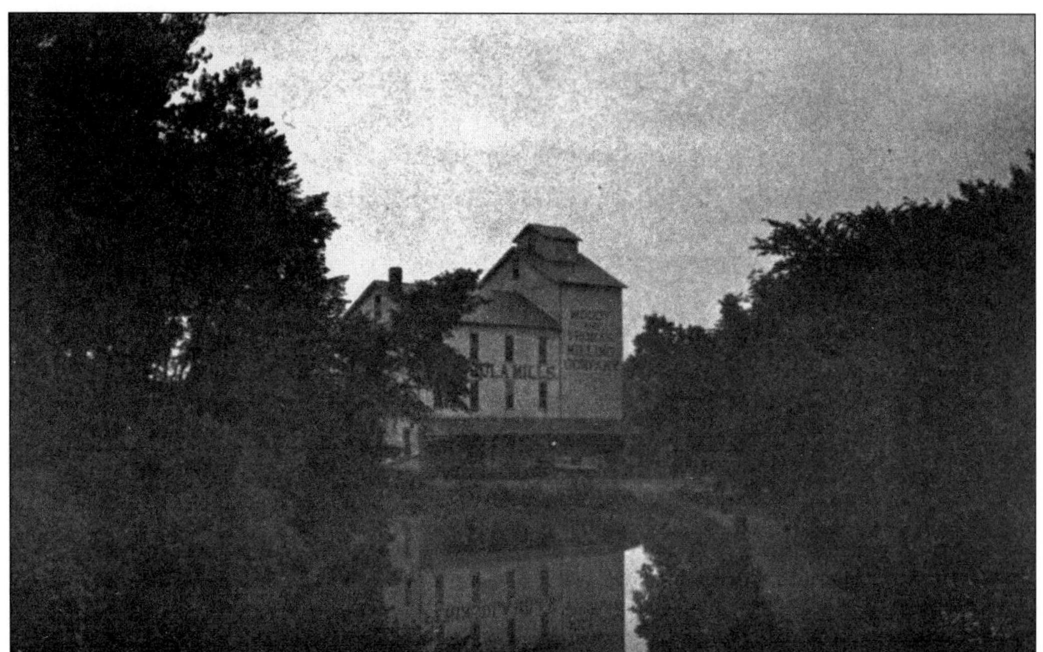

Mills were common on the lower Cuyahoga. The Peninsula Mills operated near the rollicking canal town of Peninsula, now a sedate Western Reserve village on the Ohio Canal Corridor.

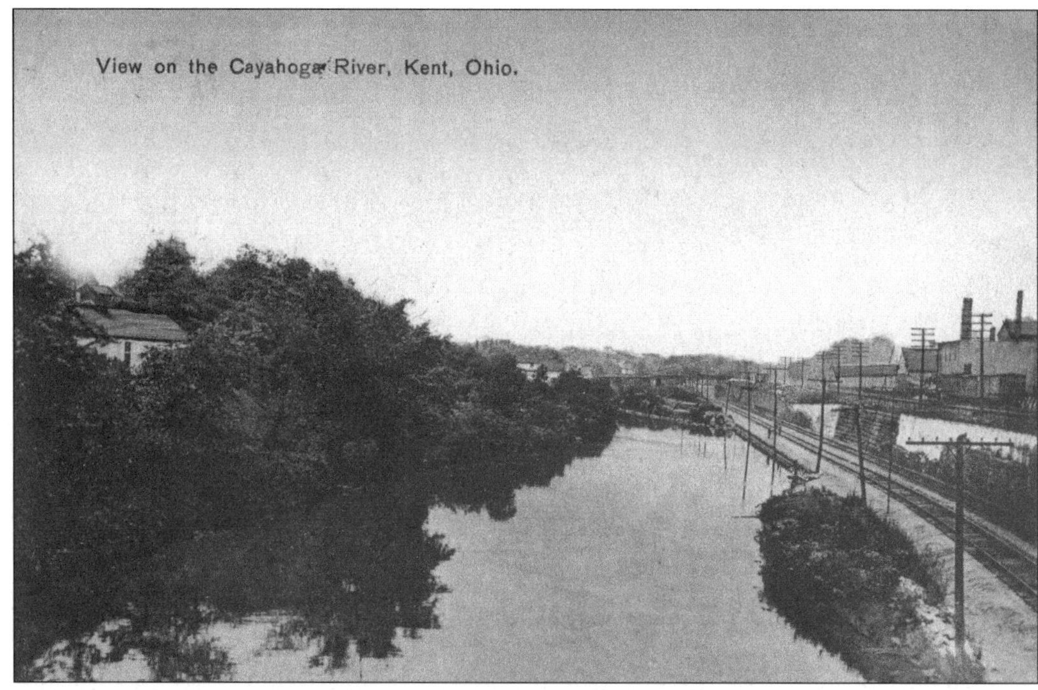

Kent, on the lower Cuyahoga, was originally known as Franklin Mills when flour and woolen mills flourished there. Two falls on the river furnished the power to run the mills. The town today is probably best known as the home of Kent State University.

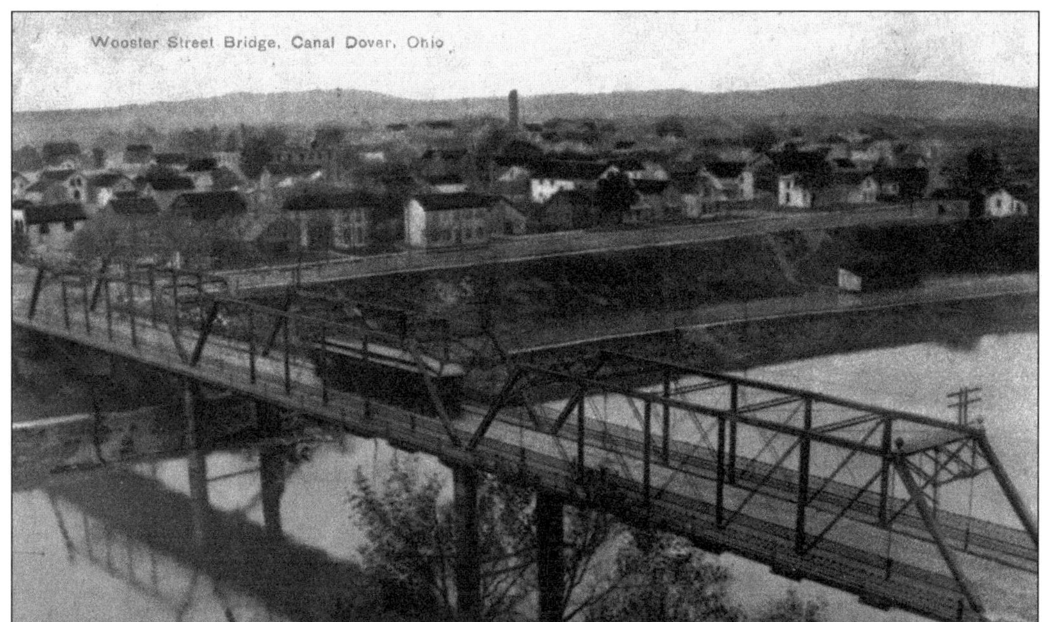

The opening of the Ohio–Erie Canal in 1825 brought Ohioans a cheap and relatively easy means to ship goods back east, via the Erie Canal to Eastern seaboard markets, or south via the Ohio and Mississippi Rivers to the great Southern emporium of New Orleans. Towns like Canal Dover, south of Cleveland, sprang up to take advantage of the canal commerce.

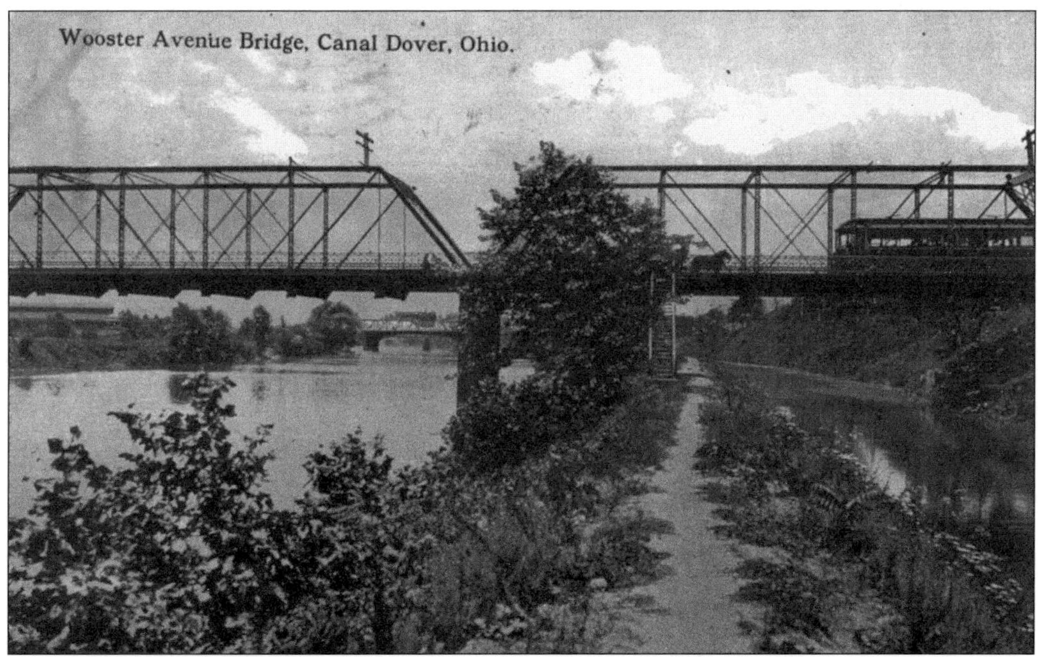

This postcard includes a view of the canal (right), with a mule towpath and the Tuscarawas River at Canal Dover.

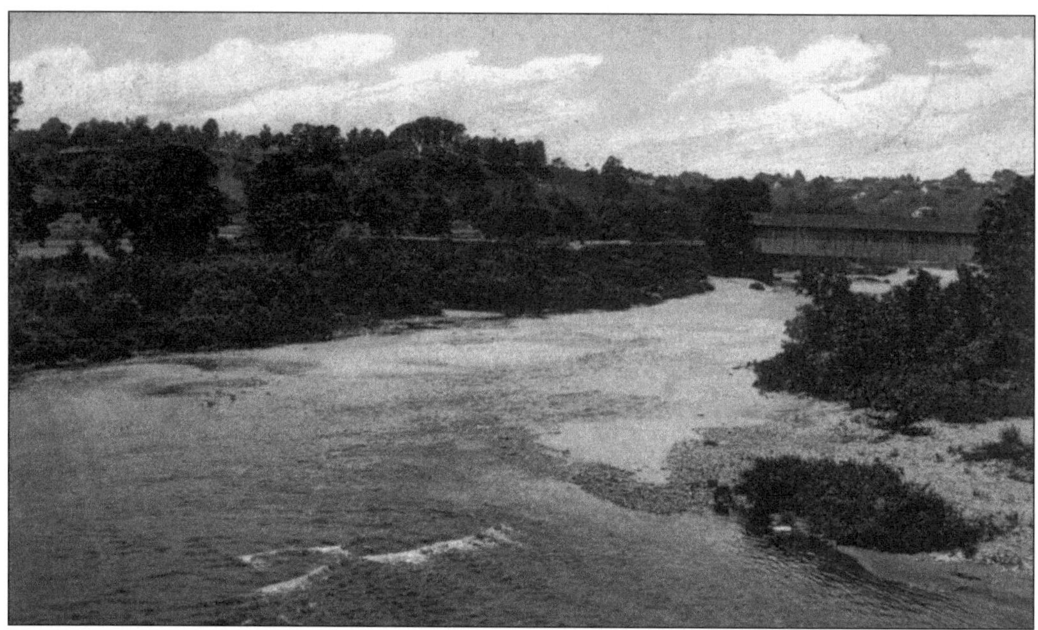

Covered bridges were common in the early days of the Western Reserve. This bridge forded the Conneaut River at Conneaut, in Ashtabula County. Ashtabula County boasts 21 existing covered bridges, the most of any county in the country. The area hosts an annual Covered Bridge Festival.

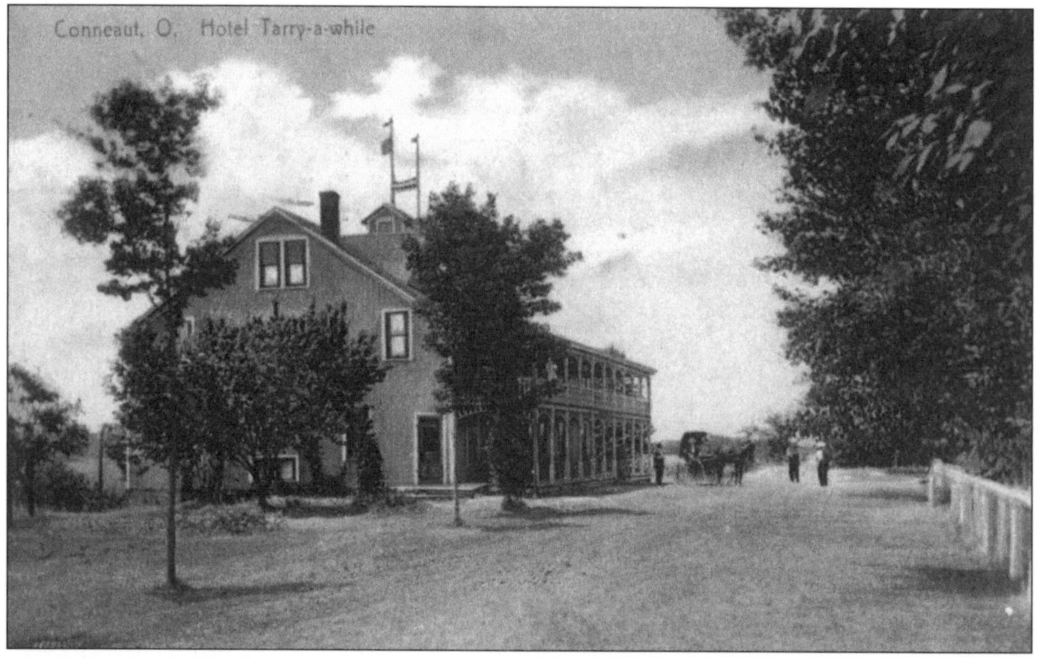

The "Tarry-a-while," two-storied with wide verandahs, was a typical early roadside hotel. It was located on the Cleveland–Buffalo Road near Conneaut, in the northeast corner of the Western Reserve near the Pennsylvania border.